2,8m

DI022781

Easy Gardening With DROUGHT-RESISTANT PLANTS

by Arno Nehrling and Irene Nehrling

DRAWINGS BY VIRGINIA HOWIE

DOVER PUBLICATIONS, INC., New York

SB 434
N 38

Donated by Micaela McGibb

Copyright © 1968 by Arno and Irene Nehrling.
All rights reserved under Pan American and International Copyright Conventions.

Published in Canada by General Publishing Company, Ltd., 30 Lesmill Road, Don Mills, Toronto, Ontario.

Published in the United Kingdom by Constable and Company, Ltd., 10 Orange Street, London WC 2.

This Dover edition, first published in 1975, is an unabridged and unaltered republication of the work originally published in 1968. It is reprinted by special arrangement with the original publisher, Hearthside Press, Inc., 445 Northern Boulevard, Great Neck, New York 11021.

International Standard Book Number: 0-486-23230-1
Library of Congress Catalog Card Number: 75-17124

Manufactured in the United States of America
Dover Publications, Inc.
180 Varick Street
New York, N.Y. 10014

3442

Dedicated to

Ruth and Oakley

In Appreciation

In preparing this book, we mailed questionnaires to all State Garden Club Conservation Chairmen and to various conservation groups in every state in the Union. The response was exceptionally good and we thank all who took the time to answer. These groups are interested in conservation in its broadest sense. They realize that through concerted effort, with enough members, pressure can be brought to bear on legislators to save our natural areas not only for ourselves but for future generations; and to pass laws reducing water and air pollution in an ever-changing industrial world.

Mrs. Lambert D. Le Maire representing the Federated Garden Clubs of New York State and Mrs. Arnold A. Morris of The Garden Club of North Carolina deserve special thanks for their useful suggestions.

For specific, concrete information in solving drought problems the U.S. Department of Agriculture with its state colleges and experiment stations were most helpful, especially in dry states where water is a problem; so too were botanical gardens and arboretums. These groups made every effort to cooperate and to be of service to both home owners and commercial growers in their respective states. They have and are conducting experiments on the problems with which this book deals.

Especially helpful in this group was the correspondence from Dr. V. T. Stoutemyer, Chairman, Dept. of Agricultural Sciences, Dept. of Agriculture, University of California, Los Angeles; Prof. D. J. Fieldhouse, Dept. of Horticulture, University of Delaware; Prof. Hendrik van de Werken, Dept. of Horticulture, University of Tennessee; Prof. J. K. Greig, Dept. of Horticulture, Kansas State University; Harold W. Pillsbury, Extension Horticulturist,

Agr. Extension Service, Wyoming; Clifford Collier, Extension Horticulturist, West Virginia; and Bernard Harkness, Dept. of Parks, Rochester, New York. We also thank John D. Lyon of Cambridge, Mass. and Orville Clapper of the Clapper's Lawn and Garden Store, West Newton, Mass. for time spent in showing us the most efficient watering devices and equipment available on the market today.

For photographs we are grateful to Joseph A. Witt, Assistant Director, University of Washington Arboretum, Seattle; W. H. Earle, Director, Desert Botanical Garden, Phoenix, Arizona; Mrs. M. E. Broughton, Santa Barbara Botanic Garden, California; Robert P. Griffing, Jr., Curatorial Consultant, Honolulu Academy of Arts. Mr. and Mrs. Herbert J. Bool, Phoenix, Arizona; Joseph S. Vilchek of the N. Y. Cactus and Succulent Society; and Prof. Clarence E. Lewis, Dept. of Horticulture, Mich. State University. Paul Genereux, formerly official photographer for the Mass. Horticultural Society (now retired), supplied many of the pictures as he did for our previous publications. George Taloumis, horticulturist, author, editor, lecturer and photographer also supplied many of the photographs used in this publication.

Muriel C. Crossman, the Massachusetts Horticultural Society's head librarian, and her staff were tireless in their efforts to be helpful as was Richard C. Hands, an assistant editor of Horticulture. His advice and help is deeply appreciated.

Virginia Howie, well known nationally in lily circles, is an artist as well as a horticulturist and it was a pleasure to have her do the drawings for this book. Betty Kelly Mellett typed the manuscript. To all of the above who were so helpful and cooperative we extend our deep and sincere thanks.

Last, but by no means least, as usual we are deeply grateful to Nedda Casson Anders, Editor of Hearthside Press, for her suggestions, advice, patience, and general helpfulness in every way in the preparation of this book.

Arno and Irene Nehrling

Needham Heights, Massachusetts

Contents

Easy Gardening
With Drought-Resistant Plants

I Why a Book on Dry Gardens?

Droughts have always been a problem in certain regions, but severe dry cycles in areas where rainfall was once adequate have widened the problem so that water conservation is now a national concern. Densely populated and heavily industrialized sections have suffered from drought for almost a decade. In the summer of 1966, water levels were dangerously low through most of New England, Virginia, West Virginia, Pennsylvania, New York, Delaware, Maryland, New Jersey, and a south central portion of Ohio.

Garden groups, women's organizations, government agencies, 4-H clubs, and wildlife associations, alarmed by the general misuse of our natural resources, have been publicizing the need for better conservation practices. It is hoped that this book will provide them with a useful reference. And since every citizen has a stake in our natural resources, we hope that gardeners everywhere will find it of interest.

WATER CONSERVATION A NECESSITY

Although the water table rose in 1967, the relief is considered only temporary, because the conditions which created the aridity—at least to the extent that Nature was not a factor—have not been improved. These conditions (increasing water consumption of an expanding population; water pollution; and inadequate facilities for storing, treating, and delivering water) and their remedies are discussed in greater detail later.

Few home owners living in communities where stringent restrictions on the use of water have been imposed are likely to forget the devastating results as grassy lawns, trees, shrubs, and flowers died of thirst. The best insurance against such devastation in the future is to garden with plants that resist drought, to increase the water-retentiveness of the soil, and to apply water more effectively. All of these subjects are covered in detail in succeeding chapters.

ARID AND SEMI-ARID SECTIONS HAVE SPECIAL NEEDS

Deserts occupy fifteen per cent of the earth's surface. In North America, there are deserts in southern California, Arizona, New Mexico, Nevada, western Texas, and north central and northwestern Mexico. Desert conditions exist not only because of lack of precipitation, but also because the rainfall which does fall evaporates quickly, as in the extremely high temperatures of some tropics.

Little of the world's land is completely barren. Mountains, boulders, and cold may make a tundra hostile to vegetation, as on the high plains of Siberia, but deserts are generally hot and capable of sustaining some plants, usually sparsely.

Desert vegetation seldom forms a continuous grasslike cover, nor is it heavy and closely matted as in most forests. The individual plants tend to be spread far apart and many remain dormant most of the year. Then after an infrequent rain, colorful flowers burst forth as the plants hurry to complete their life cycle while water is available.

All living things need some water, but the plants of arid and semi-arid regions have adapted to their environment; their structure enables them to make the best use of the water available and to store it too. By reduced transpiration they can survive with a little water and maintain their water balance through their own special combination of adaptive qualities. The plants of this type, which are known scientifically as Xerophytes, are discussed in the chapter on desert plants.

WEEK-END GARDENERS AND VACATIONERS

Many home owners are interested in gardening and are anxious to keep their grounds attractive, but, because of time limits or other more demanding interests, want a landscape job that requires a minimum of care and expense. In this category also are vacationers, some away from home for two weeks, others maybe for a month or more. Still others find it necessary to be away from home each week for business reasons. In these circumstances, it is essential that the landscape be planned carefully; hiring someone to cut the grass will not be enough to keep the grounds well-kept unless the plant material was wisely chosen to thrive under this sort of casual care.

TO MEET SPECIAL REQUIREMENTS

Drought-resistant plants are useful to gardeners even in regions where there is no special water shortage or where lack of care does not become a problem. If a particular difficulty exists such as sandy soil or a terrain where the water drains off too quickly, dry-garden plants are ideal. Patches of the garden, lacking water outlets and thus too far from the hose for convenient watering, are also places for plants which thrive with little or no water. Some sites such as this are best handled with structural materials (see Rock and Wall Gardens, Paved Gardens, and Gardens in the Japanese manner, all in Chapter II) but you can select a good plant for just about every kind of need from the descriptions given in Chapters IV and V.

TO REDUCE MAINTENANCE AND COSTS

Through dry periods, many home owners learn that the cost of water and the time spent in applying it are big items. Water is no longer free for the taking. To meet the increased demands due to the population explosion and greatly increased needs of industry, water is now stored, transported, purified and distributed for cities and industries like any other product. Marketing of this type is expensive, so choosing plants whose water needs are minimal can reduce both maintenance and maintenance costs considerably.

II Designing
Drought-Tolerant Gardens

Until the last decade or so, few gardeners except those in the South-west cared much about the drought-resistant characteristic in plants. In the heat of summer, when rainfall was inadequate there was always the hose and water to fill it.

But the years of general drought in the 1960's changed not only the garden landscape but also the requirements of its owner, who saw costly trees and shrubs dying and green lawns browning because water was not available. Today, it is unlikely that a careful gardener any-where would ignore drought-tolerance in selecting new plants, even in any given year when rainfall is adequate.

Fortunately it is no great hardship to find suitable shrubs, trees, and flowers of all kinds. Botanical gardens, arboretums, and federal and state experimental stations have been testing plants for drought-resist-ance, recommending them if they fulfilled other requirements: that they be ornamental, long-lived, easy to grow and widely available. Their recommendations run the gamut in color, form, hardiness, height, etc., so it is still left to the average gardener to select the ones which best suit his needs. This chapter points out and illustrates the various possibilities.

Does an eroding slope lose its topsoil and moisture? Is a section of soil so light and porous that it is not water-retentive? (It is surprising how the texture and quality of earth can vary from one part of the garden to another.) Or is the problem a roof overhang keeping rain away from a particular spot? There are many design solutions which will make it possible for you to bring beauty and utility to a barren site.

Designs for seashore gardens, where sand, wind, and erosion compound the difficulties, are also shown, along with suggestions for gardens in the Southwest and for container and indoor gardens.

GARDENING ON A HILLSIDE

Soil erosion can be very destructive and costly. In regions with little or no tree cover, on steep slopes and in sandy soil the washing or blowing away of topsoil can be disastrous. Where heavy rains wash out channels and carry off the best topsoil, and the wind, during droughts, whirls the soil away as dust, preventive measures must be found.

Hillsides that are to be cultivated can be terraced to break the flow of water and soil. Dig level furrows or trenches, or leave strips of sod at right angles to the slope, to prevent excessive soil and water losses.

The best control for wind erosion in dry areas on banks, slopes and beaches is a permanent planting of vegetation with strong roots.

1. A dry banking planted with juniper and heather slopes toward the sea. The berry-laden red cedar *(Juniperus virginiana)* at the right, provides a strong vertical accent at the top of the hill and continues upward the foliage texture of the spreading juniper at its base.   Genereux Photo

3. Ledges on dry bankings can be assets if carefully planted, as here with gray-blue spreading junipers and similarly colored *Alyssum saxatile* (the clumps hanging over the curb, center). Spreading yews at the right edge of the bank planting form a link with those around the house.

Genereux Photo

2. *Left:* A brick terrace and stone mulch solve the problem of what to do with a dry hill top overlooking a lovely offscape.

Taloumis Photo

4. The Sargent crabapple in the center of this driveway island is surrounded by dwarf Swiss mountain pine *(Pinus mugo mughus)* and *Cotoneaster divaricata,* all doing well with a minimum of water.

Genereux Photo

5. *Right:* Any raised terrace near a building, even in areas of high summer rainfall, is so sharply drained that extra care must be used in selecting plants. Here heather (large clump at left foreground), as well as various thymes and artemisias flourish without summer watering. The relationship between the fieldstone wall, gray-leaved plants and weathered shingles provides a subtle unifying factor.

Genereux Photo

6. The common snow-in-summer *(Cerastium tomentosum)* is generously used on a dry banking and between steps . . . a good illustration of the effectiveness of a lot of one kind of plant, even if it is a familiar one.

Genereux Photo

7. Spreading junipers at the base of the steps and rock cotoneasters (*Cotoneaster horizontalis*) above them are superior plants for dry situations.

Genereux Photo

8. Sedums and sempervivums are ideal for planting between steps. While the mat of white-flowered sedums will persist after flowering, all of the somewhat taller-flowering sempervivums will die after blooming and may be removed as soon as they have passed. Young rosettes at the base will bloom in future years.

9. Highly drought-tolerant sedums and sempervivums flourish beside and between informal steps. The blue lungwort *(Pulmonaria officinalis)* at the base receives enough water runoff from the upper area to make it grow better than it would if placed at the top; and in any case it will become semi-dormant before summer droughts arrive.

Genereux Photos

10. *Left:* Germander *(Teucrium chamaedrys)* has long been in gardens. It formed an important part of the knot gardens of Tudor, England, intertwined with lavender, santolina and other herbs. Germander remains a highly satisfactory plant for gardens in mild climates. It is evergreen; in cold areas a few cuttings wintered in a frame insures against loss. Easily divided too, it is simple to build up a stock. Reddish-purple flowers are of no importance and often sheared.

McFarland Photo

11. *Above:* A variety of textures in a small area are shown by the effective use of wooden step risers, stepping stones, a gray-leaved grass tuft, sedums and semper-vivums. This is different and a strangely appealing solution to the problem of how to plant a dry step area.

Roche Photo

12. In whatever part of the country they appear, even in areas of considerable summer rainfall, the presence of steps inevitably means a change in height, usually abrupt, which in turn creates a more or less dry situation, not only at the upper terrace area above the steps, but also at their sides and joints. Here creeping thyme is used at the upper terrace and between the steps, while long-flowering (but rather tender) glossy abelia (*Abelia grandiflora*) is placed at each side of the steps.

Genereux Photo

13. Spreading junipers thrive at the top of steps despite dry soil. Regular pruning will keep them from growing over the steps.

Genereux Photo

14. A deeper rose-colored sea pink (*Armeria maritima laucheana*) is here boldly repeated on a dry step series, in the best of the formal tradition. The rather too thick masses between the steps are thyme.

McFarland Photo

ROCK AND WALL GARDENS

In hot dry seasons, rock plants and alpines growing in crevices between stones have a great advantage over other flora, because the rocks not only prevent loss of moisture by evaporation, but also give shade and keep the roots cool. Picturesque rock formations are found all over the United States. If you do not have a natural outcropping, it is possible to make one, but it is hard work. The best site is on a downslope.

15. The large plant (top, center) is a hybrid of *Dudleya pulverulenta* and *D. brittoni*. The smaller plants are *Dudleya viscida* and *D. farinosa*. All are excellent dry wall plants but tender to freezing cold. Now listed by some as *Echeveria.*

Cornell Photo

Use large local stones, all of the same kind if available. Working from the bottom up, set each rock firmly into the slope with its broadest side down, and with more of it buried than exposed. Ideally, the exposed part (about ¼ or ⅓ of the total) should be wedged so firmly into the slope that you can stand on it—try it and see. The stone should be set at a slight upward slant so that the moisture runs into, not out of, the crevices.

The soil should be rather light and porous, but in regions where droughts are severe, less porosity is desirable. (To make the soil more water-retentive, see Chapter III.)

The best time to plant these enchanting little specimens is spring or early fall. Water in spring when growth is most active. A soaker turned on low is a good method of applying water to rock plants. Thus the moisture will seep slowly down the rock slope.

A winter mulch applied after the first big freeze is advisable in sections where the soil is alternately frozen and thawed. This mulch will prevent plants from beginning to grow prematurely. Dwarf evergreens (junipers and evergreen cotoneasters, for example) give accent and height to the alpines; many other shrubs with a dwarf or compact habit of growth are suitable for rock gardens.

16. This dry, rocky slope close to a terrace has been planted with spice pinks, thyme, dwarf pines, hen-and-chickens and other small plants. An incredibly "busy" garden, yet of interest to any family which enjoys a variety of plants and wishes them near at hand.

Genereux Photo

17. This fine small-area planting contains a number of hen-and-chickens or house-leeks *(Sempervivum)* including the popular cobweb houseleek *(S. arachnoideum)*, center. These are among the most reliably drought-tolerant of all plants, some species being so easy to grow that they are raised on roofs abroad, hence the common name houseleek. This planting is a small-scale masterpiece, with the gray-green colors and varied textures of the rock lichens repeating those of the houseleeks. The iris and ferns provide a relieving touch of airiness.

Genereux Photo

A stone retaining wall, in addition to holding a bank in place, can also serve as a stage for some of the sedums and sempervivums, ideal for a high crevice and hanging masses. A dry wall built with pockets gives one a chance to show off drought-resistant plants which often do better here than elsewhere.

Plants recommended for the rock or wall garden are cacti and other succulents, as well as the following which are also dependable: Woolly yarrow, stone cresses, basket-of-gold, pasque-flower, beach wormwood, rock cresses, purple rock cress, poppy mallows, bellflowers, pinks, creeping babys-breath, perennial candytuft, ground phlox, three-toothed cinquefoil, soapworts, saxifrages, and thymes.

WILD GARDENS

Use native dry-land and other drought-resistant material as much as possible. Informal, natural plantings using such material should require a minimum of care and watering. If you are a wildflower enthusiast plan a wildflower garden with appropriate plants in a dry habitat or a sanctuary for birds with favorite drought-resistant evergreen and deciduous berried shrubs that attract them. A planting at the edge of the woods will require little care once the plants become established. Shady gardens of the wild need less watering than those exposed to the hot sun. (This is true of all shade gardens, if the shade is caused by high walls or buildings. However, if the cause is a large hungry tree, the surrounding vegetation will need *more* water.)

EARLY GARDENS

Feature a spring and early summer garden on the premise that there will be enough water during the winter and early spring to give the plants a good start. The effects of drought and lack of water show up later in the summer during July and August. Let the foliage of drought-resistant herbs, perennials, ground covers, trees and shrubs finish out the season with the use of annuals in concentrated areas for color.

18. A spring and early June graden in the sun. Foreground is edged with perennial candytuft (*Iberis sempervirens*), snow-in-summer (*Cerastium tomentosum*), snowflake (*Leucojum aestivum*), leopard's bane (*Doronicum*), daffodils and bleeding heart. The middle ground is edged with dwarf iris (*I. pumila* and hybrids). For later bloom there are a few annuals, daylilies, platycodon, roses, phlox and drought-tolerant single chrysanthemums. Occasional spot watering is necessary during a dry spell.

Molly Price Photo

PAVED GARDENS

In climates where grass is hard to maintain, paving has long been used as a ground cover. One has only to recall the exuberant centuries-old patterns of the pebbles in Spanish patios and marketplaces to realize that paving can be a magnificent and colorful substitute for a lawn. In the Southwest, with its heat and drought, and elsewhere throughout the country where indoor and outdoor living areas are linked, paved areas outdoors are widely appreciated. So wherever water is a problem, consider making ground covers of pebbles, concrete, brick or stone.

19. Here the rectangular lines of a modern house and paving are relieved by an informal mass of spreading junipers, heather and creeping thyme. The hues of building, plants and paving are all related.   Genereux Photo

20. In city gardens where heavy traffic and dry conditions make the growing of turf or even ground covers impractical paving may be the only alternative for the "garden floor". The satisfying unity of brick paving, brick wall, brick steps and brick building is effective. Plants in pots and tubs are easily watered and add a softening touch to the abundant bricks.

Genereux Photo

21. In dry, heavy-traffic areas under trees close to a house, brick paving and beds of pachysandra make a simple and effective living area.

Roche Photo

22. One of the most dependably drought-tolerant small trees, Russian olive *(Elaeagnus angustifolia)* is shown carefully pruned, perhaps to reflect the bonsai suspended on the fence and placed on the table. Russian olive's gray leaves go well with similarly colored stone work supporting the terrace and the raked sand which also fits the Japanese-influenced theme.

Roche Photo

23. Problems of maintenance in a dry corner are reduced by the use of simply-laid brick paving and of mainly two hardy plants—extremely free-flowering, single pink floribunda rose Betty Prior and on the fence a form of *Euonymus fortunei*. Geraniums in the border are also useful. Here is a good illustration of the effectiveness of using a couple of superior plants in quantity which is much preferred to a random mixture.

Roche Photo

24. A rectangular bed of blue-flowered evergreen myrtle *(Vinca minor)* does well in a dry corner border with brick. The large-flowered Bowles variety of vinca is preferred.

Roche Photo

25. Paving effectively solves the problem of what to do with a sunbaked, dry, high-traffic area near the home. The Scotch broom at the left of the steps is among the most dependable of plants for dry locations, as are the rock cotoneasters (*Cotoneaster horizontalis*) behind the chairs.

Genereux Photo

26. With dry soil conditions you may wish to substitute a fence for a hedge, and save precious water for vines and flowers.

Taloumis Photo

GARDENS IN THE JAPANESE MANNER

The authentic Japanese garden cannot be described briefly, for it is an art form which has developed for centuries, and is complex enough to require a lifetime of study. In general, however, it may be said to be based on the use of three forms: the vertical, the recumbent, and the prostrate (called the heaven-man-earth lines). These forms may be shown in rocks, lanterns, plants, or in combinations of the three. For example, a slender dwarf conifer or a slim rock could be the vertical form; a lantern or a gnarled pine could be the recumbent one; a low rock or mounded azalea, the prostrate.

Contemporary American plantings which show some Japanese influence, primarily by their use of upright rocks as features, are shown here. Since plant material is kept to a minimum, the gardens require little water, and can be kept neat and orderly without much care.

27. Many features of the Japanese-style garden lend themselves to dry area adaptation, such as the pebbled areas shown here, which recall dried stream or lake beds.   Roche Photo

28. *Pinus mugo mughus* — A handsome simple placement of crushed stone, boulders and evergreen of oriental inspiration makes an attractive garden for a dry corner.

Lewis Photo

29. This garden corner, suggesting Japanese inspiration, uses spreading junipers and Japanese white pine *(Pinus parviflora)* at the right as softer foils for the stone mulch.

Roche Photo

SEASHORE GARDENS

Gardens by the sea have many enemies: salt, sand, cold and strong, drying winds, but even here the intelligent gardener can conquer the elements, at least to the extent of having a bit of cultivated ground. Edwin A. Menninger, in his book *Seaside Plants of the World* (also published by Hearthside), lists 1500 different species which can be used in such difficult sites. Native shrubs and trees require the least maintenance, but it is also possible to expand the list of suitable plants by building up the soil. See chapter III.

30. *Elaeagnus angustifolia* — One of the most reliably drought-tolerant of trees, Russian olive, is admired for its silvery-gray foliage. It is hardy in the coldest parts of the country, where it provides an excellent shelterbreak, and is tough enough to resist salt, sand and wind.   Taloumis Photo

Living windbreaks of trees, shrubs, fences or buildings will offer protection from the strong winds. There isn't much one can do about the salt spray (a windbreak does help, however) so set out salt-resistant plants. Fortunately, most of them like the dry, sandy soil found along the seashore.

In sandy locations where the yearly rainfall is 30 inches or more, the plants listed below are among the best and most useful. They will grow in sand and take the midday heat of summer, without additional irrigation.

Many plants for the sand garden cannot be purchased from nurserymen and must be dug from the wild. This is not always easy as many have deep taproots; even those with small tops may have roots 3 feet or more in length, some very brittle. This entails slow and painstaking digging to avoid breaking or injuring the roots.

The best plants to transform the windblown and sandy beaches into stable areas belong to a very small genus of sand binding grasses, *Ammophila*. When a planting of beach grass has become established, other plants and finally sand-garden shrubs and trees may be planted to make the area more attractive. If the sand is salty, only plants that tolerate salt spray should be selected—the plants advised for seaside gardens.

Growth in sand will be more stunted and certainly less lush but following are some of the plants that are found growing or can be planted in sand. See index for pages with descriptions.

TREES

Pinus banksiana—Jack Pine; *P. rigida*—Pitch Pine; *P. thunbergi*—Japanese Black Pine. *Prunus serotina*—Wild Black Cherry. *Quercus alba*—White Oak; *Q. ilicifolia*—Scrub Oak; *Q. velutina*—Black Oak. *Rhus* species—Sumac.

SHRUBS

Amorpha species—False Indigo. *Arctostaphylos uva-ursi*—Bearberry. *Artemisia tridentata*—Sagebrush. *Calluna* species—Heather. *Comptonia peregrina*—Sweet-Fern. *Cytisus* species—Brooms. *Elaeagnus* species. *Hudsonia tomentosa*—Beach Heather. *Hypericum* species—St. John's-Wort. *Myrica pensylvanica*—Bayberry. *Prunus maritima*—Beach Plum.

Rhus species—Sumac. *Rosa rugosa*—Rugosa Rose, Salt Spray Rose. *Salix tristis*—Dwarf Gray Willow. *Ulex* species—Furze, Gorse. *Vaccinium angustifolium*—Lowbush Blueberry.

PERENNIALS

Ammophila—Beach Grass. *Aralia nudicaulis*—Wild Sarsaparilla. *Arenaria*—Sandwort. *Artemisia stelleriana*—Beach Wormwood. *Asclepias tuberosa*—Butterfly-Weed. *Chrysopsis*—Golden Aster. *Desmodium canadense*—Bush Trefoil. *Elymus arenarius*—Sea Lyme Grass. *Eupatorium hyssopifolium*. *Lathyrus littoralis*—Pacific Coast Beach Pea. *Lathyrus*

31. Although it has become widely naturalized along coastlines, the Rugosa rose is not a true native, having been introduced from the orient about 100 years ago. While the rose-pink form is most common, a white is also available, and both are covered with immaculate deep green leaves, even in the driest locations. The Japanese are said to call it the "sea tomato" because of its bright red fruit.

Taloumis Photo

maritimus—Atlantic Coast Beach Pea. *Liatris*—Button Snakeroot. *Mesembryanthemum*—Fig-Marigold. See Succulents. *Pteridium aquilinum* —Bracken Fern. *Solidago sempervirens*—Seaside Goldenrod.

DESERT GARDENS FOR THE GREAT SOUTHWEST

Only a few woody plants are able to take the intense midday summer heat of desert areas, where the sand is so porous that it does not hold moisture, drying out and warming quickly. Here, where the annual rainfall is always low—about 4 to 10 inches—only desert plants are recommended (except, of course, for plants in containers—see index). Where yearly precipitation exceeds 15 inches, do not try to grow desert species, for they do not tolerate much winter moisture.

The desert garden is a highly specialized one, but with cacti, succulents, and other desert plants, gardens of great beauty are created. Still, no plant-life will long survive without some moisture, and artificial watering every week or 10 days during the summer must be provided (except if strictly native plants are used). Where water is given at such intervals, plantings of Mediterranean, Japanese and Himalayan species thrive. Even in Seattle's maritime climate, desert plants require water in July and August, but they need less water than the forest plants.

Succulent plants of the desert or semi-desert such as the agaves and cacti of the Americas can store water in their thick, spongy or fleshy succulent roots, stems and leaves. With water-storage tissue, they are able to accumulate large quantities of water during the rainy season.

Some of the non-succulent plants make outstanding adaptations, rapid elongation of the seedling taproots enabling them to develop an extensive root system to cope with periods of permanent wilting. The periods are short in most woody plants, but may last months in some grasses. Mesquite *(Prosopis juliflora)* develops long taproots that reach down deep for water.

Of course, drought-tolerance in general is a very relative matter, depending upon many factors of exposure, soil, and other environmental conditions.

Julia Morton, Morton Collectanea, University of Miami, Coral Gables, Florida, points this out: "I am delighted to hear that you are working on drought-tolerant plants . . . such plants are very much in my mind—I have spent so much time this year in arid regions: Curaçao, Aruba and the Los Angeles area. I will never forget the sight of *Fremontia,* so yellow, and *Ceanothus,* so blue, in full bloom side by side at the Rancho Santa Ana Botanic Garden. Such beauty in a desert!

"It is so damp so much of the time here in south Florida that one hardly thinks of any of our plants as drought-resistant . . . (but) one sees them flourishing and verdant in the devastatingly dry Netherlands Antilles."

Shrubs and trees native to arid parts are usually small in size with fewer and smaller leaves such as the sagebrush *(Artemisia tridentata).* Many have a copious supply of waxes and resins on their surfaces. The creosote bush *(Larrea tridentata)* has waxy leaves that reduce transpiration. Some like the crucifixion thorns are leafless, others soon shed their leaves.

Some desert plants like the ocotillo *(Fouquieria splendens)* slow down the life processes and become dormant during dry periods even to dropping their leaves. When rains come they put on new leaves, maybe a half dozen times in one year if necessary.

DESERT ANNUALS AND PERENNIALS

Annuals, small and numerous in arid regions, produce seeds capable of lying dormant for long periods, awaiting moisture which allows them to germinate, leaf, flower, fruit and complete their life cycle during the short period of 4 to 6 rainy weeks.

Winter rains produce these colorful spring-blooming ephemerals, and summer showers produce the summer "quickies." Following warm winters with sufficient moisture, the desert areas become alive and ablaze with the color of annuals, their extensive, spectacular displays covering sandy washes, highway shoulders, rocky slopes, hillsides, grasslands and open plateaus, growing in almost pure sand. They form attractive undercover among the taller growing plants.

Desert coreopsis spreads its yellow sunshine over vast open areas. The blue-to-violet fragrant flowers of Texas bluebonnet are a lovely sight often covering hillsides alone or intermingled with golden poppies and other desert spring bloomers. Among the handsomest is the fragrant evening-primrose with its white or yellow night-blooming

32. This garden in Palm Springs, California, combines the use of lawn, crushed rock and desert plants. The tall palm is the California fan palm *(Washingtoniana robusta)*. The Joshua-tree *(Yucca brevifolia)* is at the right and ocotillo *(Fouquieria splendens)* is the center plant. Miscellaneous yuccas, opuntias and other desert plants complete the garden picture.

Cornell Photo

flowers, making a spectacular display when seasons are favorable, often found growing with the rosy-purple or pink sand verbena.

Desert perennials are more dependable than annuals and can usually be counted on to bloom each year since many, like cacti and other succulents, have water storage tissues and many have extensive deep root systems lacking in annuals. Do not crowd desert plants; their root spreads need lots of space.

DESERT SHRUBS

Many people think of the desert as barren, but there are places in our great Southwest where vegetation is rich and diversified. A variation in growth form and species is found from one area to another due to climatic and physiographic variations although some of the more conspicious species occur everywhere. For some of the typical shrubs see Chapter VII.

DESERT TREES

Desert vegetation is unlike that in any other section of the United States. Small desert trees such as the palo-verde, desert ironwood, Joshua tree and crucifixion thorns (all these are listed in Chapter VII) are somehow able to give the landscape an appearance of woodland.

33. A motor hotel in Palm Springs, California, nestles into the natural landscape. A ground cover of pebbles and rocks and plants from the desert require a minimum of maintenance and watering. Ocotillo *(Fouquieria splendens)* is at either end of the picture, the Joshua-tree *(Yucca brevifolia)* in the left background and the palm *Washingtoniana filifera* is in the lower left of the picture.   Cornell Photo

CONTAINER GARDENS

Container gardening has long been popular in warm climates along the Mediterranean, in Mexico and in our own Southwest where comparatively few plants will survive without irrigation during the hot dry summers. Now with droughts and the scarcity and high cost of labor, container gardens outdoors are popular almost everywhere.

Mobile gardens have many advantages. For those who have little time or inclination to develop a green thumb, but want the warm inviting atmosphere which colorful plants create, such a portable set-up is ideal: you buy a few plants and get immediate results. Changes can be made easily, and the garden rearranged at will, simply by discarding a plant or two past its prime, and replacing it with a fresh specimen. Thus, at important accent points such as the garden gate or border of a terrace, the focus can be on colorful or shapely plant material in the peak of condition.

CONTAINERS

There is no end to the different shapes, sizes and materials which containers come in. Wooden tubs, buckets, planters, kegs and barrels; old copper and iron kettles, urns of earthenware or concrete, pottery jugs

34. A variety of pot plants include a peppermint geranium immediate front, rosemary to the right and rose geranium behind that. Other scented geraniums, basil and lemon verbena (*Aloysia triphylla,* syn. *Lippia citriodora*) complete the collection.   Taloumis Photo

and jardinieres, strawberry jars, hollowed-out logs, volcanic rock, even simple clay pots which take on softer, more interesting tones as they weather with usage. Simple containers which relate in color and type to the material around it are usually most successful. Black iron under a wrought iron stairway or a concrete tub against the stucco wall bring unity to the scene.

Whatever material you use, good drainage is a prime requisite as is enough depth to allow sufficient root growth. Wood is a good material

35. The containers here shown, of various sizes and shapes, were patterned to fit the area. Unity is obtained through the use of the same wood and finish for the planting boxes. The plants have not developed sufficiently to be of interest at this point.   Courtesy California Redwood Association

because heat penetrates it slowly so the roots are not likely to be scorched even in the hottest seasons. The material must be able to withstand constant wetting and drying out and should be able to resist decay, at least for a couple of seasons. And the container must be heavy enough to take storms and wind. Smaller containers are often set in holes made in platforms to secure them.

GOOD DRAINAGE

To avoid overwatering, one large hole or several smaller ones punctured in the bottom of the container are helpful although not essential. Without them more care must be exercised in watering. To avoid stoppage cover holes with large pieces of broken flower pot. A must is a thick layer of porous material at the bottom of the receptacle such as broken pieces of flower pot or bricks, large pebbles or stones, cinders or coarse sand (several inches in large containers) to allow free passage of water. A layer of sphagnum moss over this will prevent soil from washing through. Slightly raise any container resting on a solid surface, such as concrete, with cleats or set on bricks or blocks of wood to insure good air circulation underneath.

CARE AND WATERING

But there are disadvantages too to container flora. They require more frequent watering than those of the same kind set in the garden be-

36. The only plant in this terrace garden growing directly in the soil is the clematis on the post. Chief items in the display are geraniums in the sun and tuberous begonias in the shade.   Genereux Photo

cause the soil in the container warms up and dries out more quickly, and the roots have no place to go for moisture. However, with plants in pots such water as is available may be applied where and when it is needed with a minimum of loss and pots can be moved to escape extremes of climate. A plant in filtered light under a tree does not lose its moisture as quickly as one in direct sunlight.

The smaller the container, the more quickly the soil gets dry. Porous clay pots dry out more quickly than metal or glazed pots. You can reduce the danger of drought by placing the smaller pots in boxes of peatmoss kept moist but not wet. A mulch of pebbles or peat moss over the exposed soil is also useful in retarding drought. In dry areas of the Southwest permanent plumbing is often installed for watering potted trees and shrubs.

37. This small garden, obviously influenced by the Japanese styles of tray gardening reveals the variety of plants which may be grown in containers. The cacti require little water.

Roche Photo

38. A pot garden at the Chancellor's residence (University of California, Los Angeles) showing the use of echeveria, sempervivum, kalanchoe, cacti and other succulents. In effect, it becomes a portable garden which can be rearranged or moved about at will, shifted with changing sun exposure and taken inside in cold weather. Easy to care for, this type of pot garden is popular in hot dry areas of limited water.

Cornell Photo

Some plants are less sensitive to neglect. The geranium does not quickly wilt, one reason for its popularity in window boxes and planters.

Cacti, succulents and other desert plants require less water than say a hydrangea so colorful in the pink or blue form but wilting quickly without ample water. Fuchsias too are always admired as a tree or in a hanging basket, but they too wilt quickly. In the heat of summer when exposed to the sun and drying winds many pot plants will require daily watering. When growth is active and plants are flowering they need more water than at other times.

The choice of plants for potting is determined by climate, pocketbook, and personal preferences. The more tender plants commonly grown outdoors in warm regions will need some type of winter shelter, such as a cool greenhouse, pit, sunporch or plant room in the North. They are more sensitive to extremes of weather than plants rooted in soil, for all sides are exposed to air circulation and should be moved indoors before a heavy freeze.

Plants which are comparatively drought-tolerant, suitable for containers are listed elsewhere (see Index). Remember, however, that although container-grown plants have a great many advantages, they *do* need care.

HOUSE PLANTS THAT TOLERATE DRYNESS

While water is always available for indoor garden needs, house plants which tolerate drought can be very useful, particularly to gardeners who never seem to have any trouble remembering the big jobs of seasonal feeding, but all too often neglect or are too busy for routine watering of potted plants. There are an amazing number of house plants that will tolerate this kind of neglect, including bulbs, annuals, perennials, and some shrubs and trees. Under a simple fluorescent light set-up, many of these same plants will continue to thrive even in winter and even where sunlight is not available.

Select from the varieties described in the plant lists in the book the ones which most appeal to you. Be sure to supply your house plants with the drainage and moisture suggested.

Miniature indoor gardens using diminutive forms of desert growth

39. Cacti and other succulents are excellent container plants, requiring a minimum of care and watering in the heat of summer. Their intriguing foliage patterns and forms lend themselves to interesting decorative arrangements.

Taloumis Photo

40. Geraniums in formal containers are close to the house, hence easily watered. Excellent for continuous bloom from early summer until late fall. Brick paving bordered with pachysandra and myrtle were used in the design for minimum maintenance in a dry corner.

Roche Photo

41. Begonias are highly effective pot plants in a partly shaded garden. The wire fence is to restrict some beloved poodles.

Taloumis Photo

are used in all sections of the country. They require litle care or attention, and are well-suited to the generally warm, dry atmosphere of many homes. See list of Cacti and other Succulents.

42. Plants in containers here include white geraniums, wax begonias and fastigiate junipers in background. None wilt quickly. Throughout history gardeners in hot dry countries have grown plants in pots, so that such water as is available may be applied with minimum loss.

Roche Photo

GREENHOUSE AND OUTDOOR PITS

Greenhouse watering must be done with judgment and care. Not all plants need to be watered at the same time, and their requirements vary. Most plants need plenty of water when in active growth, but much less when resting. Plants that like a cool greenhouse need less watering and less humidity than those that enjoy a warm or tropical temperature.

The enthusiastic gardener should not overlook the usefulness of the sunheated, outdoor pit. Where water, maintenance and cost are items, the pit is an excellent solution for wintering-over tender plants. It can be used for any of the many cool greenhouse plants which do not need the care of the heat-loving kinds. Watering, spraying and feeding become increasingly important in direct proportion to the raising of the temperature at which the house is run.

43. The effectiveness of container grown plants for terraces and other dry areas depends upon the health, suitability and proper scale of the plants, and on well designed containers.   Roche Photo

44. Many species of podocarpus are highly effective as pot plants in dry areas. Their dark green color is highly attractive and they are readily trained to form unusual shapes.

Taloumis Photo

45. Mid-Century lilies in pots.

Courtesy Jan de Graaff, Oregon Bulb Farm
Herman V. Wall Photo

46. Court of the European art wing, Honolulu Academy of Arts. The tree is the "Kukui" or candlenut tree *(Aleurites moluccana)*, a large tree common throughout Hawaii, not grown on the mainland, and the vine is scarlet bougainvillea. Potted plants add color and a decorative interest and are frequently changed.

Courtesy Honolulu Academy Of Arts

47. Court of the Oriental art wing, Honolulu Academy of Arts. Bamboo is in the foreground. Potted plants of plumeria and *Monstera deliciosa* are used.

Courtesy Honolulu Academy Of Arts

48. Court of the Oriental art wing, Honolulu Academy of Arts — showing planting of strawberry guava trees *(Psidium cattleianum)* widely cultivated in warm regions and the ever present container plants.

Courtesy Honolulu Academy Of Arts

49. Court of the Oriental art wing, Honolulu Academy of Arts. The tropical shower tree *(Cassia)* is in the foreground. The vine against the wall on the left is petrea or the sandpaper vine *(Petrea volubilis),* native of tropical America. Beautiful bluish flowers are borne at branch tips in hanging clusters to a foot long. Bamboo clump is at the right. The potted plants are constantly changed.

Courtesy Honolulu Academy Of Arts

III Soil Improvement and Garden Maintenance

Elsewhere in this book, we deal with design and selection of plants for parched gardens; here we consider techniques for improving the soil, planting, conserving moisture in the ground, using water intelligently, and maintaining the garden in other respects.

IMPROVING THE SOIL

As old-timers and organic gardeners well know, humus and fertilizers work magic in aerating soil and making it healthy and water-retentive. If you want a good green lawn and a colorful flower border, you stand a better chance of having them, even when water levels are low, if the soil has been prepared properly. It is more economical to do this before you plant or transplant, than to struggle year after year with inferior soil. If funds are limited, improve a small section each year.

Sandy or light soil—Although many plants can be grown in this type of soil, additions of humus will replace elements which are used up and make the soil more water retentive.

Clay-type soil is hard to cultivate and at times unworkable, so stiff and heavy as to make root growth next to impossible. It becomes even more compact when wet, drying hard and solid. In so doing it shrinks and forms broad, deep cracks through which moisture from below is lost. Because of poor drainage, clay becomes water-logged from heavy rainfall and takes a long time to dry out. But it is possible to open up and aerate even clay. When the clay is dry (never work wet soil, gradually add sand and humus either as manure, compost, peat or whatever is available. This will make it friable and easy to handle.

MAKING HUMUS

Some of the sources for humus, which is used to enrich every type of soil, are leaf mold (plentiful in nature in undisturbed forests, as dead grasses and weeds which replenish meadows and pastures, or peat formed by the dying of water plants in ponds and bogs and generally sold in bales), green manure crops turned under to rot, all kinds of manure, and compost and mulches.

Leaf mold and compost can be homemade. Most experienced gardeners prefer, for the sake of neatness, to put leaves in a compost pile or in a corner of the garden, rather than allow them to decompose where they fall. Either way the leaves eventually will become humus.

Compost Pile—There are few home grounds too small for a compost pile made from fallen leaves and other vegetative waste. If you have ample space, allow a 6-by-6 foot area. With less space, use whatever room you have. A bin or 3-sided frame is helpful but not necessary. Dig a shallow pit, 1½ to 2 feet deep. Throw the soil to one side to use later on the pile. Fill the pit with wood ashes from the fireplace, leaves, grass clippings, vegetables, flower tops—any readily available organic waste material. Spread evenly and tamp well. Cover with 2 to 3 inches of soil. Sprinkle with 2 or 3 inches of manure or peat and a sprinkling of fertilizer. Add limestone at the rate of one pint for each wheelbarrow load of compost material. Then water everything down.

STORE FALLEN LEAVES

NOT UNSIGHTLY. RICH LEAF MOLD WITHIN A YEAR.

Repeat the process about every two feet, building layer upon layer. Keep the top slightly concave to collect rather than shed rain. Turn pile over about every three months to hasten uniform decomposition. During dry weather wet pile down with a hose. In a year or so an excellent compost is ready for use.

To cut labor and hasten decomposition, cover the pile with black polyethylene, holding the sides securely in place with stones or soil. This covering prevents moisture evaporation and keeps heat in the pile, hastening decay. No turning over of the pile is necessary and decomposition should take place in about 4 months.

If you have the space, humus can be made easily and quickly; dig a trench and bury all plant refuse; cover with soil, following the process described for the compost pile. It makes no difference, a compost pile or a trench, so long as you take advantage of this inexpensive source of humus.

Quick Composting—At the University of California and elsewhere a quick method for making compost has been developed. It appears to us more practical for large municipal properties than for the average small place but here is the procedure:

Reduce compost materials to small particles with a shredding-grinding machine. If material contains considerable sawdust, straw and the like unmixed with green matter, work in some high nitrogen fertilizer.

DIG A TRENCH.

BURY ALL ORGANIC
REFUSE.
COVER WITH SEVERAL
INCHES OF SOIL.

MAKE A COMPOST PILE

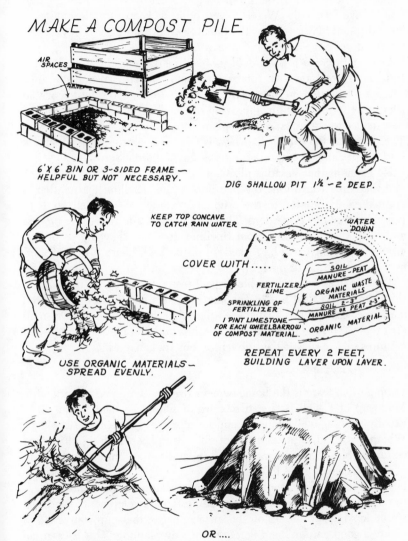

AIR SPACES

6' X 6' BIN OR 3-SIDED FRAME — HELPFUL BUT NOT NECESSARY.

DIG SHALLOW PIT 1½'-2' DEEP.

KEEP TOP CONCAVE TO CATCH RAIN WATER

WATER DOWN

COVER WITH.....

FERTILIZER LIME

SPRINKLING OF FERTILIZER

1 PINT LIMESTONE FOR EACH WHEELBARROW OF COMPOST MATERIAL.

SOIL
MANURE - PEAT
ORGANIC WASTE MATERIALS
SOIL 2-3"
MANURE or PEAT 2-3"
ORGANIC MATERIAL

USE ORGANIC MATERIALS — SPREAD EVENLY.

REPEAT EVERY 2 FEET, BUILDING LAYER UPON LAYER.

TURN PILE OVER EVERY 3 MONTHS TURNING OUTER EDGES INTO THE CENTER.

OR ....

COVER WITH BLACK POLYETHYLENE — HOLD SIDES SECURELY IN PLACE WITH STONES OR SOIL.

Make the heap no less than four feet and not over six feet high, and four or five feet wide. Water as you build to keep the pile moist but not saturated. Turn pile on the fourth, seventh and tenth days, turning the outer edges into the center to insure uniform decay.

Grass Clippings are Valuable—Mr. Robert Eddy of Fort Wayne, Indiana, recommends a rotary lawn mower with a built-in grass catcher for garden improvement. He refers to it as "the best tool that ever came to my yard for improving the garden. This rotary is not the best device to cut grass; a reel-type mower will do the job much better. The part that the rotary does best is to collect all the grass in such a way that it can be composted without any additional grinding."

He explains that he adds nitrogen and water to the grass clippings, and that time transforms the pile into "sweet-smelling"matter that is approximately one-fourth the original size and useful in all kinds of vegetable and flower gardens. The nitrogen you add to aid the process and keep the piled grass from smelling does not show up as instant nitrogen. It appears to be locked up inside each blade to be released over a long period of time.

Manure (well-rotted)—A pile of well-rotted manure in a barnyard is the farmer's greatest aid in keeping his fields fertile. But well-rotted manure is less and less available to the suburban gardener. For a small area there is on the market today odorless and non-burning composted manures sold in plastic bags under various trade names.

HOW TO MAKE TOPSOIL

Deep garden loam is the home-owner's dream, and a joy to work with. Made up of a well balanced mixture of sand, clay and humus, it is usually fertile, well drained and acceptable to nearly all plants. Whether natural or made, it is not difficult to keep such a soil in good condition but it must be maintained by addition of humus in the form of a mulch and a good fertilizer.

When topsoil has been stripped from the ground by bulldozers, as too frequently happens in new real estate developments, and the sterile-looking subsoil lies on the surface, better make up your mind to create a good garden loam before doing any planting. This is essential to aid soil in holding moisture and thus make the best possible use of available water with a minimum of waste.

Plow up the subsoil and for each 1,000 square feet of plowed ground add 2½ cubic yards of well-rotted manure or compost, 1 cubic yard of coarse sand, 100 pounds of ground limestone if the subsoil is acid and 100 pounds of a good commercial fertilizer.

POOR-STRUCTURED SOIL
WILL BREAK APART INTO
CLUMPS.

SOIL OF GOOD STRUCTURE
WILL COME APART IN
ROUNDED, POROUS CRUMBS.

BREAK-UP HARDPAN
① REMOVE TOPSOIL.
② LOOSEN HARDPAN WITH
     SPADING FORK.
③ BREAK UP BIG CLUMPS.
(IF NEEDED)
④ WHEN SOIL IS BROKEN DOWN,
     ADD —
     HUMUS
     SAND
     LIMESTONE
     FERTILIZER
⑤ MIX THOROUGHLY.

RESULT— GOOD GARDEN LOAM.

DO NOT BURY
TOPSOIL

SUBSOIL

TOPSOIL

SUBSOIL

GRADING ENTIRELY OF SUBSOIL—
ALL TOPSOIL REMOVED.

TOPSOIL REPLACED—
A VALUABLE SAVING.

Mix with a power tiller and let the soil settle for two weeks or more. A cover crop such as vetch or winter rye may be sown. Most cover crops are plowed under in the spring but some are plowed under as soon as there is danger of their flowering. This is a much cheaper and better method than buying topsoil, having it brought in and scattered in two- or three-inch layers, as is so often done for lawns in new home areas.   To improve topsoil for a small garden area, hand spade, and add one part sand and one part humus by volume to two parts topsoil, fertilize as directed on the package, add lime if necessary.

EARTHWORMS OFTEN
INDICATE A GOOD SOIL
STRUCTURE— ABUNDANT
HERE UNDER A STRAW MULCH.

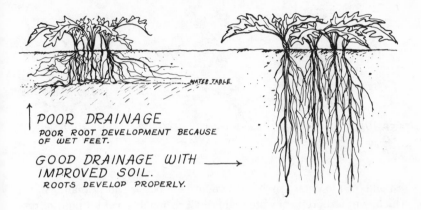

POOR DRAINAGE
POOR ROOT DEVELOPMENT BECAUSE OF WET FEET.

GOOD DRAINAGE WITH ⟶ IMPROVED SOIL.
ROOTS DEVELOP PROPERLY.

FERTILIZERS

Many soils that have good texture, having been enriched with plenty of humus, may still lack mineral plant food, which is also essential to plant growth. Commercial fertilizers supply the necessary mineral elements lacking in the soil. And mineral fertilizers supplement humus but in no way replace it.

Good all-purpose fertilizers under various trade names are on the market today. Their label numbers, 5-10-5, 5-10-10 or 6-12-6, indicate the percentages in alphabetical order of nitrogen, phosphorus and potassium (potash), the three essential elements. The numbers vary somewhat to give you a choice of minerals. A particular plant may

GREEN MANURING

TURN UNDER GROWING CROPS AT AN ANGLE – DO NOT BURY COMPLETELY.
CONVERTS BARREN SOIL TO GOOD GARDEN LOAM.

SPRINKLE DRY PLANT
FOOD AROUND BASE
OF PLANTS —

WORK IT INTO
THE SOIL —

THEN WATER
THOROUGHLY.

respond well to potash so 5-10-10 might be a better choice than 5-10-5, which contains proportionately only half as much. Avoid a high nitrogen fertilizer with annuals and perennials, as it encourages foliage at the expense of flowers. Superphosphate stimulates flower growth.

Dry Plant Food—Dry plant foods cost less than the soluble forms. Use a dry well-balanced fertilizer in quantity specified by the manufacturer; an excess may do more harm than good. Lawn foods generally cost more than the all-purpose fertilizers because a special lawn formula supplies more usable nitrogen, usually as ureaform. This is a slow-release, long-lasting fertilizer that encourages durable, healthy turf which has a better chance of surviving through summer heat and drought. It is available under several trade names, does not burn or leach away with rains, and will feed plants for 6 to 8 months from one application, so the extra cost is worthwhile.

Food in Liquid Form—Plant food in liquid form is immediately available to the plant and is valuable where the need is acute for quick results or where a booster shot is needed as in transplanting. It does not stay long in the ground however, perhaps 3 to 4 weeks, so frequent applications are required if used for regular feeding purposes. Siphoning attachments connect to a garden hose with a long tube that drops into the pail containing the liquid fertilizer. The tube sucks up the fertilizer and mixes it with the water from the hose.

Tablet Form—Tablet-form soluble plant foods are available for use with hose-end applicators, connected to the nozzle in a small jar, containing the soluble plant-food tablet.

Foliar Feeding—Use foliar feeding (a spray liquid fertilizer) over the leaves for quick results, as a supplement to normal fertilizing. Plants will sometimes show deficiencies becaues of inability to take up adequate nutrients under moisture stress. Care must be taken however not to build up excess salts in the leaves.

How To Feed Plants—When feeding perennials, bulbs and shrubs spread dry plant food around the base of the plants and work it into the soil with a hoe. Then soak the soil thoroughly and deeply to get the food down to the roots. If plants are in rows apply a side-dressing of fertilizer along each side of a row, working the material into the soil and then watering it thoroughly.

Small trees can be base-fed but larger ones need a deep feeding to get the food down in the root zone, especially during dry cycles. Use a root feeder and insert to full depth and feed at 6-foot intervals around the tree under outside drip branches. For large trees, repeat this process in a ring half the distance to the trunk. If you do not own a root feeder you can make holes by driving a length of pipe into the ground to the root area. Use sufficient water to dissolve fertilizer with each insertion.

For lawns a mechanical spreader distributes dry plant food evenly. Some prefer to split the application, using half in May or June and the other half in the fall. Limestone can be applied simultaneously, if it is needed. Fertilizer must be watered in or applied when rain is imminent. Do not apply to wet grass as burning may result.

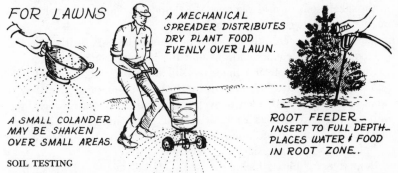

FOR LAWNS

A MECHANICAL SPREADER DISTRIBUTES DRY PLANT FOOD EVENLY OVER LAWN.

A SMALL COLANDER MAY BE SHAKEN OVER SMALL AREAS.

ROOT FEEDER — INSERT TO FULL DEPTH— PLACES WATER & FOOD IN ROOT ZONE.

SOIL TESTING

You can arrange through the local Agricultural Experiment Station to have a soil sample tested for fertility. They will interpret results and suggest what the soil needs, depending on what you want to grow—

TWO PLANTINGS OF
RADISHES MADE AT
THE SAME TIME WITH
SAME AMOUNT OF
SEED—

ONE WAS FERTILIZED   ONE WAS NOT

grass, flowers, etc. They will also run tests to find how sweet (alkaline) or sour (acid) the soil is, whether it is in need of lime. Acidity or alkalinity is a factor in plant growth. Expressed by a numerical value called pH, the scale runs from 1 to 14. The neutral point is 7, neither acid nor alkaline, a zone desirable for a good many plants. Any figure above pH 7 shows the soil to be alkaline and below acid. The entire range of soils is from around pH 3.5 in swamp peats to around pH 10 in the alkali soils of arid regions. Most kinds of plants will make reasonable growth over a considerable range.

Plants that are acid-tolerant such as blueberries, the heaths and the heathers, azaleas, rhododendrons and the mountain laurels like a low pH and succeed best on a lime-free soil. If not too alkaline soils can be made suitable for their growth by the use of generous quantities of peat, oak or pine leaf mold or well-rotted hardwood sawdust spaded into the soil and used as a mulch. Annual applications must be given or calcium from surrounding soil will permeate the treated area and the plants will become sickly.

Lime-tolerant plants include most vegetables, flower plants such as mignonette, nasturtiums, sweet peas, iris and delphinium and some of the shrubs such as *Potentilla fruticosa, Teucrium marum* and some of the acacias.

PLANT WISELY

You will have the most success with the least effort if you put the right plants in the right place. Choose plants which by nature are best suited to the soil and climate where they are to grow and then buy or grow superior transplants so they will be able to survive dry spells.

Mrs. Lambert D. LeMaire, Conservation Legislation Chairman, Federated Garden Clubs of New York State, suggests, "An important step toward solving the drought problem is stressing the use of as much native material as possible, saving the exotics that need more care and attention and usually more water for use as specimen or interest plants only."

CONSIDER HARDINESS

The first consideration in choosing plants for the South is that they be able to withstand the heat of the summer sun; in the North, winter hardiness is a prerequisite.

Cold weather is hard on most plants but if there were gradual lowering of temperature in late fall and early winter with a constant snow mulch of several inches, then a gradual thawing in the spring, many of the more tender plants would prove hardy. It is the continual weather changes as the plant goes into dormancy that most affects its winter hardiness. Those plants that go into the winter in a weakened condition may not survive, so good culture is vital to a plant's hardiness.

Winter-hardy plants have the least amount of free water in their cells, so after a dry summer deciduous kinds often show greater winter hardiness than normal since winter injury from freezing comes from ice formation within the tissues.

The hardiness of many plants is more dependent on summer rainfall than on winter cold. If they have had a steady growth rate through the growing season and there is a gradual slackening off of rainfall after late summer as September approaches, the season's growth will tend to ripen and the plant will be well prepared to go into the winter. But if there are late rains with soft, lush continued green growth, full of water, preventing ripening off of the wood, the plant may winter-kill. A temperature plunge will freeze the water and the plant cells will burst. When such is the case some winter protection is advisable. Do not promote late soft growth by feeding and overwatering after July.

Trees and shrubs that keep their leaves, as do conifers and broad-leaved evergreens, require more moisture in the soil when cold weather arrives. If the summer has been dry they should be given a few good thorough soakings in the fall before the ground freezes. A high winter temperature with warm sun and drying winds can be disastrous to evergreens, depleting the leaves of what moisture they have, and causing them to burn. The frozen, dormant roots are helpless to function and totally unable to cope with the high rate of transpiration.

EARLY BLOOMERS BEAT THE DROUGHT

Experienced growers recommend the use of the hardiest plants and the earliest varieties for the area. Early flowering bulbs, early flowering shrubs, a spring and early summer flower garden are planted in the hopes there will be sufficient winter moisture to give these plants a good start, since drought effects don't usually show up until July and August.

GROW PLANTS FROM SEED FOR DROUGHT TOLERANCE

Plants grown from seed, if they survive, are adjusted to their surroundings and can as a rule withstand the variable weather conditions. But seedlings are not necessarily like their parents. Species of plants "come true" from seed but horticultural varieties seldom do.

Advice on sowing seed in dry areas comes from Harold W. Pillsbury, Extension Horticulturist and Forester, College of Agriculture, University of Wyoming, Laramie: "One of the most effective methods of planting in dry areas is to plant at the bottom of deep (by New England standards) furrows. The covered seed should be two to three inches below the shoulders of the furrow. Of course, whatever moisture falls on the surface, it then accumulates there, but this is not as important as the fact that the drying wind action is substantially less at the base of the 'V'. In addition the shadows cast, first by one edge then the other, keeps the seeded area cooler for a longer period of time. In the more southern latitudes furrows should be run north and south while in the north furrows should be run east and west. As you can see, this gives the maximum period of shadow on the seeded area.

This procedure only works well where the soil structure will hold against the prevailing wind. In light sandy soil the furrows will fill and cover the seed too deep. Planting in back of 6 to 8 inch boards set on the sunny side of a row also keeps the immediate area cooler and more moist."

Grow or buy only the best transplants. A sickly plant will require more care and water than a robust, healthy one, will be slower getting started and many never develop into a first-class specimen.

GET PLANTS WELL ESTABLISHED

Dig a big enough hole. In general the ideal planting hole will be twice as wide and twice as deep as the roots on the new plant unless the native soil is deep and rich. Use a good rooting soil (three-fourths good garden loam, one-fourth humus and a good organic fertilizer, amount according to directions on the package). Fill the bottom half of the hole with firmed rooting soil so the roots of the plant will be at the same level they were in the nursery. Set the plant into the hole at the proper depth, look at it from all sides to be sure it is straight and with its best side forward.

Carefully remove the burlap or plastic covering so the soil and roots will not be disturbed. All roots should be spread out and down in their natural position before they are covered with the rooting soil. Use a wooden tool handle to push soil into all parts of the hole, under and around the rootball to eliminate any air pockets. When the hole is nearly filled saturate with plenty of water to settle the soil into firm contact with all the roots. If settling occurs add more soil.

WATERING NEW PLANTS

A shallow depression or saucer over the root area will guide water to the root zone; a good mulch over the area will also be helpful. New plants must have moisture at their roots at all times. Water deeply once a week. It may take two to three years before some trees or shrubs will be well enough established to survive drought without watering.

It is useless to set out a new plant unless sufficient water is available for spot watering until it takes hold and gets a good start. Plant roots anchor the plant and supply it with the necessary food and moisture

GIVE THEM A GOOD START

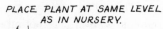

DIG HOLE BIG ENOUGH —
2X WIDE & DEEP AS ROOTS.

PLACE PLANT AT SAME LEVEL
AS IN NURSERY.

SOIL MARK

FILL BOTTOM
½ WITH GOOD
ROOTING SOIL.

CAREFULLY REMOVE ROOT
COVERING — SPREAD ROOTS
IN NATURAL POSITION.

FIRM SOIL SO THERE ARE NO
AIR POCKETS — LEAVE
SHALLOW SAUCER TO TRAP
RAIN WATER.

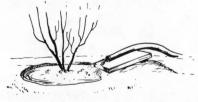

SATURATE WITH WATER.

COVER WITH A MULCH.

WATER DEEPLY, AS NECESSARY, UNTIL WELL ESTABLISHED.

which come from the soil. If the roots are allowed to dry out before the plant becomes anchored and well established and the little rootlets have recovered from being transplanted, the plant will die. Water deeply enough to wet the soil around the roots. Surface watering brings roots up in their search for moisture; these roots dry out quickly and will not withstand dry spells.

Anything you can do to make the roots grow deeper will help a plant be more resistant to dry spells. Trees and shrubs with deep root penetration will find enough moisture so no excess drying out will take place during ordinary periods of drought. As a rule, the depth of plant roots is proportionate to their top growth. There are exceptions including grass whose roots grow quite deep and bulbs whose roots are short in comparison to the top growth. Spade deeply for free root penetra-

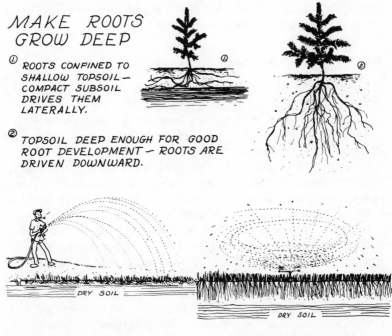

MAKE ROOTS
GROW DEEP

① ROOTS CONFINED TO
SHALLOW TOPSOIL —
COMPACT SUBSOIL
DRIVES THEM
LATERALLY.

② TOPSOIL DEEP ENOUGH FOR GOOD
ROOT DEVELOPMENT — ROOTS ARE
DRIVEN DOWNWARD.

FREQUENT LIGHT SPRINKLINGS
ONLY MOISTEN THE SURFACE.

OCCASIONAL DEEP SOAKINGS
MAKE ROOTS GROW DEEP.

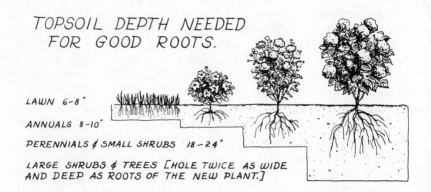

TOPSOIL DEPTH NEEDED
FOR GOOD ROOTS.

LAWN 6-8"

ANNUALS 8-10"

PERENNIALS & SMALL SHRUBS 18-24"

LARGE SHRUBS & TREES [HOLE TWICE AS WIDE
AND DEEP AS ROOTS OF THE NEW PLANT.]

tion. The plant needs ample space for roots to develop and grow and reach downward. It is amazing how far and deep roots will go in search of water with a little encouragement.

KEEP INSECT- AND DISEASE-FREE

A dry cycle will affect the insect and disease organism population. In some cases drought lessens the population, in other cases (like red-spider mite) it seems to cause an increase. Naturally healthy, fast-growing plants are less likely to be affected by this increase than those hampered in health and growth rate.

It is in the leaves that all plant foods are formed to develop the future growth of the plant. When severe insect infestations or disease infections reduce the leaf area greatly, the plant will not be able to maintain its vigor against other damage.

Effective protection is available as dusts, sprays or internal systemic materials. Trees more than 20 feet tall may require the high pressure sprayers or blowers of commercial arborists although protective pesticides may be applied at home with dusters, hose-end or pressure tank sprayers on lower growing specimens.

Insects which enter the branches, trunks or roots of plants will interfere with the necessary movement of water, chemicals and foods. They must be removed physically or promptly controlled with injected chemicals before they destroy the plant.

All pesticides must be purchased, stored and used according to the directions on the package and precautions must be taken to prevent careless handling or contamination.

A WORD FOR THE ORGANIC GARDENERS

There are plenty of organic gardeners who manage to garden successfully without using pesticides. Feeling a deep commitment to natural growth, they usually understand good cultural practices (the importance of applying composts and mulches, for example) and thus are able to keep their flora healthy without chemicals. Somehow in their

KEEP INSECT & DISEASE FREE

SPRAY BOMBS HANDY FOR SPOT INFESTATIONS.

PLUNGER TYPE HAND DUSTER IS ADEQUATE FOR SMALL AREAS.

COMPRESSED AIR SPRAYER. TO MAINTAIN PRESSURE— PLACE ON GROUND FOR PUMPING, OFTEN ENOUGH TO MAKE A FINE MISTY SPRAY.

STROLLER SPRAYER— MOVES ON WHEELS— HAS LONG BATON— TYPE SPRAYER FOR EASY REACH UNDER FOLIAGE.

JAR SPRAYER SCREWS ONTO GARDEN HOSE — WATER FLOW CONTROLLED BY TRIGGER. CONCENTRATED SOLUTION DILUTED TO RIGHT STRENGH AS DE- LIVERED.

NATURE'S SOFT CARPET OF MULCH ON THE FOREST FLOOR.

gardens there *is* a balance of nature. The birds do come to eat the (unsprayed and unpoisoned) berries and they do stay to consume their fair share of insect pests. These organic gardeners consider that the blemished leaf, the imperfect fruit, are small prices to pay for keeping their gardens uncontaminated.

MULCHING CONSERVES MOISTURE

In the forest, dead leaves, twigs, and fallen branches accumulate and cover the ground beneath the trees. Gradually, the material decays, forming a humus which contains minerals that enrich the soil, a cycle which goes on eternally. Mulching is the gardener's method of following nature. In preparing this book, we wrote hundreds of letters to garden experts and amateurs all over the country to be sure we had a cross-section of opinion from different regions about licking the drought. Every answer stressed the need and value of mulching.

Mulching conserves moisture, reduces direct evaporation, keeps plant roots moist and cool, lowers the soil temperature during the heat of summer when evaporation is high, and reduces temperature fluctuation, a stabilizing effect. Rains soak into a mulched area more readily and the effects of watering are longer lasting. A mulch helps prevent water run-off, especially on a slope.

A three-inch mulch can keep the soil underneath many degrees cooler than the surface temperature, so roots develop as they should and plants do not suffer. After the first application, a mulch eliminates the tedious work of weeding, cultivating, and hoeing, although an occasional few weeds will have to be pulled by hand.

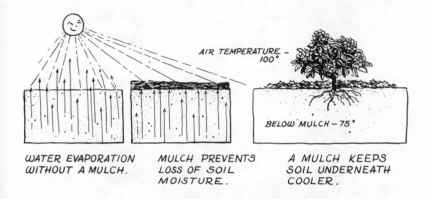

AIR TEMPERATURE – 100°

BELOW MULCH – 75°

WATER EVAPORATION WITHOUT A MULCH.

MULCH PREVENTS LOSS OF SOIL MOISTURE.

A MULCH KEEPS SOIL UNDERNEATH COOLER.

Organic mulches improve the soil texture as the decaying matter, which eventually turns into humus, works down into the topsoil and replaces the topsoil which is being constantly absorbed by the plant roots.

SUMMER MULCHING

There are no set rules for the depth of a mulch. It may vary from 2 to 6 inches. A sandy, gravelly soil needs a thicker mulch than a heavier soil. Experiment. You will want a mulch deep enough to kill weeds and prevent the soil from drying out, but not too deep to prevent air and water from reaching the topsoil. Apply a mulch well before the summer droughts and before the weeds start active growth. The time may well vary depending upon where you live. Loosen soil with a hoe removing any weeds, soak the soil well and thoroughly, then apply mulch. Some mulches last for several years, other finer ones break up more rapidly and need annual renewal.

SUMMER MULCH – REDUCES NEED FOR WATER.

STRAW – AN IDEAL MULCH
FOR VEGETABLES – ELIMINATES
NEED FOR CULTIVATING.

BUCKWHEAT HULLS MAKE A
NEAT MULCH – CUTS NEED
FOR WEEDING.

WEIGHT EDGES WITH SOIL
OR USE CROSS WIRES AND
FASTEN WITH PEGS.

SOIL

PEA
GRAVEL

PLASTIC
2 MIL

PLANTING
SLOT

BLACK POLYETHYLENE –
CAN BE SLIT FOR SINGLE PLANTS OR
LAID BETWEEN ROWS FOR LARGER
PLANTS.

COVER PLASTIC WITH
PEA GRAVEL FOR
DECORATIVE EFFECT.

JOHNNY-JUMP-UP –
A COLORFUL LIVING
MULCH.

MULCHING A PERENNIAL
BED WITH STRAWY
MANURE.

① ②

① BETTER PLANT GROWTH WITH USE
OF MULCH.
② PLANT WITHOUT MULCH – SLOWER
GROWING.

WINTER MULCHING

A winter mulch keeps the soil solidly frozen all during the winter, preventing alternate freezing and thawing, so disastrous to newly set-out plants. A mulch of snow is ideal but not always available. Apply a winter mulch after the ground freezes hard. If applied too early it may cause plants to make a soft growth during the warm days of fall, which reduces their hardiness, and may invite mice into the beds. Care must be taken to use a material that does not pack and exclude air and smother the plants.

Use a 3- to 4-inch mulch. If the mulch is light, weight it down with evergreen boughs or tree branches so the wind doesn't carry it off. Put mounds of sand or ashes over crowns of such perennials as delphinium to prevent rotting if there should be water standing.

Keep in mind that more plants are injured by removing protection too early in the spring than by winter temperatures. Loosen but do not remove winter mulch on the first warm days. Warm spells will encourage permanent growth too early. Uncover flower borders gradually. Take off mulch only after the last killing frost has passed. In the South, winter protection is used in many cases to keep plants from starting into growth too early during premature hot spells.

WINTER MULCH

PREVENTS ALTERNATE FREEZING AND THAWING — YOUNG PLANT WITH HEAVED OUT ROOTS WILL DIE OF FREEZING OR DRYING.

PROTECTION FIRST WINTER PREVENTS THIS — CUT SPRUCE OR PINE BRANCHES ARE A GOOD WINTER MULCH.

HOW TO CHOOSE A MULCH

A wide variety of mulches (organic and non-organic) is available. Many are by-products of crop residue. Select according to location, the weather, cost and soil in your area. Talk with other gardeners or your local state extension worker. Some considerations are:

Can water seep through the mulch to the soil beneath? It must never keep rain or water from entering the ground. Will it pack, cake or mat? Feeding roots need air which must seep through the mulch to the soil underneath. Will it dry out and blow away? Is it a fire hazard? If so it should not be used where careless smokers pass by. Is it too expensive? Will it look well around ornamentals? Is it suitable for the place where it is to be used? Might it harbor insects? If the garden is kept clean there is litle danger of disease spores wintering and multiplying in it. If the mulch should become infected remove and burn it. Might it attract mice or rodents? If so be on the lookout for them. Might it slow up early growth in the spring or encourage late fall growth, delaying the hardening and maturing process of the plant? Is it easily applied? How long will it last?

One kind of mulch will not do for everybody but from the many possibilities you should have no trouble finding a favorite that saves you time in watering and weeding and conserves water as well as reduces your water bill.

Asphalt—Can be purchased from road paving contractors and is used to hold soil in new construction such as roadbanks and waterways. A very light application by spraying will form a thin film directly on the soil or on top of a straw mulch, holding soil in place on steep banks until grass or a ground cover becomes established. In about a year the asphalt film completely disintegrates. For further information write the Asphalt Institute, 1270 Avenue of the Americas, New York City, New York.

Bark—Lumber companies, grinding up the bark of redwood, pine, yellow birch and other trees, have prepared for the market bark mulches of various kinds—fine (⅛ to ¼ inch), medium (¼ to ½ inch), and coarse (½ to 1 inch).

An organic ground bark mulch from soft wood trees is composed of fine aged material and some medium to large pieces. Apply at a rate of 2 to 3 inches minimum. Lets water through but holds moisture in the soil.

Another garden bark comes from western Douglas fir, is clean and in ¼ to 1 inch particles. It contains no fertile fines. There are other bark mulches, some in chunks the size of walnuts.

Tan Bark comes from white oak bark (used in leather processing) and is in long shreds and used for walks, play areas and plantings to conserve moisture. A 55 pound bag covers 40 square feet, 1 inch deep.

Burlap—A good temporary mulch to aid seed germination; often used to keep grass seed planted on an embankment from washing away during rains.

Buckwheat Hulls—At garden supply stores. Of a fine texture, good color and long life they make an attractive, satisfactory mulch for ornamental plantings. A one-inch summer mulch is good and may be retained through the winter. Do not use around small succulents that grow flat on the ground as the hulls absorb heat on a hot summer day and might burn the leaves.

Cocoa-Bean Hulls—Available wherever cocoa-beans are roasted at chocolate or candy manufacturing companies. Light and easily handled and of good color but, because they may pack and during high humidity may mold, mix them with sawdust 2 to 1. A mulch of not over 2 to 3 inches is advisable to retain soil moisture and control weeds.

Coffee Grounds—So fine that they will cake; never make an application more than 1 inch deep.

Corncobs (ground)—Available and cheap in the corn-growing and rural areas of the Midwest. They make a good mulch but are not very attractive for ornamental plantings. Apply to a depth of 2 to 3 inches. Good for roses, use 2 pounds per plant.

Cornstalks—Can be had from cornfields and harvested gardens but since they are very coarse they are most useful for holding down other mulches. Make certain they do not harbor borers or any other pests before using.

Cranberry Vines or Clippings—On Cape Cod and in parts of Wisconsin where cranberry vines are plentiful they are used as a winter mulch held in place by evergreen boughs. Wiry and light, they never pack.

Crushed Stone or Gravel—Most lumberyards or building contractors carry a supply. Of limited value but some find stone or gravel a useful mulch for alpine plants.

Evergreen Boughs—Where plentiful, evergreen boughs are excellent in winter. They do not mat down so provide adequate aeration.

Grass or Lawn Clippings—If used too green and too deep may heat up and form a dense mat. They are perhaps better on the compost heap. Unless so long that they smother the grass, clippings may be left on the lawn.

Hay—Widely available from farms, feed stores or cut from one's own property. Spread around young trees and shrubs. Rain-spoiled hay unsuitable as cattle feed can be bought cheaply. Near the coast, marsh grass or hay (salt hay) is used successfully as a winter mulch. Light, yet dense, it is a favorite with commercial pansy growers. Rake off in the spring and store for future use or burn it.

Hops (spent)—Available near breweries for the hauling. The odor may be objectionable but the beery smell disappears after a few weeks. Of a very light color and fire-resistant, which is a great advantage. Never apply this mulch wet, on a real hot day of 90° or above, as the material heats noticeably. Keep it about 12 inches away from the basal stems of plants. A 4- to 6-inch mulch will last a couple of years before disintegrating appreciably.

Leaf mold—Made by composting leaves raked in the fall. Sometimes available from the woods. Excellent for the wildflower garden.

Leaves—Nature's own mulch, a good source of humus and free to gardeners because they are so readily available wherever deciduous trees grow. Dried leaves are combustible, may blow away, and the larger kinds may be unsightly, so many gardeners prefer to grind, chop, or compost them first.

Do not use a deep mulch of soft leaves such as poplar, willow and maple as they tend to pack. A few inches of oak or beech leaves are ideal because they do not pack so tightly. They are used mostly around shrubs and small trees where any smothering effect is not harmful. Leaves can be piled to a depth of 8 to 10 inches. Twelve months later they will be quite well rotted. No weeds emerge except bindweed. With Norway maple hundreds of seedlings may push up. Elm and maple leaves may have a slightly alkaline reaction.

Living Mulches—An underplanting of ground-hugging plants such as thyme, myrtle, pachysandra, violets, Johnny-jump-ups, or similar suitable ground covers will form an attractive, dense, living, green mulch; it will reduce evaporation of moisture from the surface soil.

Manure (strawy)—Obtainable from farms or stables, will provide some nutrients but if used too fresh may burn the plants.

Mushroom Compost (spent)—In commercial mushroom-growing areas in Pennsylvania, growers sell this as a mulch. It has a slight nutrient value and is dark in color.

Paper Mulch—Made up in rolls of various widths, paper mulch is efficient for large-scale planting in rows and was originally used on Hawaiian pineapple fields. It is also sold in squares provided with a slit in the center for slipping over individual plants. Now largely replaced by plastic sheeting.

Paper Pulp—This is made at home from newspapers and sawdust but a special mixer is needed to prepare it. F. W. Schumacher of Sandwich, Massachusetts uses all wastepaper products from the house and kitchen, in deep holes he digs for trees and shrubs. He adds a layer of paper, then a layer of soil, until the bottom portion of the hole is filled. The paper disintegrates adding humus to the soil. It could of course be added to the compost pile and be used as compost.

Peanut Hulls—Used in southeastern parts of the country. They are lightweight and easily handled, a good mulch but not too attractive.

Peat Moss—Available in most garden supply stores. Fine textured and of good color but has a tendency to dry out and then become impervious to water, so water runs off it to other areas. If it is moist it absorbs much of the water itself. Peat is used for acid-soil plants. It decomposes slowly and adds some nutrients.

Pine Needles—Plentiful in areas where conifers grow and easily lifted and applied as a mulch with rake and fork. Use a depth of 3 to 4 inches. Attracive and useful, they are excellent for acid-loving plants. White pine has soft flexible needles which make a very fine mulch. Red pine needles are coarser and may not deteriorate for 3 or 4 years. No weeds will grow in them, yet rain and air will filter through to the soil.

Plastic Sheeting—Some people complain that it blows no matter what you do and splits too easily, others recommend it highly. In California and Texas, considerable research has been done with plastics to reduce evaporation during hot dry periods. The plastic is cut in strips to fit between the rows of plants or around single plants, then the edges must be held down to keep the wind from getting under.

Black polyethylene has all the properties of clear plastic except that it excludes light so prevents weeds from growing. Since it does not let water into the soil, after it is placed on the ground, punch holes at 6-inch intervals with an ice pick or make a few knife cuts in depressions to allow rain water to drain through into the soil. The plastic strips can be lifted in the fall and stored for reuse.

H. Granville Smith, Field Biologist, U. S. Department of Agriculture, Soil Conservation Service, Columbus, Ohio, writes "Recently I visited the Hawaiian Islands . . . the Dole Pineapple Company conserved moisture while raising the pineapple crop, since there are areas in the Hawaiian Islands where there is as little as 10 inches of rainfall per year. There are also areas where there is an exceptional amount of rainfall.

"Water is conserved by placing a 36-inch plastic strip on the ground between every other row. The young pineapple plants are spaced along the edge of these plastic strips. This allows the space between two rows to be open so that it can receive and absorb rainwater. The space between the alternate row is covered with plastic so as to conserve moisture by preventing heavy evaporation."

Mrs. Robert B. Henn, a Cornell graduate in floriculture back in the days when we taught there, and now Librarian and Educational Consultant at the Garden Center of Greater Cleveland in Ohio, comments that in the Fine Arts Gardens at the Museum of Art mulch is being used more and more each year in July and August, when Cleveland is so dry and hot. "They prepare the bed, cover it with black plastic, plant through holes they make in the plastic, make more holes for rain water to flow through to the soil, and then put a good-looking mulch over the plastic. This method. . . keeps the weeds from growing . . . keeps the earth moist and the water coming up from underneath." She adds that mulching is practiced at Kingwood Center in Mansfield, Ohio, to cut down on manpower usually needed for weeding and also at the Park of Roses of the American Rose Society, Columbus, Ohio where chopped-up corncobs are used. She also comments: "Some of my roses are mulched and some are not, a matter of time. . . . The ones that are mulched are in much better growth condition and the soil around them is soft and the soil is aerated by the worms and other insect cultivators."

Rose Mulch (Terralite)—Finger-tip-size pieces of exploded mica or vermiculite. It does not rot, holds moisture, yet allows drainage through it.

Sand—F. W. Schumacher, Sandwich, Mass., who sells seeds for the nurseyman and forester, uses a mulch of sand over his clay loam. The rains seep quickly through, leaving no time for the water to run off or evaporate before entering the topsoil.

Sawdust—Use hardwood or softwood, fresh or rotted, from a nearby sawmill, lumberyard or other woodworking operation. It is cheap. Apply a generous application of a complete fertilizer to the soil first, otherwise the sawdust might result in a nitrogen deficiency causing yellow foliage and stunted growth. Use a 2- to 3-inch application. After several years it will break down and become humus; then apply more fertilizer and sawdust. Some gardeners feel it takes too long to decay and that a gusty wind whisks the top dry sawdust away. Good for bulbs which push through it easily in the spring. Sawdust protects low-growing flowers from splattering mud during hard rains. The sawdust that splashes falls off readily as the flowers dry. An effective summer mulch for many plants.

Seaweed (kelp, etc.)—Practical near the shore, and adds mineral elements to the soil but is not too attractive.

Stones, Pebbles, Granite—Small flat stones, stone chips and clean white pebbles may be used around newly planted trees and shrubs. Fine-grained granite produced in Stone Mountain, Georgia, is frequently used there.

Conklinite is the trade name for lime or marble pebbles that come in small, medium and large pieces. It gives a formalized appearance when used as mulch, stops splashing or rolling onto buildings and is used for roofs, garden paths, driveways, shrub borders along buildings and for tree trenches. Use 8 pounds a square foot, 1 inch deep.

Straw—May be obtained at feed stores or from farms. It is coarser and more durable than most kinds of hay; wheat straw is commonly used as a mulch in our wheat-growing states.

Sugar Cane—Ground cane, where cheaply obtainable, may be used as a mulch; use about 2 inches thick. Like all organic mulches it will decompose into humus.

Tobacco Stems (chopped)— Available in tobacco growing areas. They are coarse and thought by some to discourage insect attacks.

Wood Chips and *Wood Shavings*—Chips and shavings are available from tree companies. Use them two to three inches deep. They will last two years or longer. As with sawdust, fertilize first but because they are coarser than sawdust they are less apt to cause any nitrogen deficiency. Chips are preferable to shavings since they are coarser, less flammable, less subject to blow away in high winds and less apt to pack. Avoid elm wood if there is any danger of Dutch elm disease. Chips can be made from prunings if a chipper is available, a useful method of disposing of waste twigs and branches.

OTHER PRACTICES

ELIMINATE SUPERFLUOUS GROWTH

When setting out new plants, prune or cut away any unnecessary vegetative growth to stop early flowering or fruiting, as commercial growers do when water is at a premium. Eliminate weeds and all other competitive plants. Apply selective herbicides in the lawn to destroy weeds without killing the grass. You can control most weeds in the flower borders with a mulch.

PROTECT PLANTS FROM HOT SUN AND STRONG WINDS

Light or partial shading from the afternon sun is a practice used by some florists and nurserymen for certain crops that can be partially shaded. This shading reduces the amount of water used and given off by the plants. Different weaves of cloth and overhead protection made of lathing are shading materials sometimes used.

If the plants in question are to be part of a garden for landscape purpose then the garden itself may be located in an area where the plants will be partially shaded by natural growing trees during some of the day.

High winds, especially dry ones with high temperatures, take moisture both from the plants and the soil and can be quite devastating. Strong winds are especially harmful to large-foliaged plants. Screens or windbreaks constructed or planted on the windward side will protect the garden area and prove useful. A row of trees or shrubs in an exposed situation will reduce wind velocity, prevent the drifting of snow and even the blowing of unplanted soil; or design and place

ELIMINATE UNNECESSARY VEGETATIVE GROWTH

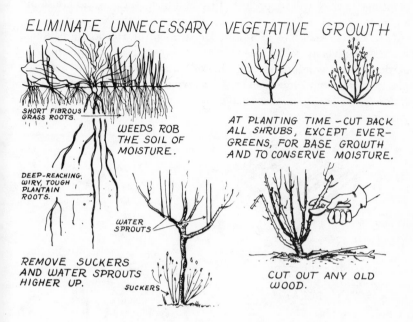

SHORT FIBROUS GRASS ROOTS.

WEEDS ROB THE SOIL OF MOISTURE.

AT PLANTING TIME – CUT BACK ALL SHRUBS, EXCEPT EVER-GREENS, FOR BASE GROWTH AND TO CONSERVE MOISTURE.

DEEP-REACHING, WIRY, TOUGH PLANTAIN ROOTS.

WATER SPROUTS

REMOVE SUCKERS AND WATER SPROUTS HIGHER UP.

SUCKERS

CUT OUT ANY OLD WOOD.

A FENCE USED AS PROTECTION.

PLANT A SCREEN OF TREES OR SHRUBS TO PROTECT FROM THE WIND.

plantings so they will be protected by buildings, such as the house or a garage.

J. K. Greig, Associate Professor, Department of Horticulture, Kansas State Universiy writes "Some of the aids to conserving moisture in gardening are windbreaks and shelter-belts which are used around plantings; also snow fences to break the wind, cut down on the transpiration rate. These practices have been used historically by Kansas gardeners."

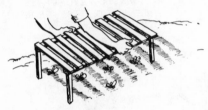

A PRACTICAL MOVABLE LATH SHADE FOR SMALL PLANTS IN A SMALL AREA.

A WOODEN FRAME FOR TALLER PLANTS - HINGED LEGS FOR EASY FOLDING & STORING - CAN BE COVERED WITH CHEESECLOTH OR BURLAP.

TRANSPIRATION SUPPRESSANT SPRAYS

From their work at the University of Delaware, Department of Horticulture, D. J. Fieldhouse and J. C. Ryder write "Water loss from all plants is extravagant and serves no real purpose beyond some cooling of the leaves and providing a moist surface for absorption of carbon dioxide. This water loss could be reduced to a small fraction of the total without harming the plants. This would reduce the need for irrigation and plant growth would not be as likely to be limited by a water stress.

"Anti-transpirants have been tested and sold for many years. The fact that a very small amount is actually used testifies to the rather poor results and/or high costs. . . . This does not mean that there cannot be a good anti-transpirant sold at a reasonable price."

IDEA TO CUT WATER LOSS

Frederic Heutte, retired Director of the Norfolk (Va.) Botanical Gardens, comments: "I am much involved at the present working out a system which I believe will save about 50 percent water, besides reducing temperatures. I call it a 'Mist Irrigation System.' My contention is that we propagate by mist and we foliar-feed, so why not go a step further and irrigate by mist? If you will read the article entitled 'Mist, Fog and Dew' by Dr. Went in the 1955 U. S. Department of Agriculture Yearbook entitled *Water* you will see what I mean."

The desire and need for conserving water has set many interested gardeners and manufacturers busy thinking and working along conservation lines.

WETTING AGENTS

Now on the market are soil-wetting agents such as Aqua-Grow and Turf-Wetter. Initially developed for a golf course connected with Yale University, these agents are used to insure the immediate penetration of water to a greater depth, thereby reducing somewhat the water needs. It is now advocated for use by the home gardener on tight soils or on banks with wasteful run-offs, but it is fairly expensive and hence its major application is on golf courses and in irrigation water, to reduce surface tension and thereby increase the speed of penetration.

USING WATER EFFECTIVELY

Whether you live in a drought area where water is restricted or in a section where it is plentiful, water conservation should be your concern, not only for good citizenship but for personal rewards. With proper watering, you not only save time and money, but also improve soil conditions, decrease the amount of fertilizer needed, lessen disease, insect and weed problems, and improve the lawn and garden.

REDUCE WATER WASTE

There is no line of demarcation between the intelligent use or conservation of water and good gardening. Conserve it in the following ways.

TO CONSERVE MOISTURE

PLANT ANNUALS & SMALL
PERENNIALS IN CONTAINERS –
WRAP IN PLASTIC & SINK IN
GROUND – DIRECT WATER TO-
WARD POT – MULCH.

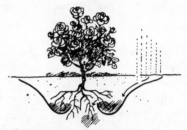

DEVELOP SUB-TERRANEAN CATCH
BASIN FOR SOLITARY PLANTS TO
LEAD WATER TO THE ROOTS.

1. Repair leaky valves and watering equipment that leaks or is wasteful in any way.

2. Avoid surface runoff that often flows into gutters and storm drains.

3. Avoid frequent, shallow watering. A relatively large fraction of this water is lost by evaporation. Every watering is accompanied by some loss so the fewer waterings the less the loss. Allow a drying-out period between good deep waterings for deep root growth, giving a slow drenching every 2, 3 or 4 weeks depending upon the range of temperature and rainfall.

4. Apply water only when it is actually needed. Too much water will cause water-logging, forcing air out of the soil that is vitally needed by plant roots to survive. Also wet soil compacts easily when heavy objects such as power lawn mowers are rolled over it. Thorough waterings develop strong, deeply-rooted plant systems that can go for long periods without moisture until soil is almost dry.

5. Do not apply water faster than the soil can take it up.

6. Water uniformly without missing sections.

7. Water when the air is still.

8. Generally the best time of day to water is in the early morning when humidity is higher and temperatures are usually lower. Appreci-

able water losses occur when evaporating conditions are severe. With early watering, water has time to soak into the ground before the heat of the day. Avoid watering late in the evening as excessive moisture remaining on leaves and grass overnight tends to promote disease.

9. Most home gardeners use more water on their lawn than anywhere else. If the water supply is inadequate, to save a valuable tree or shrub, let the grass go. If deep-rooted, the turf can be allowed to wilt and turn almost brown without much danger. You will be amazed at the way it comes back and greens up with the first rains.

10. Improve the soil, mulch, make roots grow deeply and select those plants that have proven most drought resistant.

WHEN TO WATER

Take a sampling of soil to know exactly how moist or dry it actually is, to a depth where the plant roots are. Use a sampling tool such as a sharp pointed probe or soil auger to reliably test soil moisture. By turning the handle and pressing down on the auger it will bore into the ground. The soil it passes through collects in the grooves so when the auger is lifted you have a good sampling of the soil, layer by layer, as deep as you probe. It will show you how well the water is penetrating and when you have watered deeply enough.

Then use the squeeze test. A soil that is wet enough will form a tight ball when squeezed in the hand while one that is dry will not hold together. Best results are obtained when extremes of either wet or dry soil are avoided. The root zone should never become either very dry or excessively wet at any time.

The soil auger also makes good holes for conducting water and plant food to deep rooted plants.

After plants shed their leaves in the autumn and become dormant they use practically no water and moisture begins to collect. Usually there is enough to carry plants during the early spring months. Allowing them to be on their own and forage for this moisture develops a bigger, stronger and deeper root system and better prepares them to find water during the drier hot summer months.

In April and May comparatively little water is used because of cooler temperatures, but consumption soars during the high temperatures of July and August.

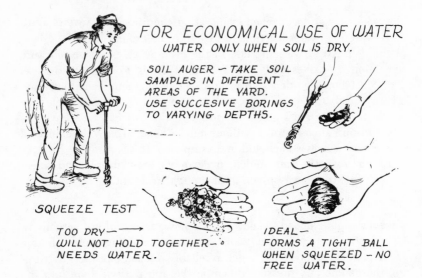

FOR ECONOMICAL USE OF WATER
WATER ONLY WHEN SOIL IS DRY.

SOIL AUGER — TAKE SOIL
SAMPLES IN DIFFERENT
AREAS OF THE YARD.
USE SUCCESIVE BORINGS
TO VARYING DEPTHS.

SQUEEZE TEST

TOO DRY —
WILL NOT HOLD TOGETHER —
NEEDS WATER.

IDEAL —
FORMS A TIGHT BALL
WHEN SQUEEZED — NO
FREE WATER.

HOW OFTEN AND HOW MUCH TO WATER

The length of intervals between watering will depend on the timeliness of the rain and how well the plants draw moisture from the reservoirs in the soil. In addition the penetration and absorption of water is determined to a large degree by the type soil. A fine, slow spray over a longer period of time with less frequent waterings is advisable for clay soils. The rate of penetration for sandy soils is high, a coarser spray may be used and less time is necessary but sand dries out quickly requiring more frequent waterings. For loam a procedure half way between the two above recommendations works well.

Turn on the water and let the sprinkler or soil soaker run for half an hour. Then check with a hand trowel or soil probe to see how deep the water has penetrated. This will give you an idea of the time it takes to wet the soil to root depth.

The amount of water being applied to a lawn can be measured quite simply with a few 1 lb. coffee cans or other wide-mouthed straight-sided container. Mark the inside off in inches and set several containers at intervals out from the sprinkler. Observe the measurements inside the cans to determine how long the sprinkler must operate to produce any set amount of water. Then check the soil penetration to set up a watering schedule tailored to your particular soil. Except during periods of extended drought, the soil below 12 to 18 inches usually holds sufficient moisture so it can be disregarded in figuring your needs.

The following chart will serve as a guidepost based on average conditions.

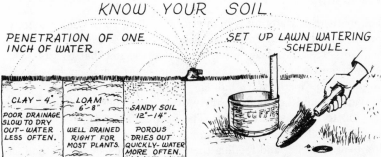

KNOW YOUR SOIL.

PENETRATION OF ONE INCH OF WATER.

SET UP LAWN WATERING SCHEDULE.

CLAY - 4"
POOR DRAINAGE SLOW TO DRY OUT - WATER LESS OFTEN.

LOAM 6-8"
WELL DRAINED RIGHT FOR MOST PLANTS.

SANDY SOIL 12"-14"
POROUS DRIES OUT QUICKLY - WATER MORE OFTEN.

MEASURE WATER THAT FALLS IN CAN AFTER ONE HOUR - PROBE SOIL TO FIND DEPTH OF WATER PENETRATION.

Type Soil	Average Rate of Absorption	Water Needed To Penetrate 1 foot	Under Average Summer Conditions, Water
Light Sandy	1½"- 2" per hr.	¾" water	every 5 days
Average Loam	½"-¾" per hr.	1½" water	every 10 days
Heavy Clay	¼"-½" per hr.	2½" water	every 17-18 days

Some plants are naturally more drought-resistant than others. In addition the demands for water of any plant depend upon its size, the weather conditions and its exposure. The amount needed will vary from place to place and day to day according to the amount of sunlight, temperature, wind, humidity, shade and nearness to competitive plants. Once transplants become established it is not the stage of growth so much as these factors that determine their water needs.

HOW TO WATER

The method of watering is highly important in conserving water and saving on water bills. To be beneficial, water must reach the root area of plants. It is how deep water soaks into the soil that counts, to get the water to where the roots are. By spacing several outdoor faucets around the property you'll lighten your watering chore.

Water should be applied slowly over a long period of time to wet the soil to an adequate depth. The deeper the roots, the larger the supply of soil moisture and nutrients they can draw on and the less frequent watering and feeding they will need. Select the method that does the best job for you. Hand watering, furrow irrigation, the sprinkler and porous or perforated hose soakers are all means by which your garden may be watered.

Hand Watering—Old-time gardeners understood the "know-how" but this method is just too time-consuming for our modern age. Failure to apply a sufficient depth of water and the lack of uniform distribution may result from improper hand watering.

For spot-soaking, water by hand or fasten a water breaker at the end of the hose. Tie a piece of bagging or other cloth such as an old glove or sock over the hose outlet making a bag for the water to run through. These devices break up the water flow and keep it from splashing on the leaves and washing away soil.

Furrow Irrigation—The old, still satisfactory method of furrow or border irrigation is practical when contours are appropriate and the soil is not sandy. Soil must hold water well without excessive amounts soaking in toward the end where the water is delivered. If the slope is satisfactory, furrow application causes less packing and crusting of the soil. If water penetration is slow, water may be applied in the furrows precisely where it is needed without waste or washing away of the soil. Shallow furrows carry water close to the base of the plants.

SHALLOW-FURROW IRRIGATION

LETS WATER FLOW
ALONG SIDE OF
PLANT ROW.

Sprinklers—The most popular method of watering with homeowners is the sprinkler but the experienced gardener relies on both sprinkler and soil soaker.

Efficient sprinklers distribute large quantities of water so effectively that all the water which reaches the ground has time to soak in without puddling or running off onto drives and walks. Although water should be applied slowly enough to penetrate the soil, many of the fine- or mist-spray sprinklers do not supply water rapidly enough to penetrate the soil and much is lost in evaporation.

The type or style of applicator, whether revolving, oscillating, pulsating or of a fixed-pattern, makes little difference. Several adjust to square and rectangular shapes, handy for getting into corners and efficient on lawns bordered with walls or drives. Those with size droplets that deliver the right amount of water at the right speed and in the right place are best for you. Visit garden centers and talk with knowledgeable gardeners to find out what types are most efficient and effective.

Will the applicator apply water uniformly over the entire lawn? Some tend to have a conical pattern of distribution, the greater amount of water falling near the head and tapering off to a mere trace at the edge of the area to be covered so the water is not uniformly spread over the entire wetted area.

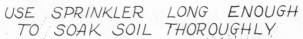

USE SPRINKLER LONG ENOUGH TO SOAK SOIL THOROUGHLY

SIMPLE
PERFORATED
RING TYPE.

WHIRLING
TYPE

AUTOMATIC
OSCILLATING
WATER-FAN TYPE

FAN-SPRAY TYPE-
SPIKE PLUNGED
IN GROUND.

CONTOUR SPRINKLER-
ADJUST RING OF WHEELS
TO THE SHAPE OF YOUR
LAWN - SPIKE SOCKET FOR
SAME PLACEMENT.

ROOT-IRRIGATOR FOR LARGE TREES
& SHRUBS· INSERT TO FULL DEPTH
½ DISTANCE FROM OUTSIDE DRIP
BRANCHES INWARD TOWARD
TRUNK AT 6 FT. INTERVALS AROUND
THE TREE.

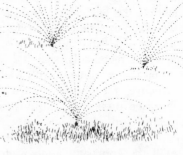

OVERHEAD SPRINKLER SYSTEM
USEFUL FOR VEGETABLE GARDEN.

UNDERGROUND SPRINKLERS
WITH ONE CONTROL FAUCET
ARE TIMESAVERS.

Do not leave sprinklers untended for long periods as surplus water may be wasted carrying away plant nutrients at the same time. Sprinklers must be moved when the soil in a given location is sufficiently moist, to prevent waste and harmful results.

Soil Soakers—Soil soakers make efficient use of water and are a practical method of applying water on small flower and vegetable gardens and on lawn areas that are smaller than the spray pattern of your sprinkler. They are perfect for deep watering of shrub borders and ideal for irrigating steep banks.

Laid directly on the ground, water oozes from the porous or perforated soaker going deep to the roots of the plantings without runoff or harmful puddling and without wetting the foliage, a decided advantage with plants subject to foliage diseases. Little if any water is lost through evaporation, an important consideration when water is scarce or restricted in time of drought or in areas where water meter rates are high.

SOIL SOAKER FOR SHORT ROWS or IRREGULAR BEDS

"DEW-HOSE" TYPE
① CUT "DEW-HOSE" WITH SCISSORS.

② JOIN WITH TEES OR ELBOWS WITH AID OF PLASTIC TAPE.

③ PLACE PRESSURE REGULATOR DISC IN HOSE COUPLING.

④ PLACE UNDER MULCH OR ON SURFACE— WATER OOZES FROM EDGE SEWN WITH NYLON THREAD.

MULCH

There are several types of soakers on the market. Some are for spot watering, excellent when you wish to water a single shrub or tree. Others will cover quite large areas. As with sprinklers, they must be moved to another location as soon as the soil becomes sufficiently moist. Soaker-sprinkler combinations now on the market are useful.

WATERING A SLOPE

On a bank or slope, terracing prevents runoff and gives the soil a chance to absorb all possible moisture. It holds water on the land long enough to permit most to soak into the soil. When applying water on a grade do so slowly to avoid runoff. Turn down the pressure and adjust the sprinkler for a finer spray and then if necessary alternately turn the water on and off, for intervals, until the soil is watered the necessary depth. A soil soaker is excellent for irrigating sloping land. A bank or abrupt slope may be necessary to take care of differences in grade but properly handled it can become an asset.

WATERING THE FLOWER BORDER AND SHRUBS

Most annuals and perennials appreciate extra water when they are in bud and starting into bloom, and the long canvas soil soaker is excellent for watering the flower-border. It may be used as one long strip or coiled around group plantings. It is ideal for watering flowers subject to mildew because it does not wet the foliage. With a soaker you are less likely to have runoff or soil washing away and there is less evaporation while watering. Generally, annual roots go only about 8 inches deep, perennials 12 to 18 inches.

Shrubs may be watered in the same manner. The roots of small shrubs stretch down 18 to 24 inches, those of larger shrubs go deeper. For large shrubs, during dry cycles, use the water-spike or irrigator advised for established trees.

The soaker-sprinkle combination may be used right side up for gentle sprinkling or turned upside down to make a satisfactory soaker. The water oozes into the soil along the full length of the porous hose.

WATERING VEGETABLES AND BERRIES

Nearly all vegetables require relatively large amounts of water for their profitable production. Most of them have only shallow or medium depth roots; consequently the supply of soil moisture available to their roots is limited and the shallow roots dry out quickly during droughts. They must be supplied with ample water during the growing season for satisfactory results. Berries also need adequate moisture to develop with flavor and have the taste that makes them worth growing.

Mrs. Lambert D. LeMaire of Scotia, New York, comments: "Watering done during dry spells seems to go for the vegetables when they are raised. One frequently sees a few grown in the regular flower garden . . . the cherry and plum tomatoes are being used for flower arranging and it is logical to grow them in with the flowers. The cherry tomato plants sometimes winter over and will frequently seed themselves for me."

WATERING TREES

Young transplants need frequent watering until they become well established, about every 3 to 4 weeks during the growing season for the first 2 or 3 years.

Usually established trees take care of themselves. The roots of trees and large shrubs go deep and as the soil below 12 inches or so is generally moist, only in lengthy periods of drought will they need watering. Then they need plenty of water at their roots where it counts. Deep rooted, well-established trees and shrubs can go longer without supplemental water because they draw on a much larger and deeper soil area for their supply.

Root spikes, root feeders and irrigators on the market today provide feeding and watering. A tree's feeder roots are located in an area that extends from the outside drip branches half the distance inward to the trunk. In this area, insert the water spike or irrigator to full depth, directly into the root zone, at 6 foot intervals around the tree. For large trees, repeat this process in a ring half again the distance to the trunk.

WATERING LAWNS

An inch of water a week will be sufficient to keep lawns green and attractive. It is time to water when you can see footprints on the lawn or when the surface soil appears dry.

To keep lawn watering to a minimum sow seed on a well-prepared garden loam, choose a grass adapted to your area, and keep the lawn well fed and free from weeds. All this encourages deep healthy roots and a lawn is as good as its roots. Such a lawn will survive summer dryness and heat.

New lawns need constant care until turf is heavy. Warm dry windy days in spring can kill off new tender grass unless a light misty spray is applied daily. For this use a mist nozzle.

Maintain a mowing height of at least two inches during the hot months of July and August. Non-fed lawns, cut short with shallow roots, dry out quickly and soon suffer from lack of moisture and encourage the spread of crabgrass. The taller cut, two-inch grass acts as a mulch and shade to conserve the soil water.

Frequent light sprinklings cause harm and are better omitted. It cannot be over-emphasized that a lawn, like other plantings, requires a good deep soaking. Anything that causes roots to grow deeper so they can draw on water reserves during dry periods is helpful.

Lawns seem to be the sites that cause most concern among homeowners. Summer heat and drought will cause bluegrass to go partly dormant and turn brown. This should not cause alarm because cooler weather and seasonable moisture will stimulate new green growth. Don't worry about the brownness of the grass at this time. If water is scarce, instead of sprinkling the lawn, use the water on plants that will not survive without it.

UNDERGROUND IRRIGATION

You can install an underground irrigation system equipped with risers containing pop-up sprinkler heads, spaced to distribute water without wasteful overlap. A more recent innovation involves underground low-pressure or micro-watering that keeps the soil moist from below. This means little or no water loss through evaporation.

Such systems work well where soil is not filled with rock, land is level and the landscape design is open—without large trees that fill the soil with their roots or flower and shrub beds scattered over the lawn. You can understand that a system which makes watering a lawn as easy as turning on a faucet will be expensive. Properly designed and installed it certainly is convenient and should be efficient. If this is your choice see that you have good workmanship because hunting for leaks can prove expensive. So do not necessarily sign a contract with the lowest bidder. Investigate before investing.

Several do-it-yourself installations make it possible for homeowners to put in an underground system. Most use flexible plastic polyethylene pipe buried in narrow trenches in the lawn. Various methods are used to join the pipe, connectors and spray heads such as stainless steel clamps and threaded or cemented joints.

Many automatic controls may be added. Automatic timers can be installed to turn the water on and off. A zone-hopping system controls the watering of each zone in sequence, then shuts off until the next watering. The latest in robot controls includes moisture sensers which trigger the sprinkling system when the water content of the soil becomes low. To double check water needs, some systems use two such sensers, one near the surface, the other buried with the root system.

Clifford W. Collier Jr., State Extension Specialist, Landscape Architecture, West Virginia University, Morgantown, writes "There is one water conservation practice which has not been investigated but is quite feasible. That is applying water underground through a perforated pipe or clay tiles, laid 12 to 18 inches underground. This would certainly minimize water lost through evaporation and the water would be placed within the root zone of the plants. We often use drain tile placed vertically in the soil around newly planted trees. I have used this method (using one- and two-pound cans when planting banks). This minimizes the loss of water through run-off and places the water in the root zone of the plants.

"There are those avid gardeners to whom expense means nothing and who are willing to go to any extremes to have a beautiful garden. These gardeners may wish to construct a reservoir in the vicinity from which they may pump water. A couple here in Morgantown is doing this very thing. I know of others who have drilled their own well for this purpose. Another approach is to construct a small filtering system in which laundry water may be cleaned and used in the garden."

WATERING DEVICES AND EQUIPMENT

Watering gadgets and equipment that aid in conserving water and make the chore easier should be studied and considered if they fit your needs. Visit a well-equipped garden center to see what is available. Generally you can find a helpful salesman who can answer your questions and show you the various choices obtainable for the problem you have.

An underground water pipe extension with two or three handy outlets for hose connections may be one of your best investments, saving pulling the hose around corners and across flower beds. Survey your grounds and decide whether the time and labor you will save is worth the investment.

Hose—A good garden hose is one of the most essential of garden tools. Basically there are three kinds—reinforced rubber, reinforced vinyl and non-reinforced vinyl. Reinforced rubber is the most durable of the three. Reinforced vinyl has the advantage of being light in weight. Non-reinforced vinyl is inexpensive and considerably less durable.

The inside diameter of a garden hose may vary from three-eighths of an inch to 1". The larger its inside diameter the faster the water goes through. If you keep all hose on the property of the same size then there is no trouble with hose menders and fittings.

Hose may be purchased in 25-, 50-, 75-, 100-foot (less common) and 250-foot lengths. For the small home 25-foot lengths are satisfactory; elsewhere 50-foot sections are long enough. All hoses come with standard connections for attaching to taps and various kinds of nozzles, sprinklers, etc.

FOR HOSE SPOT WATERING

PRESSURE BREAKER NOZZLE WILL BREAK FORCE OF FLOW.

SECURE NOZZLE IN NOTCHED BLOCK ON A BRICK WITH ½" SECTION OF OLD INNER TUBE.

Take care of a good hose and do not leave it out in the hot sun unnecessarily. If it is so left on a hot summer day leave it full of water. Avoid kinks and when they do occur untwist them patiently, with no jerking and pulling.

Quick Coupling—The gardener who seeks efficiency and labor-saving methods will want some of the handy accessory connections that simplify the attachment of hose to faucet. There are couplings that snap together quickly and easily and with a single twist or the flip of a lever make a tight, leakproof fit. Made of metal or plastic, with male and female parts, any coupling should be carefully attached so as to be leakproof and not waste water.

Shutoff Valve—A shutoff valve near the point of operation to regulate and shut off the flow of water can save time and needless steps making it unnecessary to walk back to the faucet where the hose is attached to stop the flow of water.

Twin Or Siamese Connection—This is used to convert a single faucet to a double unit so two hoses can branch out from a single faucet, yet function as two independent units as there is an independent shutoff for each arm.

Water Bubbler—Garden club members have written us enthusiastically about the water bubbler. A past generation "put the hose on a flat board to break the flow of water" or would tie a piece of sacking on the end of the hose to break the flow and prevent washing. The bubbler was designed to do this job better, to water quickly, gently and deeply without washing away soil or digging holes around the roots of precious plants. Place the bubbler on the soil, turn the hose on and water flows over the area in a gentle flood and does not wash any soil away. No water gets on the leaves of the plants causing leaf burn or other plant diseases.

The bubbler is excellent for roses subject to blackspot, or for newly planted annuals or perennials, or for any sort of spot watering. It puts the water where you want it, quickly and without waste.

Lightweight yet durable, the aluminum head is screwed on to the end of the hose. A series of patented bubbles breaks the water up as it flows through the bubbler. There are no moving parts; it does not clog and lasts practically forever. Originally designed for desert areas where deep watering is essential and water precious, its use has spread to other areas because of its adapability to other gardening problems.

Nozzles—Most gardeners do not find one all-purpose nozzle sufficient to meet their needs. It is a convenience to have at least three types The *fog or mist type* applies water in a mist-type spray and is useful for watering seedlings or newly planted grass seed. Because of its gentle action it will not wash away seed, seedlings or soil. *The water or pressure breaker* attachment breaks the force of the flow of the single solid stream into many tiny ones which flow out without force. The bubbler is fast taking its place. Both are useful for spot watering. *The regular sprinkler nozzle* has several adjustments by which water may be fanned out or gradually changed to one heavy spray.

Soil Auger—A tool for testing soil moisture, to probe the subsoil and find out where the water you apply to your plants and lawn goes. You can improvise your own auger with a pipe and a carpenter's ⅞" wood auger but garden supply dealers sell soil augers that are most efficient and cost little more than a good shovel. By turning the handle and pressing down on the auger it bores into the ground. The various types of soil it passes through collect in the grooves. When you raise the auger you have a visual account of your soil, layer by layer deep into the ground.

Water Rod, Lance or Root Irrigator—This device injects water directly where it is needed in the root zone. It couples directly to the garden hose and a thumb-control shutoff valve controls the flow of water right at the point of operation. A cone point makes for easier penetration and there is a grip handle to lean on when probing into the ground. Especially useful for trees and shrubs to get the water where the roots are.

Root Feeder—Some water irrigators feed at the same time. You open a top-loading fertilizer cup and fill it with essential plant nutrients, often in the form of special food pellets. As with the irrigator the plant food is put in the root zone, the plant feeding area, where it will do the most good and will help develop strong roots, improve the quality of the plant and thereby build up resistance to drought and disease.

KEEP SEED BEDS MOIST.

SPRAY DAILY WITH A HAND-HELD HOSE - USING FOG OR MIST NOZZLE.

OR - USE PERFORATED PLASTIC HOSE WHICH EMITS A GENTLE SPRAY.

Soaker—Especially useful for irrigating narrow places, as parking areas, flower and shrub borders, and between plant rows or coiled around individual plants, to soak a special tree or shrub. A soaker does not wet foliage. The older type is made of porous canvas and comes in 15-, 30- and 50-foot lengths and does a commendable job. The length of hose permits a steady but slow flow of water, thoroughly soaking the soil without runoff or soil washing away and with a minimum of evaporation.

Dew-Hose Soaker—Made of durable polyethylene, this plastic tube has one edge sewn with nylon thread which lets moisture seep out slowly. Available in 25-, 50- and 100-foot lengths which easily attach to the house spigot or yard hose. The 100-foot length comes in a kit with all necessary fittings, tape and a pressure reducer.

Useful for the shrub or flower bed, it can be placed under a mulch or on the surface and used in one long length to water single rows or joined with other lengths to water multiple rows or large areas from one sillcock. For short rows or irregular beds cut the Dew-Hose with scissors and join with ½" plastic tees and elbows with the aid of plastic tape.

A pressure regulator disc may be placed in the hose coupling next to the tap. Select the flow best suited for the bed or border you want to water.

Placed under mulch this makes a good semi-permanent installation which can be left in place all season. It makes the best possible use of water with practically no waste or evaporation.

Soaker-Sprinkler Hose—Three or triple tubes lie flat on the ground, and are flexible and can be curved. They make a fine spray, soaking without fast runoff, and have a special flush-out end cap and solid brass connections if another length is needed. It is marketed under various trade names. Water pressure can be regulated so soaking and spraying are even. Can be used on the surface or as a fixed installation below ground.

Sprinkler—Sprinklers are of many patterns and types, from adjustable hand nozzles in which the opening can be changed to emit any kind of stream, to mechanical devices that automatically operate by water pressure, revolving or otherwise throwing fine streams over a wide area without needing further attention. The type should be chosen according to the nature and amount of work to be done and the money to be invested.

Whatever its type, a lawn sprinkler is valuable only if the rain-like drops adequately cover the area to be watered without runoff or puddling or other waste and if used long enough in one place to soak the soil thoroughly. Most sprays can be regulated from coarse to very fine with a speed from 0 to 35 feet per hour.

Overhead Sprinklers—In sections where rainfall is generally sufficient overhead sprinkling systems are frequently installed to meet drought emergencies or to improve crop quality or hasten growth, both on truck gardens and in some home gardens. Water is conducted in pipes under pressure and distributed through tiny nozzles to fall in rain-like drops. This system saves time and puts the water where it is needed when it is needed and is especially desirable in vegetable gardens where water may be needed all summer.

Irrigation For Arid Regions—In arid regions of the western United States elaborate and costly construction and equipment including dams, reservoirs, flumes, ditches, furrows, etc. are often used in irrigating field crops and orchards.

To Measure Water—Various gadgets on the market take the guesswork out of watering.

Moisture Meter—This tells you immediately how damp a soil is. You can tell how much water you are putting on per hour so as not to overwater. You can buy extra 5-inch or 12-inch electro-chemical probes.

Rain Gauges And Sprinkling Indicators—Tell how much water you are putting on per hour. It is freestanding with a 10 inch cap.

Water Timer—This is a conservation device which measures and controls the gallons or hours of water flow.

IV Hardy Trees

When choosing trees that will survive dry conditions in your area many factors must be considered. August P. Beilmann, manager of the Arboretum, Missouri Botanical Garden, Gray Summit, Missouri, writes in a bulletin "What Tree Shall I Plant": "Trees which will stand dry weather in New England may not be happy during a dry period in Missouri. In the first case, a droughty period may last for only three or four weeks; even then, the nights are cooler, and the humidity quite high. A tree which shows some distress under those conditions may be seriously injured during a Middle Western summer which may be rainless from eight to thirteen weeks. During this time, night temperatures may approach ninety degrees; day temperatures exceed a hundred. To this add a thirty-mile-an-hour wind and a humidity reading of fifteen percent, and the term 'dry spell' takes on an altogether different meaning."

During its first year in the garden any young tree will need to be watered at least every week or ten days, if there is not sufficient rainfall, but once established it will need to be watered only during extended dry spells. Always be sure watering is necessary before you soak the soil around a plant. Many of our native trees and shrubs have survived over the years on water from the normal rainfall. Encourage their tolerance for less water by giving them the opportunity to search deep for the moisture available to them.

In regions where rainfall is ample but soil is poor, the condition can be remedied by improving the soil with the addition of organic matter in the area where the tree is to be planted. Dig a hole of sufficient size, use the improved soil and then mulch the area above the tree roots to help retain the soil moisture.

Where rainfall is insufficient—less than an inch a week, the equivalent of twenty inches of rainfall or a little more during the growing season—and watering is restricted, one must turn to drought-resistant plants. Dry soils are fairly prevalent throughout the Middle West and the alkaline soils in southwestern United States are mostly dry. The Northeast has been suffering through seven years of dry weather so lists of drought-resistant trees are more and more in demand.

ACER—Maple. Among the best of our ornamentals, valuable as shade, street, lawn and specimen trees, and many with ornamental foliage turn bright hues in autumn. Through recent dry seasons, maples have shown ability to survive. *A. campestre, A. ginnala* and *A. platanoides* will take considerable abuse and are recommended as city trees since they withstand smoke, dust, heat and lack of moisture.

A. campestre—A Eurasian round-headed tree growing to 30 ft. or less with branches slightly corky; hardy from zone 2 southward. It is quite heat and drought-tolerant.

A. ginnala—Amur Maple. Hardy from zone 3 southward, this graceful shrubby tree grows to 20 ft. with smooth slender branches. It is from north China and Japan. The foliage turns a brilliant crimson in the fall. It may be planted where the Japanese maple *(A. palmatum)* would be killed by winter.

A. negundo—Box-Elder. Valuable because it withstands dry situations where nothing but sumacs, the Siberian elm and the tree-of-heaven will grow. It is planted for shelterbelts in the West as a temporary quick-growing screen to protect slower growing but longer lasting trees while they are becoming established.

A. platanoides—Norway Maple. A large handsome European tree hardy from zone 2 southward. It grows to 100 ft. in height. The bright green foliage turns yellow in the fall and remains on the tree for a long time. Used extensively as a street tree in the Middle West. Many varieties and cultivars are available. 'Crimson King' keeps its deep red foliage color throughout the season and 'Globosum' is a lower, round-headed form.

AILANTHUS ALTISSIMA—Tree-Of-Heaven. A native of China and a

rapid grower that may attain a height of 60 ft. It grows so fast the wood is weak and splits readily in heavy windstorms or with the weight of snow or ice. A well rounded form but open, offering little shade. Coarse textured with leaflets about 5 in. long, prominently toothed toward the base. It has small greenish-yellow flowers in large pyramidal clusters in late June. Only female flowered trees should be cultivated as the odor of the male flower is objectionable. The bright reddish fruits of the female tree are effective in late summer and add to the interest of the tree. Cut saplings back to the ground every so often, when they reach around 10 ft. in height and they will sprout up vigorously from the base producing a luxuriance of foliage in one year. They can be used to create semi-tropical effects in gardens. No other tree will stand smoke and city conditions as well. It will thrive on nothing but ashes or may be seen growing out of cement blocks, seemingly enjoying such growing conditions. The tree thrives in wet or dry soil and is not susceptible to any serious diseases or insect pests. It can withstand submergence in salt water. Easily propagated from seed, root cuttings and from suckers.

ALBIZZIA JULIBRISSIN—Silk Tree. A tropical tree of the pea or legume family which is native to Asia. It resembles and is related to the acacia. In the South, it is attacked by mimosa wilt; the tree is incorrectly known there as mimosa. Flat topped and spreading, it grows to a height of from 15 to 30 ft., its dainty, lacy foliage casting a light shade. From midsummer until early September it is covered with dainty pink flowers; its long blooming period is unequalled by any other northern ornamental tree. The leaves do not take on fall coloring and they drop with the first frost. The tree is used for shade as well as for its color, when in flower, and for its wide range of hardiness. In frost regions use care in the selection of species. Variety *rosea* survives as far north as Boston but should be protected the first 2 or 3 winters. It is easily propagated by seed or 3 in. root cuttings made in

50. The box-elder (*Acer negundo*) thrives in the poor dry soils of the Great Plains area in the Midwest. Wide spreading, rather open and quick growing, it is weak-wooded, splitting easily in storms. Valuable because it withstands dry situations where little else will grow. This picture was taken in Utah.

U. S. Forest Service Photo

early spring. All tend to reseed. Although its life span is fairly short
it starts to bloom at an early age and will do well on poor, dry gravelly
soils. Any but small specimens resent transplanting.

ALMOND—See *Prunus amygdalus.*

AMELANCHIER CANADENSIS— Shadbush. Ranges in size from a
shrub or small tree up to about 30 ft. It is rounded at the top and more
or less elliptic in outline and native to eastern and southern United
States. Other native species have appeal and are worthy of investiga-
tion. Billowy masses of small white flowers in nodding racemes appear
in late April, either before or with the leaves. In warm weather they

51. *Albizzia julibrissin rosea*—The silk tree is one of the best long-flowering small
trees for areas where it is hardy. The var. *rosea* is generally considered hardier
than the typical form, and does especially well even in the Boston area on dry
bankings. Pinkish feathery blossoms are borne all summer and fall. The tree is
especially attractive when viewed from above. Unfortunately it is prone to attacks
of insects, is extremely late to leaf out in spring and is fragile-wooded and likely
to split at the crotches.

McFarland Photo

fade and fall quickly. Its purple fruits in summer are well liked by the birds. Both sides of the young foliage are covered with short, dense, woolly hairs giving the tree a very silvery appearance for a short time. It is attractive in the fall because of the brilliantly colored foliage which ranges in color from red to yellow. A desirable ornamental for naturalizing at the edge of a woodland or used at the edge of a lawn or in the border. It does best in a well-drained loamy soil but is quite tolerant of varied soil conditions, doing well in dry areas. Relatively free of pests and diseases but it is occasionally attacked by fire blight, red spider and various scales so keep alert and spray or dust with the first indication of any trouble.

ARALIA ELATA—Japanese Angelica Tree. A stout growing shrub or small tree native to eastern Asia, it is hardy from zone 4 southward. Of wide spreading, open habit with several trunks, the main stems have sharp triangular thorns and the tree often suckers from the base. Large compound leaves, sometimes 3 ft. long, are dark green above and paler beneath, usually clustered around the ends of the stems. Large feathery spikes of small, whitish flowers are produced above the rather horizontal leaves in August, followed by small black berries in early fall, quickly eaten by the birds. The autumn coloring is reddish-orange. A very striking tree giving a marked sub-tropical effect, conspicuous all season, but rather difficult to use properly and out of place in the small garden. It will withstand dry, poor sterile soil and is the hardiest member of this genus. All do well under trying city conditions.

ASH—See *Fraxinus*.

BETULA—Birch. Hardy deciduous trees, generally medium to tall and of narrow form. Their delicate flexible branches and conspicuous bark, ranging from white through shades of orange to almost black, give them a special charm and appeal during the dormant winter months. They are attractive grouped with evergreens and especially suited to natural woodland plantings. The characteristic bark colors do not show until the trees are several years old. All bear catkins and soft cones. Only the following birches do well in dry locations. Unfortunately they are rather short-lived.

B. *davurica*—Dahurian Birch. Grows remarkably well on a comparatively dry, gravelly hillside. It has wide spreading branches, open foliage, and reddish-brown ragged bark, interesting in the way it peels or flakes off in regular pieces. Grows to 60 ft. in height and is a native of northeast Asia.

B. papyrifera (B. papyracea)—Canoe or Paper Birch. Our native white birch that grows in the cooler parts of North America, preferring zone 4 and northward. It will reach up to 90 ft. or more. With its chalky white bark and thick dark green leaves it is probably the most showy of the birches and highly decorative. Short-lived, it is not particular as to soil, frequently offered in nursery catalogues as *B. alba*.

B. pendula—European White Birch. It resembles our canoe or paper birch but does not grow as tall, hardy from zone 2 southward; short-lived. The most commonly grown birch in cultivation, it is found in many attractive forms, not fussy as to soil.

B. populifolia—Gray Birch. Useful where other trees will not thrive, in very poor, stony soil or on sandy wastes. It is short-lived, sometimes incorrectly offered as *B. alba* or *B. papyrifera*.

52. *Betula papyrifera* — The paper birch is a much more desirable species than gray birch, but the same miner problem exists in growing it.

Taloumis Photo

53. *Betula populifolia* — Gray birch, a familiar colonizer, with red cedar of abandoned fields, is a short-lived, drought-tolerant small tree suitable in wild areas or gardens where better things will not survive. Like other birches, it is prone to leaf miner attack, which must be controlled by frequent lindane spraying or use of new systemic insecticides.   U. S. Forest Service Photo

BLACK CHERRY, WILD—See *Prunus serotina.*

BOX ELDER—See *Acer negundo.*

BROUSSONETIA PAPYRIFERA—Common Paper-Mulberry. A native of China and Japan, the paper-mulberry grows into a wide spreading tree with a broad rounded-head and to a height of 50 ft. It has smooth gray bark and dense, large oval leaves usually lobed. The trunk grows into irregular shapes. The female catkins are globular and interesting in May, followed in June and July by round, orange to red fruit, ¾" in diameter. It is a neat tree, used as an ornamental in the South, occasionally as a street tree. It does well on poor, sterile, gravelly soil where other trees will not survive and does equally well in areas where heat, smoke and dust are prevalent. A reliable tree where growing conditions are difficult. Hardy from New York south.

CEDAR—See *Cedrus, Juniperus.*

CEDRUS ATLANTICA—Atlas Cedar. A most interesting evergreen with a picturesque upright habit of growth, broadly pyramidal, reaching a height of 40 to 100 ft. With maturity it becomes somewhat flat-topped. Clumps of short needles on twiggy branches leave the trunk or trunks open to view at all seasons. It should be planted as a specimen tree where there is adequate room for growth. It withstands wind and drought, cannot take soggy soils, hardy to zone 6. There are several fine horticultural forms with silvery white leaves and drooping branches. 'Glauca' is best known, its somewhat bluish needles give it added interest. 'Pendula' is a weeping form and deserves to be better known.

   C. libani—Cedar of Lebanon. This is difficult to distiguish from the Atlas Cedar; a dwarf compact form is called 'Comte de Dijon'.

CELTIS OCCIDENTALIS—Common American Hackberry. A round-headed tree 50 to 100 ft., native to eastern North America and hardy from zone 2 southward, standing poor soil, high winds, smoke and dust. It is frequently planted in the East and Middle West states.

CERCIS—Redbud, Judas-Tree. These are deciduous shrubs or small trees belonging to the pea family, grown for their very showy abundant rose-pink flowers opening before or as the leaves unfold in early spring. Clusters of flowers are produced on the old stems as well as on younger growth. The handsome foliage is not compound as with most pea family members. Of easy culture in open, rather sandy loams they like the sun and do not like heavy, moist sites; transplant when small. Their early bloom makes them useful for color in the shrubbery while most other plants are still dormant. Propagation is by seeds, layers or greenwood cuttings.

54. *Cedrus atlantica* — This Atlas cedar is an old mature tree, now somewhat flat-topped. It withstands wind and drought but needs adequate room for growth. There are several fine horticultural forms.

U. S. Forest Service Photo

C. canadensis—American Redbud. Found from New York and Ontario to Florida and Texas, this tall shrub or sometimes tree of 30 ft. or less has a broad round head and is hardy from zone 3 southward, the only redbud really hardy North. There is a white form, also one with double flowers.

CHERRY, FLOWERING—See *Prunus serrulata.*

CHOKE-CHERRY—See *Prunus serotina.*

CLADRASTIS LUTEA—Yellow-Wood. A member of the pea family, this decorative native tree has attractive dense foliage and a beautifully smooth gray bark, deservedly popular for its showy bloom and adaptability. In late spring and early summer it produces white flowers

55. *Cladrastis lutea* — Yellow-wood, an attractive native tree of the Kentucky-Tennessee area, is notable for its long, fragrant panicles, which are produced rather erratically—in good quantity some years, not so good in others. Its gray, smooth bark is handsome.   McFarland Photo

56. Close-up of the fragrant pea-like flowers of the yellow-wood *(Cladrastis lutea)* in long racemes resembling those of wisteria.

McFarland Photo

in racemes a foot long resembling those of wisteria. They fill the air with fragrance for a great distance. Flowers sometimes are borne only every 2 or 3 years. The shiny leaves turn a rich yellow in the fall. Rounded in form and growing 40 to 50 ft. its open branches give an airy effect, a fine specimen tree. Deep-rooting and drought-resistant the yellow-wood will stand extremes of heat and cold as well as drought but needs a sunny location. It is tolerant of varied soil conditions and relatively free from pests and diseases. Prune in summer if necessary or in the autumn rather than in the spring to avoid excessive loss of sap. It will grow much farther north than its native range which is southeastern United States. May be propagated from seed sown in the spring and root cuttings kept cool and moist over winter.

COCKSPUR THORN—See *Crataegus crus-galli.*

COTINUS OBOVATUS—American Smoke Tree. Formerly *Rhus cotinus* and sometimes listed as *C. americanus.* Native in the southern part of the United States but hardy north from zone 5 southward, perhaps in zone 4 with protection. Belonging to the sumac family and of easy culture the smoke tree prefers soil not too rich or moist. Easily raised from seed, needing water and attention to get started, later requiring scant care. A large shrub or small tree 15 to 30 ft. tall. The fruiting clusters in August and September form a plumed, silky attractive feature and the leaves turn a brilliant orange and scarlet in the autumn.

CRABAPPLE—See *Malus.*

CRAPE-MYRTLE—See *Lagerstroemia indica.*

CRATAEGUS—Hawthorn, Thorn-Apple. A member of the rose family this group includes many native species widely distributed over North America valuable for ornamental purposes; all attractive in habit of growth, blossom and fruit; slow growing and long-lived. Common in pastures or along old hedgerows. All are dense, twiggy trees or bush-like shrubs with thorns often an inch or more long. In some areas they encounter pest problems where they require annual attention. Many are difficult to transplant. Attractive the year round and valued for their picturesque shapes, their dense twiggy habit and sharp thorns; some for glossy foliage and most for their bright red fruits in the fall and clusters of small white flowers, sometimes pink, in early spring. The species and varieties that do well locally are the ones to grow as they are the easiest to establish and will require less pampering. They are excellent specimen, hedge and barrier plants. The following will tolerate poor, dry soils.

Crataegus crus-galli—Cockspur Thorn. This is a round-headed tree, sometimes flat, with wide-spreading horizontal thorny, dense branches. The definite flat spreading form makes it a striking specimen plant. It can be sheared to make a fine hedge or unsheared will grow to 30 ft. Its lustrous, dense foliage turns orange to scarlet in autumn. White flowers ½ in. in diameter in late May are followed by bright red fruit ¾ in. in diameter during most of the winter. Native to eastern North

57. Close-up of a Washington thorn (*Crataegus phaenopyrum*) branch showing the attractive red fruit which remains on the tree throughout the winter.

McFarland Photo

America it grows from Quebec to Michigan and South Carolina. Var. *splendens* is considered more ornamental than the species and has very glossy leaves.

C. *oxyacantha*—English Hawthorn. This is a native of Europe and North Africa, often confused with C. *monogyna*. A dense thorny, rounded tree of attractive habit it grows to 25 ft. or more, useful as a specimen or as a hedge plant. It does not develop autumn coloring. The species is best known for its white flowers, but has pink and red varieties of greater interest. The dense, fine textured foliage gives the plant a distinctive character. Red fruits are colorful in the fall. English hawthorn has about the same growing requirements as the Washington thorn. It needs periodic care to combat pests. There are several worthwhile forms—'Coccinea' has crimson flowers, 'Pauli' (Paul's Scarlet) is double red-flowered and the showiest of the hawthorns and 'Plena' has a double white flower. They are hardy from zone 4 southward.

C. phaenopyrum (C. cordata)—Washington Thorn. A dense upright tree to 30 ft., it is useful as a specimen planted near the edge of the lawn, also valuable along the highways. Considered one of the best of the hawthorns and of interest at all seasons of the year. The foliage is dense and lustrous turning orange or scarlet in the fall. White flowers are borne in clusters in early summer. The small bright red fruits remain attractive throughout the winter. It grows well in rich well-drained sandy loam but will tolerate alkaline conditions and drought and thrives where winters are fairly cold and dry. For this reason it may not reach its best development in coastal areas although it will grow there. Native to southeastern United States it is hardy to zone 4 and needs full sun.

C. punctata—Dotted Thorn. A low growing species growing from 20 to 30 ft. with horizontal branches which give it a flat, open top effect. Native to eastern North America, its range is from Canada to Georgia and westward to Illinois. White dots appear on its yellow-red fruits. *'Aurea'* has yellow fruit.

ELAEAGNUS ANGUSTIFOLIA—Russian Olive, Oleaster. A hardy, vigorous grower this tree was used in early colonial times and prized for its outstanding silvery gray-green foliage and ease of culture. Its unique crooked trunk and branches, covered with a brown shedding bark, give it interest and character making it especially ornamental during the winter. Deciduous in the North, it grows up to 20 ft. in height. Spicy, fragrant, inconspicuous small greenish-yellow flowers bloom in June followed by inconspicuous yellow coated berries with silvery scales in early fall. The Russian olive is useful in backgrounds of large

58. *Elaeagnus angustifolia* — Russian olive trained as an espalier against a wooden fence near the seashore.

Taloumis Photo

shrub borders; severely pruned it will make a dense plant suitable for screens and windbreaks and may also be trained espalier style. Care should be taken in selecting plants for good silver color. There are varieties with spiny branches and some with larger, greenish leaves. It does best in light sandy loam but can be grown in most any soil and will withstand seacoast conditions; enjoys a sunny position and good drainage. Easily propagated by seed or by cuttings of mature or half-ripened wood. *E. umbellata* is quite similar but a little smaller and has more ornamental red fruit; also useful for seashore plantings.

ELM—See *Ulmus.*

FRAXINUS—Ash. Most of the ashes prefer ample moisture but the following two are quite drought-resistant.

F. pensylvanica lanceolata—Green Ash. A deciduous tree of the olive family and a variety of the red ash found wild over much of eastern North America, hardy from zone 2 southward, from Maine to Florida and Texas. It is well suited to the windswept, dry regions in the prairie states, growing to about 60 ft.

F. velutina—Arizona Ash, Velvet Ash. A round-headed tree with foliage more or less open, frequently used as a street tree in southwestern United States and Mexico. Of value in these semi-arid regions with dry alkaline soils where little else will grow. Although it likes some fertility it grows quite rapidly almost anywhere. It grows from 20 to 45 ft. 'Coriacea' (Montebello Ash) has leathery leaves that are much roughened. 'Glabra' (Modesto Ash) has smooth glossy leaves appearing late in spring and turning a good yellow in autumn. Both are refinements of the type.

GINKGO BILOBA—Ginkgo, Maidenhair Tree. This hardy, deciduous tree from China and Japan grows to 120 ft. with attractive foliage that resembles that of the popular maidenhair fern; it turns yellow in the fall. Of upright form, branching is often irregular and spreading in old specimens. Its interesting habit of growth and beautiful foliage make this most ancient of living trees a desirable specimen subject where a picturesque effect is desired. Used in parks and as a street tree it will withstand wind, smog and other tough city conditions. It tolerates a wide variety of soils, wants good drainage, is fairly drought-resistant, will grow in sun or shade and is practically free of pests and diseases. It will grow in such diverse climates as California, New England and Canada. Grow only the male plants as the odor of the decaying fruits of the female plant is objectionable. 'Aurea' has yellow leaves in youth; 'Fastigiata' (Sentry Ginkgo) has a narrow columnar habit making it useful where space is limited; 'Pendula' is a weeping form, and 'Variegata' has yellow-blotched leaves.

GLEDITSIA TRIACANTHOS—Honey-Locust. Sometimes called black locust or three-thorned acacia and found growing from Pennsylvania to Texas. It may reach 130 ft. at maturity, less under cultivation, and is a broad-headed, open tree of the pea family, excellent for light shade. Attractive in habit of growth, somewhat similar to the elm, it has fine textured, light green lacy foliage. Inconspicuous greenish flowers produce the brown, sickle-shaped, twisted pods 12 to 18 in. long that persist after the leaves fall. The trunk and branches have long, usually branched, thorns, sometimes as much as 4 in. in length.

59. The Ginkgo or Maidenhair tree *(Ginko biloba)* shown growing in Wooster, Ohio, is one of the finest street and specimen trees in the temperate world. It wants good drainage but will withstand wind, smog and other tough city conditions.
Courtesy Secrest Arboretum

60. *Gleditsia triacanthos* 'Shademaster' — The many thornless, podless forms of honey locust are worth considering for difficult locations. They have numerous assets: desirable grasses grow well under them, whereas crabgrass does not; the small leaves mulch into the turf and do not require raking; the trees grow in a variety of soils. However, they need generous summer watering and annual fertilizing to get well started. In some areas they are a favorite of insect pests.
Lewis Photo

A handsome tree, it makes a splendid street or lawn specimen. Easy to grow, it withstands drought, sun and smoke and is not particular as to soil and relatively free of pests. A perfect tree to withstand city conditions.

Cultivar 'Inermis' (Moraine Locust) is thornless, believed to be sterile, rarely producing pods. Widely used as a substitute for the American Elm as it can be grown in so many situations. It can be a long-lived tree. The foliage appears late in the spring and falls early.

GOLDEN CHAIN—See *Laburnum*.

GOLDEN-RAIN TREE—See *Koelreuteria paniculata*.

GYMNOCLADUS DIOICUS—Kentucky Coffee Tree. A deciduous tree scattered from New York to Pennsylvania to Nebraska, Oklahoma and Tennessee; a member of the pea family growing to 90 ft., less under cultivation. It is hardy only from zone 3 southward. Male and female flowers are on separate trees. Propagated by seed and from root cuttings. Of easy culture it will withstand droughts. 'Variegata' has variegated foliage.

61. *Gymnocladus dioicus* — The Kentucky coffee tree was given its common name because of an inferior coffee substitute made from the beans produced in the large pods, which remain on the tree in winter. A strange, sparsely branched tree, it is worth considering only for its ability to withstand poor dry soil and its fairly rapid growth rate.

U. S. Forest Service Photo

HACKBERRY—See *Celtis.*

HAWTHORN—See *Crataegus.*

HONEY-LOCUST—See *Gleditsia triacanthos.*

HOP-HORNBEAM—See *Ostrya virginiana.*

IRONWOOD—See *Ostrya virginiana.*

JAPANESE ANGELICA TREE—See *Aralia elata.*

JAPANESE PAGODA TREE—See *Sophora japonica.*

JUNE-BERRY—See *Amelanchier canadensis.*

JUNIPERUS—Juniper. —See also Shrubs. Ornamental evergreens belonging to the pine family of widely recognized merit, perfectly adapted to permanent plantings in dry exposed areas. They include some of the best hardy small and medium sized trees and shrubs. the majority hardy even in the coldest parts of the United States with a wide distribution in the northern hemisphere, from the Arctic regions to the sub-tropics. Most will develop better color and form in dry sandy, alkaline or gravelly soils and are generally comfortable at the seashore under exposure to sun and wind. They resent shade, are easily moved when young; sexes are separate. Varied in form from dense columnar trees to the trailing ground covers, the erect forms are of value in formalized plantings or as accents in natural settings. Their small leaves are mostly gray-green, and berry-like fruits are blue or reddish.

J. chinensis—Chinese Juniper. (40 to 60 ft.) Pyramidal in habit with evergreen, pointed scale-like leaves; the sexes are separate, the female plants bearing fruits ⅜ in. in diameter; hardy from zone 2 southward. Var. *columnaris* is columnar with silvery green, sharp leaves; var. *mas* is an excellent densely columnar form and var. *pyramidalis* is narrow, compact, with upright branches.

J. scopulorum—Western, Rocky Mountain or Colorado Red Cedar. A round-topped tree, usually low, but may grow to 35 ft. The bark is red-brown and shredding, the short trunk often dividing near the ground. It is hardy from zone 3 southward, from British Columbia and Alberta south to Texas and northern Arizona in the mountains. It stands dry and difficult situations. The western equivalent of *J. virginiana,* it differs mainly in habit, bark and nature of its fruit. Var. *argen-*

62. *Juniperus virginiana* — Red cedar, commonly seen colonizing old abandoned fields throughout the eastern half of the country, forms an impressive tree with age. Although one of the finest evergreens for dry soil and available in many forms of various needle coloration, it quickly forms a tap root and is therefore best transplanted when young.

U. S. Forest Service Photo

tea is of a narrow, upright habit with glaucous silvery leaves. Var. *viridifolia* is of upright habit with bright green leaves.

J. virginiana—Eastern Red Cedar. A native columnar or pyramidal tree when young, becoming broader and spreading with age. Usually growing 40 to 50 ft., sometimes to 100 ft. A splendid evergreen, its red-brown bark peels off in long strips and has considerable interest ornamentally. Common in dry, rocky fields from Canada to Florida, east of the Rockies. Hardy from zone 1 southward, perhaps the hardiest and most popular of the tree junipers. Usually dense, but can easily be pruned. Grows slowly. Does well in poor gravelly soils. A variable species it has many varieties and cultivars. 'Canaerti' is a compact, pyramidal form with dark green foliage. In 'Elegantissima,' Gold-tip Red Cedar, the tips of the branches are golden-yellow; var. *glauca,* Silver Red Cedar, has silvery-gray foliage; 'Keteleeri' is compact, upright with dark green scale-like leaves; var. *pendula,* Weeping Red Cedar, has pendulous branches; 'Schotti' is small, narrow, upright; for 'Tripartita,' see Shrubs; var. *venusta* is upright with shiny leaves, light to sometimes bluish-green.

KOELREUTERIA PANICULATA—Golden-Rain Tree. A deciduous tree native to Japan, China and Korea which grows from 30 to 40 ft. in height. Flat-topped with a compact habit of growth and twisting branches, it bears compound leaves which form broad masses of bright green foliage, dull red before they unfold. Small yellow flowers in large conspicuous upright pyramidal clusters merge in early summer followed by bladder-like pods which change from whitish through pink to brown by October with the falling leaves; then the crooked character of the stem and branches lends a picturesque effect. Sometimes it is used as a street tree and is excellent as a specimen tree near the edge of a lawn or in a woodland border.

Hardy as far north as Massachusetts in sheltered positions, it is rather short-lived and likely to be killed back by severe cold spells. Much planted in the southern central states because of its adaptability to a large range of soils and its resistance to drought. It withstands both drought and hot winds and will take city smog, likes full sun, becomes straggly in the shade and is quite free from pests and diseases.

63. *Koelreuteria paniculata* — The golden-rain tree is noted for its profusion of deep yellow flowers in early summer, which are followed by odd-looking conspicuous seed capsules.

McFarland Photo

LABURNUM—Golden Chain. These are small deciduous trees growing to a height of 20 ft. or more belonging to the pea family. Where hardy they are among the most beautiful of the spring flowering trees with 3-part leaves and long pendulous clusters of bright yellow flowers in May and June, to 15 in. in length. Closely allied to the brooms they thrive in even poor soil if it is well drained; they take city conditions well, flowering profusely. They even grow on rocky slopes and will take some shade. Useful trees as specimen plants and effective in shrub borders.

L. alpinum—Scotch Laburnum. A small, stiff, upright tree growing to 20 ft. or more. Hardy from zone 3 southward.

L. anagyroides—Sometimes listed as *L. vulgare*. It is the common laburnum which grows about 20 ft. in height, often branching close to the ground; hardy from zone 3 southward. It has shorter racemes than *L. alpinum* and blooms 2 weeks earlier. 'Aureum' has yellow leaves.

L. watereri is a cross between the two above species and is sometimes listed as *L. vossi*. A handsome tree not too different from *L. alpinum* but very free-flowering, leaves and stems of flower clusters are hairy, the flower clusters are longer and a near golden-yellow. It is hardy from zone 5 southward, in protected sites in zone 4.

LAGERSTROEMIA INDICA—Crape-Myrtle. A small shrubby tree native to China and belonging to the loosestrife family. It reaches a height of 20 to 25 ft. in the South where it is widely grown; it becomes more shrub-like northward. Reliably hardy as far north as Baltimore, although it will grow successfully in sheltered spots farther north. Its abundant and attractive flower panicles, resembling the lilac, continue to bloom into early fall, a real asset. Useful for large hedges, as specimen plants or for accent and in some places they have been naturalized. It is grown in the North in pots or tubs in the cool greenhouse. Considered by many as the most spectacularly showy deciduous summer-flowering shrub. It grows best in hot, dry climates, in fertile well-drained loam but will tolerate a wide range of soils. It needs the sun. Flowers are borne on current season's growth so prune severely if necessary in early spring for a compact specimen. There are several forms with white, purple, pink and red flowers.

LINDEN—See *Tilia cordata*.

LOCUST—See *Robinia*.

MACLURA POMIFERA—Osage Orange. Recommended mostly for the Midwest where it withstands the cold winters and summer drought. Of vigorous growth with stout thorns it quickly grows into a dense thorny hedge valuable for confining stock and also serves as an excellent windbreak. It will grow to 60 ft. and belongs to the mulberry family. The sexes are separate, only the female plants bear the large orange-like greenish-yellow fall fruits which are around 3 in. in diameter. The Osage Indians valued the wood for making bows and called it bow-wood. Because of its durability in the ground it is used for fence-posts and railroad ties.

MAIDENHAIR TREE—See *Ginkgo biloba*.

MALUS—Flowering Crabapple. Ornamental flowering crabs are of the rose family and valued for their year round interest, their beautiful

64. *Malus sargenti* — Sargent's crabapple growing on a dry hillside in the Arnold Arboretum. Many of the arboretum's crab apples are planted on sharply-drained slopes, indicating that these trees do not mind dryness.

Genereux Photo

flower display in spring, attractive fruit in fall and early winter, and interesting form of growth which makes the tree skeleton itself a decorative asset during the winter months. There are many fine kinds available, a good color range and varieties in scale for the small property. Visit a nearby arboretum or nursery to see the trees in bloom so you will understand just what you are getting and find out how large the tree will be when fully grown. Inquire about the best crab for your location and dry situation. Crabapples grow well in almost any well-drained soil whether poor or fertile and will stand considerable drought.

MAPLE—See *Acer.*

MORUS ALBA—White Mulberry. A northern hemisphere deciduous tree not over 50 ft. high, round-topped and dense. It varies considerably so far as its bright green foliage is concerned and is cultivated in eastern Asia for its leaves, the food of silk worms. Fruit is similar in size and shape to blackberries, usually white, sometimes pinkish or purplish. Useful in hot climates where it grows fast and well in almost any soil, even gravel, and it also does well in drought areas. With its rapid growth it creates quick shade, has no autumn color. The falling fruit makes a continual clutter although attractive to birds. There are one or two fruitless clones now on the market. It is hardy from zone 1 southward.

'Pendula' (Weeping Mulberry) has slender pendulous branches and 'Tatarica' (Russian Mulberry) is a smaller tree and very hardy with small red fruit.

MOUNTAIN ASH—See *Sorbus.*

MULBERRY—See *Morus.*

OAK—See *Quercus.*

OSAGE ORANGE—See *Maclura pomifera.*

OSTRYA VIRGINIANA—Hop-Hornbeam, Ironwood. A small or medium sized deciduous American tree of the birch family, very slow growing but should be considered as an ornamental for dry places. It has bright green attractive foliage turning yellow in the fall and light green cone-like fruiting clusters, its most attractive feature. A native in eastern North America it grows to around 30 ft., taller in the wild; hardy from zone 2 southward. Propagation is by seed best sown in the fall.

PAPER-MULBERRY—See *Broussonetia papyrifera.*

PHELLODENDRON AMURENSE—Amur Cork-Tree. A native of northern China, Manchuria and of the rue family it grows 40 to 50 ft. in height. Of rapid growth when young it develops into a shapely, round-headed tree with gray, deeply fissured, corky bark. Its decorative dark green foliage turns yellow in the autumn. Clusters of black berry-like fruit hang on the tree for several months and are interesting in winter. It will grow in almost any soil, withstands droughts and is hardy from zone 2 southward.

PINUS—Pine. For year-round effectiveness, pines are hard to beat. Some of the older trees under stress of seashore winds develop a picturesque quality with age. All are drought-enduring and adapt to varied climatic conditions. In poor but well-drained sandy loam, they develop long tap-roots that anchor them well and increase their ability to withstand drought. Many will grow to 100 ft. or more; some are medium-sized, others dwarf in habit. All pines enjoy light so never shade them and they will not reach their typical form if crowded.

P. banksiana—Jack Pine, Scrub Pine. Sometimes known as *P. divaricata*. A shrubby tree usually less than 60 ft. with a loose and open habit and evergreen foliage, 2 needles in a bundle, mostly 1 to 2 in. long and oblong cones 1 to 2 in. long. One of the hardiest pines and although not as ornamental as many it does well on dry sandy banks where few evergreens and deciduous plants will thrive. Native to northeastern North America and west to Alberta, useful as a soil-binder on our northern sand dunes.

P. cembra—Swiss Stone Pine. A slow growing Eurasian tree so its size is not a problem under cultivation in a home garden. It has a narrow, pyramidal form with very dense, short thick branches. Its dark green narrow needles are in bundles of 5 and of a soft texture. An upright regular habit makes it suitable for formal plantings or as an accent plant. It grows best in a well-drained loamy soil on hillsides in full sun, hardy from zone 3 southward.

P. coulteri—Coulter Pine or Big Cone Pine. This is a slow growing magnificent forest tree 40 to 80 ft. at maturity, with a somewhat asymmetrical crown, very dark bark, long blue-green needles in bundles of 3, and pendant cones whose heavy scales are curved into hook-like spurs at the tips. It has the largest of all the pine cones, they weigh 4 to 5 lbs. when green. This native of California is hardy from zone 4 southward.

P. griffithi—Himalayan Pine. Also called *P. excelsa* and *P. wallichiana*. A wide-spread, fast growing tree it may reach 70 to 150 ft. in height. It makes an excellent specimen tree where space is ample. The blue-green leaves, soft in texture, in clusters of 5, drooping from 5 to 8 in. long give a cascade effect to the tree. It grows satisfactorily as far north as Long Island and the Connecticut shore and in temperate areas of the Northwest.

P. koraiensis—Korean Pine. A pyramidal tree with dark green leaves, 5 in a bundle, 3 to 4 in. long, and oblongish cones 4 to 6 in. long. It is hardy from zone 3 in sheltered places and zone 4 southward. It grows 50 to 80 ft. in height.

P. mugo—See Shrubs.

P. nigra—Austrian Pine. Long known as *P. austriaca* and *P. laricio*. A pyramidal tree up to 90 ft., hardy from zone 3 southward. It is one of the most widely cultivated pines in the country and along with *P. thunbergi* the best for city conditions. There are many horticultural varieties; var. *calabrica*, Corsican Pine, forms a narrower crown than the typical species.

P. parviflora—Japanese White Pine. Under cultivation it is generally a grafted tree, low with wide spreading branches. The egg-shaped cones are 2 to 3 in. long. Hardy from zone 3 southward.

P. pinaster—Maritime Pine, Cluster Pine. Well adapted to seaside planting where hardy. If sand dune areas at the seaside are to be planted, this should have first consideration. It is difficult to transplant so young seedlings should be used whenever possible. It will grow to 90 ft.

P. rigida—Pitch Pine. A scraggly native and picturesque at maturity with its open branching, valuable for planting on dry and rocky soil where little else will grow. Used extensively for exposed wind-swept dunes along the Atlantic Coast, from New Brunswick to Georgia and inland to Kentucky.

65. *Pinus thunbergi* — The Japanese black pine has become one of the most popular pines for seaside planting as it tolerates drought as well as most other pines, and salt spray better than many. However, in extremely exposed locations it needs the protection of other trees or a heavy fence. A larger colony of pines than the one shown would be better able to withstand the gales.

Taloumis Photo

P. strobus—Eastern White Pine, Northern White Pine. Known as the Weymouth pine in England. Native to eastern North America and perhaps the most beautiful of all the eastern species; tall, rounded or pyramidal, often reaching 150 ft. at maturity. Old trees frequently take on an asymmetrical picturesque appearance. A superb specimen tree or it may be used as a background for other plantings, it also may be used as a hedge with judicious pruning. It will grow in most well-drained soils whether fertile or poor, but needs full sun and is hardy from zone 2 southward. There are many horticultural forms of this popular pine, some with variegated foliage and others dwarf. 'Fastigiata' is good for screen planting with its columnar, erect habit.

P. sylvestris—Scots Pine. This is a Eurasian tree hardy from zone 2 southward. With maturity it becomes an irregular, round-topped tree up to 75 ft. Its bark is cinnamon-brown. There are many horticultural

66. *Pinus sylvestris* — The Scots pine is especially admired for its reddish-brown bark. It is highly adaptable to a variety of poor, dry soils. The specimen shown has lost its leader either in a storm or by insect damage which gives the tree a picturesque appearance.

Taloumis Photo

varieties with different colored foliage including golden, yellow, white and variegated; one has pendulous branches and 'Fastigiata' is columnar in form.

P. thunbergi—Japanese Black Pine. This is perhaps only a form of the Austrian pine with somewhat shorter, darker colored leaves, rarely over 4 in. long, 2 in a sheath and cones 3 in. long. Hardy from zone 3 southward, it is far quicker growing and does well in exposed, windswept places along the northeastern seacoast, very well on Martha's Vineyard and Nantucket.

P. virginiana—Virginia or Scrub Pine. Used only for planting in poor, dry soils where other pines will not grow. Open, with sparse branching, it often has a very wide top. It may grow to 45 ft., hardy from zone 4 southward, a useful soil-binder on dry sandy slopes.

PLATANUS ACERIFOLIA—London Plane Tree. A hybrid between *P. orientalis* and *P. occidentalis* the tree is hardy as far north as Massachusetts and quite free from disease. Tall and widely spreading, up to 100 ft. or more in height, it is much planted as a street tree and characterized by bark that peels off in large patches and dense maple-like foliage. One of the best all-around street trees widely planted in London, Paris and American cities in the temperate region. It will stand considerable abuse including smoke, dust, wind and drought. It is hardy from zone 3 southward.

POPULUS—Poplar. This genus of soft-wooded deciduous trees belongs to the willow family. Because of their rapid growth they are planted in dry prairie regions for windbreaks and as avenue trees, also as ornamentals. Some are widely planted as street trees because they grow well under adverse conditions but they are not long-lived and since their long roots can be a nuisance finding their way into drains, water pipes and sewers they should be placed with care. Their graceful trunks and light airy leaves rustling in the slightest breeze attract notice, especially when planted with contrasting darker-leaved deciduous trees or before evergreens. Weak-wooded and brittle, they are easily broken during heavy snowstorms. As rapid growers they can be used as fillers until better trees become established.

P. alba—White Poplar. The white poplar withstands very dry growing situations, so is used extensively in parts of the Middle West where few other ornamentals can take the trying growing conditions. A good specimen tree where there is room, it is an ornamental columnar tree that is a good substitute for the Lombardy poplar (*P. nigra italica*) which is susceptible to trunk canker. Irregular and rather open, this Old World tree has whitish-gray bark. The only poplar with lobed leaves, the upperside is grayish-green, the underside white and downy making an interesting contrast; there is a tendency to have red autumn coloring. The tree will grow to 60 ft. and is hardy from zone 2 southward. Var. *nivea* has leaves still whiter beneath and 'Pyramidalis' with its columnar habit is a valuable accent plant, sometimes known as *P. bolleana*.

PRUNUS—The Stone Fruits. An important group of mostly deciduous shrubs and small trees belonging to the rose family including all the plums, cherries and apricots; the peach and almond are sometimes included too. Found chiefly in the north temperate zone, many are hardy in the North and very decorative for their superb flowering in early spring, some before the leaves expand. They thrive best in a well-drained loamy, limy soil and are of easy culture.

P. amygdalus—Almond. This is a deciduous tree of moderate size, up to 24 ft. with a bushy habit and dense foliage, good for shade, exceptionally clean and with blossoms that rival those of the peach. Grown in southern California, it is best with heat in a light well-drained soil, drought-resistant and quite frost hardy. It blooms early with pink and white 1 to 2 in. flowers in February and March. 'Alba-plena' has flowers double and white; 'Nana' is a dwarf compact form grown in California; 'Pendula' is represented by pendulous branches and 'Rosea-plena' has double pink flowers.

P. serotina—Wild Black Cherry, Choke-Cherry. Found throughout eastern and central North America and hardy everywhere. It will live considerably longer than most *Prunus*. It is the best of the native American species for ornamental planting, a good general purpose tree with its dense long, lustrous peach-like foliage and slightly drooping branches. It is useful for seashore planting. Profuse small, single white flowers in terminal drooping racemes, 4 to 5½ in. long, appear in late May followed by small conspicuous red fruits in August, later turning black. The choke-cherry is widely planted by birds along fence rows where they are quite weedy in character; the juice of its foliage is poisonous.

P. serrulata—Flowering Cherry. The Japanese flowering cherry grows up to 30 ft. tall, much smaller in some of the varieties, and is hardy from zone 3 southward. The most commonly cultivated variety is a double white.

P. sieboldi. This resembles *P. serrulata* but the twigs and under side of the leaves are softly hairy. Long cultivated in Japan it is hardy from zone 3 southward.

P. subhirtella—Rosebud Cherry. A showy Japanese tree that grows 20 to 30 ft. and is hardy from zone 3 southward. 'Pendula' is weeping, a particularly fine form with gracefully hanging branches, more cultivated than the typical form. 'Autumnalis' is fall-flowering.

PYRUS—Pear. This genus belongs to the rose family and contains the pear of commerce as well as a few other ornamental plants. The white clustered flowers bloom with or before the expanding of the leaves. Of easy culture in well-drained soil they do not mind warm, dry summers.

P. calleryana—Callery Pear. Hardy from zone 3 southward, this Chinese free-flowering species is showy when in bloom in early spring and its glossy leaves are very colorful in the fall. Used as grafting stock for the common pear but also planted as an ornamental because the tree withstands droughts.

P. salicifolia 'Pendula'—Weeping Pear. A small tree with slender, more or less drooping branches, it has silvery willow-like leaves and creamy-white flowers.

QUERCUS—Oak. Among the most dependable of our ornamental trees, the oaks are mostly deciduous and characterized by the capped nuts called acorns. The genus includes some of the finest trees of the north temperate zone. Listed below are some fairly drought-resistant species.

Q. alba—The white oak is native to eastern North America, hardy from zone 2 southward. It is a round-headed tree that grows from 60 to 100 ft. tall and is perhaps the largest of the native oaks, used by the Cape Cod National Seashore Park, for planting stabilized dunes.

Q. coccinea—Scarlet Oak. An upright, open, round-topped tree with ascending slender branches that grows to 75 ft. or more, the lower branches may droop almost to the ground. It is an excellent specimen or street tree, the bright green glossy foliage casts a light shade and turns a brilliant scarlet in the fall. The scarlet oak will do well in most soils, tolerating rocky and sandy soils and drought. It is excellent for dry situations and hardy from zone 2 southward. 'Splendens' has more glossy leaves than the species.

Q. ilicifolia—Scrub Oak. Native to eastern United States, the scrub oak grows to 10 ft., is much branched and of a shrubby habit. Very hardy everywhere, it is useful for dry banks or seaside planting. See *Q. prinoides.*

Q. imbricaria—Shingle or Laurel Oak. This tree grows to 50 ft. more or less and is native from New Jersey to Tennessee and westward. In youth it has slender drooping branches but becomes round-topped with age. The foliage is glossy dark green above, downy beneath and becomes russet-red in autumn. It is hardy from zone 3 southward.

Q. laurifolia—Laurel Oak, Darlington Oak. A half evergreen tree with a glistening, rounding top that grows 60 ft. more or less and has slender branchlets. It grows from New Jersey to Florida and Louisiana along the South Atlantic and Gulf area and in California in sandy soils. It likes heat. The Darlington oak is a fully evergreen form used in the South as a street and shade tree. Some consider *Q. hemisphaerica* the correct name.

Q. macrocarpa—Bur Oak. A tree up to 100 ft. which is native to eastern North America and west to Texas, hardy from zone 2 southward.

Q. marilandica—Black Jack Oak. Found in eastern and central United States. A slow-growing small tree to 30 ft., it is well adapted for planting on poor, dry sterile soil. Of irregular growth, it has stout branches and attractive leathery glossy foliage that turns yellow or brown in the fall. It is useful where more ornamental oaks will not grow.

Q. montana—See *Q. prinus.*

Q. palustris—Pin Oak. Native to eastern North America, the pin oak is hardy from zone 3 southward. A valuable street or lawn tree, it grows to 80 ft. more or less and forms a symmetrical pyramidal head with branches conspicuously horizontal; the much cut, shining leaves turn bright red in autumn. Of fairly rapid growth once the pin oak is established it thrives without extra watering.

Q. prinoides—Scrub Oak. A shrubby oak found from Maine to Alabama and Texas, hardy from zone 2 southward, quite similar to *Q. ilicifolia.*

Q. prinus (Q. montana)—Chestnut Oak, Rock Chestnut Oak. Grows up to 70 ft. and more. The chestnut-like leaves, yellowish-green above, are 5 to 7 in. long. Found growing in eastern North America it has deeply ridged bark in age which turns dull orange in autumn. Hardy from zone 2 southward it grows well in dry ground.

Q. rubra — Red Oak. The more northerly red oak is sometimes known as *Q. borealis*. It is the better of the two and widely planted for ornament from zone 3 southward. The southern form is hardy from zone 4 southward. Both are tall growing, to 80 ft., and relatively quick growing trees. Handsome and round-topped the red oak has spreading branches and foliage becoming dark red in the fall.

Q. stellata—Post Oak. A round-headed tree that grows from 50 to 100 ft., native from Massachusetts to Florida and westward, especially common along the edges of the salt marshes and on the dunes where it becomes a picturesque, wind-swept bushy tree. The post oak is hardy from zone 3 southward.

Q. velutina—The black oak is found native from Ontario to Florida and west to Texas and is hardy from zone 3 southward. It is a columnar tree up to 100 ft. or more in height. Used by the Cape Cod National Seashore Park for planting on stabilized dunes.

RED CEDAR—See *Juniperus.*

RHUS—See Shrubs.

ROBINIA—Locust, False Acacia. A member of the pea family, the locust is ornamental both in leaf and flower. It is characterized by its graceful, feather-form leaves and showy pea-like blossoms, in long drooping clusters, in late spring after the foliage is fully developed. Flattened almost black pods follow. The locusts grow well under ordinary conditions, and are valued for their ability to grow in poor sandy and dry soils. Propagation is mainly by seed, though they may be multiplied by suckers, and certain varieties are grafted. Use these trees in areas where the leaf miner and borers are not a pest or plan to spray to keep them clean.

R. 'Idaho' Locust. This hybrid of unknown origin is much used in the Midwest on poor, dry soils where other trees seem to have a struggle. Of open habit, it grows to 40 ft., with open compound leaves and dark reddish-purple pea-like flowers in pendulous clusters in early June, followed by pods.

R. neo-mexicana—Thorny Locust. A small tree or spiny, branched shrub, that is native to Colorado, Utah, New Mexico and Arizona and hardy from most parts of zone 3 southward.

R. *pseudoacacia*—Black Locust. Found from Pennsylvania to Oklahoma and often naturalized in its native habitat and elsewhere in North America, hardy from zone 3 southward. An open upright tree, with few branches, it grows to 70 ft. or more and has furrowed brown bark. It has open foliage and fragrant white pea-like flowers in pendulous clusters appearing in early June, followed by pods. 'Decaisneana' is handsome with rose colored flowers and 'Umbraculifera' develops a dense, rounded head, known as the umbrella black locust. The black locust is a good street tree, resistant to dust, smoke, drought, wind and salt spray and much liked by the bees.

ROSEBUD CHERRY—See *Prunus subhirtella*.

RUSSIAN MULBERRY—See *Morus alba tatarica*.

67. *Robinia pseudoacacia* — Black locust is a common native tree in many parts of eastern United States. It is extremely hardy and can be grown in the coldest parts of the country, even on poor dry soil. Although its pea-like blossoms are attractive in June, the tree is suitable only for the largest gardens or where more desirable trees will not survive.   U. S. Forest Service Photo

RUSSIAN OLIVE—See *Elaeagnus angustifolia.*

SALIX PENTANDRA—Laurel Willow. This is a tree growing to 50 ft. with shining green leaves 3 to 5 in. long and finely toothed. Native to southeastern Europe it sometimes is an escape in eastern United States and is hardy from zone 2 southward. The golden-yellow catkins are showy. It is one of the willows that can withstand dryness.

SALIX TRISTIS—See Shrubs.

SASSAFRAS ALBIDUM—Sassafras. An aromatic deciduous tree of the laurel family long known as *S. variifolium,* the familiar common native sassafras of the eastern United States. Usually a small slender tree to

68. *Sassafras albidum* — Though appealing because of its oddly-shaped leaves, which are aromatic when crushed, and its orange-scarlet fall color it is seldom seen in gardens, mainly because it is not easy to transplant. However it is native throughout a large part of the East and any large wild garden ought to include it.

U. S. Forest Service Photo

60 ft. but large specimens to 100 ft. are to be found on Gardiner's Island, Long Island. It usually has a long trunk with short, sparsely-spaced branches and irregularly shaped aromatic leaves which turn a brilliant orange to scarlet in autumn. Almost no other native tree has such gorgeous fall coloring. Bluish-black berries under ½ in. in diameter on a bright red stalk appear in early fall. Sexes may be separate or some trees may have both male and female flowers. It will grow in dry, poor gravelly soils, is rather difficult to transplant, at least when large. Grown individually out in the open it makes a fine tree. Grown in groups on the border of a woodland or along an old fence row it tends to be narrow and upright.

SERVICE BERRY, SHADBUSH—See *Amelanchier canadensis.*

SIBERIAN ELM—See *Ulmus pumila.*

SILK TREE—See *Albizzia julibrissin.*

SMOKE-TREE—See *Cotinus obovatus.*

SNOWBELL—See *Styrax japonica.*

SOPHORA JAPONICA—Japanese Pagoda Tree, Chinese Scholar Tree. One of the world's finest ornamentals, native to China and Korea, a rounded tree with wide spreading branches growing from 40 to 60 ft. in height. Its feathery, rather open, dark green foliage is attractive from the time of its appearance until the leaves drop in the fall although they take on no autumn coloring. Last of the large trees to bloom, in late summer, its cream colored pea-like flowers are in large conspicuous pyramidal, upright clusters. They are highly ornamental as are the handsome yellow-green pods which follow and frequently remain on the tree all winter. The tree grows well under almost any conditions including poor, rocky, dry soils and withstands city and seacoast conditions. It is practically free of pests and disease. The plant makes a handsome, excellent wide spreading specimen, street or shade tree and is hardy from zone 3 southward. 'Fastigiata' is erect and columnar in habit and 'Pendula' (Weeping Japanese Pagoda Tree) is a picturesque form with pendulous branches.

SORBUS—Mountain-Ash. These are ornamental trees and shrubs grown for their attractive feather-fashioned foliage, showy clusters of white flowers and decorative fruits, mostly red or orange. A member of the rose family they are mostly hardy North, not fussy as to soil, but like the sun and are able to endure dry conditions. Propagated by seed, or layers, the rare kinds by grafting. The mountain-ashes, especially in the East, unless properly protected from the borer, may be short-lived. The trees are frequently seriously infested with borers near the base of the trunk which weaken and eventually may kill the infected tree. Protective paints may be used or better, control by an application of a 12 percent spray of DDT to the trunks just prior to the time the borer insect eggs are known to hatch (April to June) and again about 3 weeks later. This preventative measure should be practiced each year.

S. *americana*—American Mountain-Ash. Its native range is from Newfoundland southward to North Carolina and westward; it likes a pH 4-5 soil and is hardy from zone 2 southward. Growing to 30 ft. it flowers in May and June, and is showy in the fall with its bright red fruits. S. *scopulina* is a shrubby western form of S. *americana*, rarely reaching over 10 ft., hardy from zone 3 southward.

S. *aucuparia*—European Mountain-Ash, Rowan Tree. A round-headed European tree that grows to 50 ft. or more, hardy from zone 2 southward. Its leaflets are shorter and more rounded than the American species but equally showy in fruit. It has long been in cultivation. 'Fastigiata' is of a narrow, pyramidal habit; 'Pendula' has long drooping branches and var. *xanthocarpa* has orange-yellow fruit.

S. *decora*—Showy Mountain Ash—is another native species, a tree 30 ft. tall or shrubby, hardy from zone 2 southward. It has fewer leaflets and larger, showier bright red fruits.

STYRAX—Storax. This is a genus of ornamental trees and shrubs; most species are found in tropical or warm regions but some are hardy in the temperate zones. There are several native species in the southern states which may be transferred to home grounds. They will withstand considerable dryness. Propagation is by seed or by layers, cuttings are difficult.

Styrax japonica—Japanese Snowbell. This is a small tree or shrub that grows 20 to 30 ft. high, frequently less under cultivation, a native of China and Japan, hardy from zone 3 southward. White fragrant flowers, in drooping terminal clusters in June and July, are followed by ½ in. long egg-shaped fruits. It does best in light, well-drained soil in open situations and is a good showy small specimen tree or useful for the back of the shrub border.

S. obassia—Fragrant Snowbell. A native of Japan with a more or less columnar habit and of considerable beauty while it is in bloom in early summer.

SUMAC—See *Rhus* under Shrubs.

THORN-APPLE—See *Crataegus.*

TILIA CORDATA—Small or Little-Leaved Linden. A slow growing shapely tree to 90 ft. in height, that is much taller in its native Europe. Small yellowish to whitish inconspicuous flowers appear in early July, it is the last of the lindens to flower. A densely pyramidal tree with compact, heart-shaped leaves, giving perfect shade. A good street tree that grows unusually well under adverse city conditions and as far north as Manitoba, Canada. This is one of the hardiest of the lindens.

TREE-OF-HEAVEN—See *Ailanthus altissima.*

ULMUS PARVIFOLIA—Chinese Elm. Sometimes known as *U. chinensis.* This is a small, quick growing tree, to 40 ft., round-topped with dense, dark green small leaves. The flowers are borne in small clusters in August and September. The mottled bark, often flaking off in irregular spots, exposes a much lighter colored bark underneath. The beautiful bark of the older tree is of ornamental interest the year round. Hardy from zone 3 southward, the fall foliage is red or purple North, and remains on the trees late into the fall; they are evergreen southward. An excellent ornamental used as a permanent tree in the landscape or as a screen or to provide quick growth.

ULMUS PUMILA—Siberian Elm. An elm somewhat resembling the Chinese elm but much taller. It grows to 80 ft., the bark is rough, and the flowers appear before the leaves unfold; the branches are more inclined to fork. It is hardy from zone 3 southward. Both of the above species are frequently used for shelterbelt planting in the West. Of rapid growth, rugged and hardy in extremes of heat or drought, they can grow in any soil. Serviceable trees for the drought areas of the

Midwest and valuable in the arid Southwest. Currently they are resistant to the Dutch elm disease.

WASHINGTON THORN—See *Crataegus phaenopyrum*.

YELLOW-WOOD—See *Cladrastis lutea*.

ZELKOVA SERRATA—Japanese Zelkova. This is a graceful elm-like Asiatic tree, a fast grower reaching 50 to 90 ft. It has a roundish top, wide spreading branches and dense foliage much like that of the elm which turns russet to reddish in the autumn. It is nearer in growth habit to the American elm than almost any other tree. Because of this similarity and its resistance to the Dutch elm disease it is being used as a substitute for street and lawn plantings. Hardy from zone 3 southward it grows well in a variety of soils. It will tolerate alkaline soil and drought and withstands sun and wind. For persons who like the graceful vase-shape habit of the elm this tree is recommended.

V Hardy Shrubs, Ground Covers and Vines

Shrubs grown under mulch with plenty of good humus in the soil will withstand periods of drought, even when watering is prohibited. By improving the water retaining properties of a poor soil the variety of shrubs that can be grown will be greatly increased. Where soil is poor and for one reason or another it can not be improved and where rainfall is below normal, a list of shrubs that will suffer from drought less than others should be carefully studied and selections made that will best serve under the circumstances.

By using native dry-area species and their varieties it is possible to diversify plantings and have an interesting landscape job. The value of winter silhouette, bark, fall coloring and berries, as well as leaf texture and pattern in summer should not be overlooked in choosing either trees or shrubs resistant to dryness.

AARON'S-BEARD—See *Hypericum calycinum.*

ABELIA GRANDIFLORA—Glossy Abelia. This is a half-evergreen, dense shrub of hybrid origin belonging to the honeysuckle family. It grows 3 to 5 ft. in height with small lustrous leaves turning bronze to purple in the fall, with loose flower clusters. The pinky-white, funnel-shaped flowers have reddish bracts and bloom from June or July until frost. Prune away a few of the older branches to the base each spring. It may be used as far north as New York City and even Boston with some protection. Hardy from zone 4 southward, it is the hardiest and most free flowering of the abelias and a good hedge plant. Although not generally listed with drought-resistant shrubs, the glossy abelia withstands a reasonable amount of dryness. Var. *sherwoodi* is a more compact form and it grows to only 3 ft. in height. It can be grown in a cool greenhouse.

ACANTHOPANAX SIEBOLDIANUS—Five-Leaved Aralia. A deciduous, bushy, densely foliaged shrub from Japan with slender arching branches grown in America for its handsome ornamental foliage and prickly stems. The leaves are compound with 5 to 7 nearly stalkless leaflets, generally wedge-shaped and arranged fan-fashioned. They do not drop until late into the fall. It grows from 6 to 9 ft. tall, will tolerate shade, dry soil, smoke and city conditions and is relatively free of pests. Sometimes listed in the trade under *A. pentaphyllus*. Hardy from southern New England south, makes a good hedge or a good accent plant in the shrub border. Propagate by seeds which should be stratified or by root cuttings over bottom heat.

AMELANCHIER. Shrubs and trees of the rose family found throughout the north temperate zone. They are attractive in early spring for their profusion of white bloom and later for their abundant small, brightly colored berries.

A. alnifolia—Serviceberry, Juneberry. Native to central and western North America and hardy most everywhere, from zone 2 southward. An upright, dense shrub growing to 15 ft. tall and almost as wide, it has white flowers, in 6 to 8 in. clusters, appearing in May, followed by edible blue-black berries. It is very hardy and drought-resistant, makes an excellent screen or untrimmed hedge and spreads by suckers.

A. canadensis—Shadbush; see Trees.

A. stolonifera—Running or Dwarf Serviceberry. Native in northeastern North America, it is hardy most everywhere. A low, sprawling shrub of dense growth it grows from 3 to 4 ft. high but is likely to form wide patches because of its underground stolons. Attractive upright flower clusters appear in May and are followed by edible blackpurple fruit. Hardy and drought-resistant.

AMORPHA—False Indigo. North American shrubs of the pea family, they are not especially showy but are used in the shrub border or as specimen plants in cool regions; they do well in poor soils. Not reliably hardy. Grown from zone 2 south.

A. fruticosa—Bastard Indigo. This shrub is native from Connecticut to Florida and west to the central United States, hardy from zone 3 southward. A fine-leaved bushy shrub with an open habit it grows 10 to 20 ft. Flowers dull purplish or bluish, in clusters 6 in. long, appear in June. There are varieties that come in pale blue, white and crisped-foliage.

ARCTOSTAPHYLOS. Drought-resistant evergreen shrubs of the heath family, mostly natives of California and the West Coast but the best known is *A. uva-ursi*, the bearberry, widely spread throughout the northern hemisphere and native in sandy areas in northern United States from coast to coast. One of the best of all the evergreens for ground cover and as a binder for dry sandy banks and slopes, it will trail nicely over walls and take the salt, wind and sun required of seaside plantings. Broad sheets of handsome small dark olive-green leaves form a dense carpet which covers the sandy dunes of Long Island and north-ward along the Atlantic coast. Small bell-shaped white or pink flowers

69. Flowering branches of manzanita (*Arctostaphylos manzanita*) on a young plant. The white or pink flowers in profuse clusters appear in April and May. A drought resistant, native evergreen shrub found growing on the Pacific coast, here growing in the University of Washington Arboretum.

Mulligan Photo

appear in May and June. Bright red berries are decorative in September and attract the birds. The foliage turns a bronzy red cast, attractive throughout the winter months. The plants are effective all year. This neat, hardy ground cover should be planted 18 to 24 in. apart, using only pot grown plants from the nursery for best results. Bearberry will not flower or fruit in rich soil nearly as well as in a dry sandy soil slightly on the acid side and it prefers and should have full sun or only light shade. Cuttings of mature growth may be taken in late summer. Grow and establish in pots previous to outdoor planting.

70. The hooker manzanita *(Arctostaphylos hookeri)* is a low growing west coast shrub, colorful the year round. Useful as a ground cover or in the rock garden, it needs sun and a well-drained soil and is quite drought-tolerant.

Shuster Photo

ARUNDINARIA—Bamboo. Although bamboos are associated with wet soils, certain species will grow like weeds on acid, sandy, dry soils where they can become a nuisance. They are tall growing, tree-like, woody members of the grass family.

A. japonica is the hardiest; can be safely planted from zone 4 southward. The leaves, green and shiny above and whitish and hairy beneath, are 4 to 12 in. long and 1½ in. wide. The stems die down each winter in the North. They make a dense, impenetrable screen of broad foliage carried on 6 to 10 ft. canes or stems. Other bamboos good on sandy dry soils include. *A. auricoma* and *A. fastuosa.*

AUCUBA. Asiatic evergreen shrubs of the dogwood family tolerant of shade, smoky atmosphere and poor dry soils, not reliably hardy north of Washington, D. C. It can be wintered safely in a cool place if kept on the dry side. Popular as foliage plants grown in the cool greenhouse and used in the North in pots or tubs for porch or terrace decoration during the summer months. Also used in city window boxes in the North.

A. japonica—Japanese Laurel. The most generally grown is this shrub from 4 to 15 ft. tall, usually much smaller; its glossy dark-green, toothed leaves are 4 to 8 in. long. The large waxy scarlet berries need both male and female plants. 'Variegata'—Gold-Dust Tree—has yellow spotted leaves.

BAMBOO—See *Arundinaria.*

BARBERRY—See *Berberis.*

BASTARD INDIGO—See *Amorpha fruticosa.*

BAYBERRY—See *Myrica pensylvanica.*

BEACH HEATHER—See *Hudsonia.*

BEACH PLUM—See *Prunus maritima.*

BEARBERRY—See *Arctostaphylos uva-ursi.*

BEAUTY BUSH—See *Kolkwitzia amabilis.*

BERBERIS—Barberry. A large genus of evergreen and deciduous spiny shrubs valued for their good habit and handsome foliage, many with beautiful autumn coloring and attractive fruit. Of easy cultivation and adapted to various soils and situations they are useful shrubs for dry banks and sandy soils and are tolerant of lime. They resent transplanting so plant them when small.

B. aggregata is a densely branched, deciduous shrub 5 to 6 ft. tall. The flowers open late, in close panicles toward the end of the branches, the fruit is coral-red. The species is hardy from zone 4 southward. Var. *pratti* is more profuse in flowers and fruits with longer, sometimes toothless, leaves.

B. mentorensis—Mentor Barberry. This is a spiny hybrid, evergreen in the South. It grows from 3 to 5 ft. tall and is hardy from southern New England south, will survive the cold winters as well as the hot dry summers of the middle west better than most barberries. It makes an impenetrable thorny hedge, a fine barrier planting in dry areas. Dark, dull red fruit are effective in the fall.

B. stenophylla—Rosemary Barberry. A hybrid, this is a fine textured, graceful shrub with slender arching branches, growing to 8 ft. or less in height with glossy dark green, very narrow leaves dark green above, whitish beneath. It is evergreen south of Washington, D. C., semi-evergreen or deciduous farther north. Attractive golden yellow flowers are followed by black fruits covered with a waxy bloom. Spiny branches make it an excellent barrier hedge. It does well in a variety of soils especially light sandy ones and is resistant to disease and pests. It is too large for the small garden.

B. thunbergi—Japanese Barberry. A popular hedge plant it is noted for its ability to withstand dry conditions. Of dense, thorny habit its bright red fruits remain on all winter and in autumn the leaves turn a brilliant scarlet. When mature the shrub is from 4 to 6 ft. tall. It is hardy from the southern part of zone 3 southward and is not attacked by rust.

There are several horticultural forms, some with variegated leaves. 'Minor,' the box-bayberry, is a dwarf, dense form about 3 ft. tall with smaller leaves; smaller in every way than the species, it makes an excellent low hedge. 'Erecta' is erect in form, excellent as a hedge demanding little trimming. 'Atropurpurea' has bronzy red leaves and is an excellent ornamental shrub.

B. verruculosa is of low dense habit, not over 3 ft. tall, with glossy evergreen leaves, whitish beneath turning a lovely bronzy tone in the autumn. The golden flowers are solitary or in twos and larger than in most barberries. The fruit is bluish-black with a bloom. Hardy from zone 4 southward.

B. *wilsonae* is a compact prostrate or erect, half-evergreen shrub of 4 to 6 ft. with brilliant autumn coloring and a mass of coral-red berries. Birds do not bother the berries as they dislike the prickly spiny leaves. Hardy from zone 5 southward. 'Tom Thumb' has slightly toothed leaves and prolific red fruit.

BITTERSWEET—See *Celastrus scandens* under Vines.

BLUEBEARD—See *Caryopteris*.

BLUEBERRY—See *Vaccinium*.

BLUE SPIREA—See *Caryopteris*.

BROOM—See *Cytisus*.

BROOM CROWBERRY—See *Corema conradi*.

BUCKTHORN—See *Rhamnus*.

BUDDLEIA—Butterfly Bush, Summer Lilac. Mostly tropical shrubs native to China, they are some of the most attractive of the late flowering plants. Attractive blooms are borne in panicles resembling the lilac, mostly lavender or purple in color. Fast, rather coarse growers, they enjoy a sunny position in a well-drained rich but not heavy soil. Nearly all have a prominent orange eye and are sweetly fragrant. Easily propagated by cuttings of half-ripe wood.

B. *alternifolia*—Fountain Buddleia. This is a beautiful Chinese shrub that grows up to 10 ft. It is the hardiest of all the buddleia species with wide-spreading arching branches, a vigorous grower. Clusters of small lavender-purple flowers on last year's branches bloom in early summer. It needs room to expand as it may become 15 ft. in diameter, making a colorful showing if given adequate space. With this species, branches do not die to the ground in winter and its light green foliage is made up of comparatively small, narrow, willow-like leaves. Shoots of the current season may flower later in the summer. It thrives in poor, but well-drained, gravelly soils and although the hardiest species, it is only hardy from zone 5 southward.

71. The orange-eye butterfly bush *(Buddleia davidi magnifica)* flowers from late July until frost; one of the most attractive of late flowering plants and sweetly fragrant. Fast, rather coarse growing, it needs ample room. Dies to the ground most winters. The above growth was made during the current summer and carries a wealth of attractive bloom.

U. S. D. A. Photo

B. davidi—Orange-Eye Butterfly Bush. From China, it is one of the most popular species of the group. The plant grows 4 to 10 ft. in height, often much less. The foliage is coarse in texture, the plant open in habit, with large pyramidal white, pink, red and purple flowers in upright spikes that appear from late July until frost. The plants die to the ground during most winters so cut them back to the ground and give some winter protection with a mulch.

BUFFALO-BERRY—See *Shepherdia.*

BUSH CLOVER—See *Lespedeza.*

BUSH HONEYSUCKLE—See *Diervilla* and *Lonicera.*

BUTTERFLY BUSH—See *Buddleia*.

CALLUNA VULGARIS—Scotch Heather. Calluna is the genus that comprises the true, hardy heathers. The heaths or florists' heather belong to the genus *Erica*. The different forms of heather have all been derived from the one species *C. vulgaris* which is hardier than any of the heaths and well adapted to clothe dry sunny slopes in cool areas. If kept sheared in the spring the plants make compact clumps, mostly less than 18 in. high. By planting several forms together in drifts pleasing foliage effects are possible as well as flower color variations during the summer. Tiny numerous, evergreen leaves completely clothe the twigs and a profusion of small, nodding, rosy-pink flowers bloom from July to October. The heather has become naturalized in northeastern United States, notably Nantucket where it covers sandy banks and slopes. The many horticultural varieties and cultivars of *C. vulgaris* include 'Alba', white-flowered; 'Alporti', crimson-flowered and taller than the typical form; 'Aurea' with golden-yellow foliage; 'Carnea', with pink flowers; 'Coccinea' has deep red flowers; 'Cuprea', has golden foliage in summer, bronzy in winter; 'Hammondi', has white flowers and is taller than the typical form; 'Hirsuta,' gray-hairy foliage; 'Nana', has purple flowers and is scarcely 6 in. tall; and 'Searlei' has white flowers and a looser growth habit than the typical form.

CARAGANA—Pea-Shrub or Tree. Hardy, deciduous, decorative shrubs or small trees of the pea family, mostly native in central Asia, they thrive in sunny places and light soils. Few plants are better planted as a hedge for use as a windbreak or snow trap in regions of severe cold. They are grown for their bright yellow, typically pea-like flowers and interesting habit of growth. The leaves are compound with numerous leaflets arranged feather-fashion.

   C. arborescens—Siberian Pea-Shrub. Hardy in the north half of the country, from zone 1 southward, it grows 16 to 18 ft. tall. A stiff coarse shrub, upright in habit, becoming leggy unless it is kept well pruned. Cut back severely when young to encourage branching. Yellow pea-like flowers appear in mid-May. It is one of the best hedge and shelter plants for the prairies and Northwest, very drought-resistant.

   There are dwarf forms suitable for hedges and valuable in regions where privet is not hardy. 'Pendula' is a weeping form with stiffly hanging branches and 'Nana' is a stunted, dwarf form with contorted branches.

C. *maximowicziana*—Maximowicz Pea-Shrub. With an interesting form, and densely branched, of spreading habit, this shrub grows 3 to 4 ft. high but spreads to 12 ft. in diameter. It has bright green leaves and bronzy-yellow pea-like flowers appear in late May, hardy from zone 2 southward.

C. *microphylla*—Littleleaf Pea-Shrub. A graceful Chinese shrub growing to 10 ft. with long spreading branches it has yellow pea-like flowers in Mid-May.

C. *pygmaea*—Pygmy Pea-Shrub. Usually a prostrate spiny shrub it makes an excellent low clipped hedge, a barrier 2 to 4 ft. tall and 3 to 5 ft. wide. With attractive arched, spreading branches and fine foliage, it has bright yellow flowers in May and June. It is hardy from zone 2 southward and drought-resistant.

CARYOPTERIS—Bluebeard, Blue Spirea. These deciduous shrubs from Asia belong to the vervain family and are valuable for their colorful lavender or white flowers late in the season when any new flower in the garden is most welcome. The tops are generally killed back during northern winters but new young shoots come up from below as the weather becomes warm and flower the same season. They like a sunny location and a well-drained light limey soil. The leaves are of an attractive grayish tone and aromatic. Hardy from zone 5 southward, they winter kill further north, where they are popular cool greenhouse plants. Good shrubs where hardy for the modern small garden. Prune hard in early spring for best results.

CEANOTHUS AMERICANUS—New Jersey Tea. A low deciduous shrub growing to 3 ft., of slender, upright growth bearing white flowers in flat-topped small clusters in June. The least showy of the species. Grown where something better will not survive. Found growing from Canada to Florida and westward. Hardy from zone 3 southward. Can be carried over where not hardy by digging them up in the fall and wintering them over in a frost-proof place. Propagate with stem or root cuttings in the fall.

CHAENOMELES LAGENARIA—Flowering or Japanese Quince. Often listed as *C. japonica* or *C. speciosa,* this is a vigorous spiny shrub growing to 6 ft. or more in height and a member of the rose family from east Asia. Because of its ornamental lustrous dark green leaves held late and large showy scarlet flowers in early spring the flowering quince is useful in the landscape in the shrub border, as a hedge or trained against a wall. There are many named varieties with flowers of varying shades from pure white and pink to deep scarlet, some with semi-double flowers. They all do best in sunny locations and are in demand on limey soils where azaleas will not grow. Hardy from zone 3 southward. Propagated by cuttings, root cuttings or layers. The ornamental quinces were previously known as *Pyrus* or *Cydonia.*

C. japonica alpina—Alpine Flowering Quince. The lowest growing of all the quinces, it makes a good ground cover suckering readily. It grows to 1 ft. in height and is not fussy about soil.

CHASTE TREE—See *Vitex agnus-castus.*

CHERRY—See *Prunus.*

CHINESE or HORNED HOLLY—See *Ilex cornuta.*

CINQUEFOIL—See *Potentilla.*

CLERODENDRON TRICHOTOMUM. A tall Japanese deciduous shrub or small tree growing from 7 to 20 ft. it is hardy from zone 4 southward. A good berrying shrub for sandy limey soils. With its large soft leaves it is conspicuous in late summer with loose clusters of fragrant white flowers set off by persistent red calyxes. These contrast pleasingly with the bright-blue fruits. Var. *fargesi* from China has smaller leaves, also the calyx which is green when the flowers open, later turns a reddish-purple to set off the turquoise-blue berries. If further north the tops are killed back in severe winters, the plant usually comes back.

COMPTONIA PEREGRINA—Sweet-Fern, Sweetbush. Also known as *C. asplenifolia* and *Myrica asplenifolia.* A sweet smelling, deciduous, native shrub of the bayberry family, found in dry sandy and rocky soils throughout eastern North America. It is a hairy shrub that grows 4 to 5 ft., although often much less, with finely cut fern-like leaves and bears inconspicuous flowers in catkins. Valuable in naturalistic

72. A close relative of bayberry, the sweet fern, *Comptonia peregrina* is unfortunately equally difficult to transplant. Small plants under a foot high are the best risks for moving. Sweet fern grows on the driest, gravelly slopes and its beautifully lobed leaves are most distinctive.

Taloumis Photo

plantings, the wild garden, as a ground cover or a soil-binder on dry sandy slopes or banks. Attractive planted at the base of sumac bushes. Easily grown from seed, division or layers.

COREMA CONRADI—Broom Crowberry. An evergreen heath-like bushy, low shrub of the crowberry family cultivated in the rock and the wild garden and useful as a ground cover in poor soil. Native from

New Jersey to Newfoundland, found in acid sandy or rocky soils. Of an upright, twiggy habit to 2 ft. it has tiny crowded, narrow leaves and inconspicuous flowers.

CORNUS—Dogwood. Most dogwoods are not drought-resistant, some prefer a moist, moderate rich loam, but those listed below adapt well to dry soils.

C. baileyi—Shrubby Dogwood. Useful for seaside plantings and found from Ontario to Pennsylvania. It has reddish branches and takes on vivid coloring in winter. The leaves are whitish beneath and brilliantly colored in the fall with white fruit.

C. mas—Cornelian Cherry. A large bushy shrub or small spreading deciduous tree of vigorous growth from Eurasia, hardy from zone 3 southward and takes city conditions. Conspicuous in early spring with small clusters of yellow flowers appearing in March or April before the lustrous leaves which remain green until late in the fall. Large red fruits appear in late summer. 'Aureo-elegantissima' has creamy-white and pink variegated leaves.

C. racemosa—Gray Dogwood. This gray-branched attractive shrub of dense habit is found from Maine to Georgia and grows from 6 to 10 ft. tall. A vigorous grower it sprouts readily from the base, withstands pruning and can be cut back as necessary. Effective in early summer with its small creamy-white flowers followed by early white fruit on red stalks. Gray twigs are attractive throughout the winter. Good as a barrier planting. Thrives in almost any soil, in the shade or open.

C. stolonifera—Red Osier Dogwood. A native of North America, found from Newfoundland to Virginia. This shrub rarely is taller than 6 ft., but since it spreads by underground prostrate stems it makes large clumps. It has dark red erect branches with small white flowers in flat-topped clusters in May and June. Its fruits are bluish-white. Var. *flaviramea* has yellow twigs.

COTINUS—Smoke-Tree. A member of the sumac family including two species cultivated for ornament. Both specis are of easy culture, thriving in well-drained soil, not too rich or too moist.

C. americanus is now known as *C. obovatus*.

C. coggygria—European Smoke-Tree. Often known by its old name *Rhus cotinus*. This European species is the hardiest and produces the best "smoky" effect. A bushy shrub it grows 10 to 15 ft. An old fashioned plant, it stands out because of its large feathery fruiting panicles borne in profusion that last for weeks and are effective all summer. They give the plant its "smoky" appearance and later turn grayish or brown. The foliage takes on good coloring in the fall. 'Purpureus' has purplish leaves and plumes with dark purple hairs. Hardy from zone 4 southward.

73. *Cotinus coggygria* — The smoke tree is a favorite old-fashioned shrub, conspicuous in summer with its showy plumes and in fall with its yellow to deep purple foliage. As the plant is hard to transplant, the purchase of small potted specimens is recommended.

Taloumis Photo

C. obovatus—American Smoke-Tree. Sometimes known as *C. americanus* or *Rhus cotinoides*. A native in the southern part of the United States but fairly hardy north, from zone 5 southward, in zone 4 with protection. It is a large shrub or small tree growing from 15 to 20 ft. Its fruiting panicles make very litle show but it is a brilliant plant in the fall when its leaves turn orange and scarlet.

COTONEASTER. Shrubs belonging to the rose family, most of them hardy North and among the most useful for ornamental planting. They are outstanding for their attractive habit of growth and colorful fruits and thrive in open sunny sites in well-drained soil with an alkaline rather than an acid reaction. Plants from pots are most easily transplanted and once established they succeed well in dry situations. There are species of sizes, habit and other characteristics to fit most any need. Those dwarf or prostrate and of a spreading habit, with small dark green leaves (some evergreen) and red fruit are well suited for planting on slopes, for use as ground covers and in rock gardens. The taller kinds make excellent bed or specimen plants.

C. acutifolia is a deciduous shrub of compact habit, growing to 10 ft. tall, from northern China, hardy from zone 2 southward. It has dark-green glossy leaves, light red in the fall, makes a good untrimmed or clipped hedge.

C. adpressa—Creeping Cotoneaster. This is a low prostrate shrub from western China that hugs the ground, the stems often rooting. It has pink flowers and the leaves turn dark red in the fall. Useful for planting on slopes, used as a ground cover and in rock gardens. Hardy from Philadelphia or zone 4 southward. 'Praecox' is a more vigorous form, a little taller, with distinctly pink flowers and larger fruit.

C. dammeri is a low evergreen with long trailing branches that often root at the joints and small white flowers and red fruit. A valuable rock garden plant. Hardy from zone 5 southward or zone 4 with protection.

C. conspicua, an evergreen spreading shrub from 4 to 6 ft. tall is smothered with white, solitary flowers in May and June, followed by winter-persisting, bright red berries. Hardy from zone 5 southward. Var. *decora* is practically prostrate and widely grown. Not over 2 ft. but has a spread of about 6 ft.

C. dammeri, an evergreen prostrate shrub from China, its trailing branches rooting at the joints, valuable used for retaining walls, as a ground cover or for the rock garden. Hardy from zone 5 or with protection from zone 4 southward.

C. divaricata makes a dense upright wide-spreading bush 3 to 6 ft. with shining dark green leaves. Flowers are pinkish, fruits red, very showy in the fall. Hardy to New York, from zone 4 southward.

C. horizontalis—Rock Cotoneaster. This is a low shrub, its branches forked and almost trailing. It makes a good wall plant and is effective sprawling over a boulder in the rock garden. It has pinkish flowers and red fruit. Hardy from Philadelphia south or zone 4 southward. 'Perpusilla' is a dwarfer form. Its foliage turns orange-red in autumn.

C. hupehensis is a medium sized deciduous shrub of graceful arching habit growing 4 to 6 ft. tall with conspicuous white flowers in spring and large red berries which drop in September. The leaves remain green late and finally turn yellow. Hardy from zone 4 southward.

C. lactea has whitish hairy twigs and crimson fruits which appear late and last a long time. Hardy from Washington, D. C. southward. Excellent trained against a wall.

C. lucida—The hedge cotoneaster is a strong upright grower 6 to 8 ft. tall holding its lustrous green leaves till late in the autumn, they turn red in the fall. Flowers are pinkish, fruits bluish-black, hardy from zone 3 southward. Excellent as a hedge, trimmed or untrimmed.

C. microphylla—The rock spray cotoneaster is perhaps one of the toughest, a dwarf dense evergreen of spreading habit, tolerating poor soil and a windy site. White flowers are followed by red berries. Hardy from zone 4 southward. 'Thymifolia' is a dwarf, compact form with very narrow leaves and smaller flowers and fruit.

C. salicifolia is an upright specimen 6 ft. or more in height, hardy from zone 5 southward. Var. *floccosa,* the willowleaf cotoneaster, is considered one of the best of the tall evergreen species, found growing as far north as Massachusetts; it is half evergreen northward. It has narrow dark green leathery leaves, the underside of the young ones densely hairy, and white flower clusters about 2 in. across. 'Fructu-luteo' has yellow berries and is tall and graceful.

C. simonsi, a handsome upright, semi-evergreen grower, is hardy from zone 5 southward, it is a good hedge plant.

CRATAEGUS CRUS-GALLI—See Trees.

CURRANT—See *Ribes alpinum.*

CYTISUS—Broom. Members of this genus make a good showing, (where shrubs such as rhododendrons and azaleas will not grow), with their profusion of bright yellow pea-like flowers in early spring. Deciduous or evergreen spineless shrubs, mostly from the Mediterranean region and western Asia, they belong to the pea family. In some cases they are almost leafless. Several can be grown outdoors in the North if given suitable conditions. They prefer full sun, will stand a lot of wind and like a poor soil with perfect drainage. The taller kinds should be pruned back to keep them from becoming straggly. Considerable pruning keeps the brooms attractive, compact and in good shape, of value even when not in flower. They transplant poorly when mature, small plants are much easier to establish.

C. kewensis—Kew Broom. Of hybrid origin, not reliably hardy north of zone 4. A low plant not over 12 in. Nearly prostrate with a spread of about 4 ft. Excellent for covering a hot, sandy bank and among the earliest to bloom, covered with a mass of creamy-yellow flowers.

C. praecox —Warminster Broom. A handsome hybrid plant hardy from Washington, D. C. south growing from 4 to 5 ft. Unlike many brooms it is a compact grower about 3 ft. tall, not leggy but clothed to the ground with a mass of sulphur-yellow flowers in spring. Tolerates hot dry sites and a poor soil.

C. scoparius—Common Scotch Broom. A European shrub 4 to 9 ft. that has become naturalized in some parts of North America on Cape Cod, Nantucket Island and the Pacific Northwest. It makes a good showing with its bright green stems and brilliant yellow flowers in May or June covering a dry, gravelly bank. Effective from a distance, reseeds itself. Plant from pots. Hardy from zone 3 southward. 'Moonlight Broom' is a lower more compact form with sulphur-yellow flowers. 'Andreanus' has very striking flowers of yellow and crimson but is more tender. There are many other color forms.

DAPHNE. Slow growing, small deciduous or evergreen shrubs, to 3 ft. in height, valued for their fragrant flowers, sometimes resembling those of candytuft. They do best in a loose, loamy, well-drained soil with a fair amount of sand, preferably somewhat alkaline. Not all are hardy North. Although uncertain plants which may fail completely the two listed below are grown successfully by some gardeners under hot, dry and poor conditions.

74. A flowering branch of Scotch broom (*Cytisus scoparius*) clothed with brilliant yellow flowers in May or June when it is a lovely sight covering a dry, gravelly bank; very effective from a distance.

Marten Photo

D. mezereum—A neat little upright deciduous shrub that has become naturalized in some parts of eastern North America. Fragrant lilac-purple flowers appear early in March or April before the leaves and in the summer are followed by scarlet fruit. 'Alba' has white flowers and yellow fruit. Hardy from zone 3 southward. Prefers some shade.

D. odora 'Aureo-variegata'—An evergreen shrub from China and

Japan growing from 3 to 4 ft. with dense, head-like terminal clusters of very fragrant soft rosy-purple flowers in January or later. Leaves are heavily margined with yellow. Hardy from zone 5 southward.

DEUTZIA. Deciduous shrubs native in Asia and members of the saxifrage family. Attractive in early summer with an abundance of flowers, mostly white, some tinged pinkish. Two of easy culture that may be grown on rather poor, light soil are listed below.

D. *pulchra* is a spreading 6 ft. shrub with gray-green leaves and a profusion of panicles of pearly colored flowers in June.

D. *scabra* is widely cultivated. A branching more or less arching shrub, 5 to 8 ft. in height, it has reddish-brown shedding bark. Spire-like clusters of white flowers, sometimes pinkish on the outside, appear in June and July. Hardy from zone 4 southward. Will take city conditions. There are many horticultural forms, dwarf ones and others with white-dotted or marbled leaves. 'Plena' (Pride of Rochester) is a popular double-flowered form, rosy purple on the outside of the corolla. 'Candidissima' has white double flowers in late June. Both are the latest deutzias to flower.

DIERVILLA—Bush-Honeysuckle. Deciduous low shrubs of North America, not particular as to soil, that do well in partial shade and are propagated by suckers or increased by division.

D. *lonicera* is native from Newfoundland to North Carolina and westward, hardy everywhere and from 2 to 3 ft. in height. Oval, long pointed leaves to 4 in. and small yellow flowers usually in threes in early summer. It spreads rapidly by stolons and is useful for holding banks.

DOGWOOD—See *Cornus.*

DWARF GRAY WILLOW—See *Salix tristis.*

ELAEAGNUS. A genus of hardy ornamental wind-resistant shrubs and small trees useful as windbreaks particularly in the prairies states and valuable for seaside plantings. They grow easily in a variety of dry sites. Many have beautiful foliage and are useful on dry, well-drained limy, sandy coastal areas where evergreens are difficult. They are slow growing to about 8 to 10 ft. in height. Easily propagated from cuttings. Also see *Elaeagnus* under Trees.

E. commutata—Silverberry. An erect, deciduous shrub native to North America growing 8 to 10 ft. Formerly known as *E. argentea*. Excellent on a dry bank where its silvery foliage glistens in the sunlight, hardy.

E. multiflora (E. longipes)—Gumi. A spreading Asiatic shrub growing to 6 ft. with fragrant yellowish-white flowers but most conspicuous for its long stemmed, spotted, scarlet edible fruit. Hardy from zone 3 southward. There are several varieties with minor foliage differences but none superior to the typical form. Tolerates city conditions.

E. pungens is a fragrant fall-flowering, usually spiny, spreading, sometimes sprawling Japanese shrub much grown in the South. An evergreen from 10 to 15 ft. with reddish fruit. It is hardy from zone 5 southward where it is frequently used as a vine for arbors. There are many variations with leaves blotched or margined yellow, white, etc. *E. pungens* and varieties are greenhouse grown in the North. 'Aurea' has yellow-margined leaves, 'Reflexa' wavy-margined leaves and 'Variegata' has white or yellowish-white margined leaves.

E. umbellata is a branching spiny shrub from eastern Asia, that grows from 10 to 15 ft. tall and is hardy from zone 3 southward. It has silvery foliage and small but fragrant yellowish-white flowers which appear in May and June. One form has silvery twigs.

EPIGAEA REPENS—Trailing Arbutus. Also called Mayflower, this attractive spring-blooming, creeping evergreen is native from Massachusetts to Georgia and west to Ohio and Tennessee. A member of the heath family and one of the choicest wild flowers of the eastern United States. Not commonly grown in cultivation because it is difficult to establish successfully. It likes a peaty sandy soil in shade. If you want to try it buy nursery grown plants from a reliable firm that specializes in wild flowers. It is an excellent ground cover, useful in the rock garden and in woodland plantings if you can once get it to growing well. Its white to pink flowers are small and very fragrant, the evergreen leaves 3 in. long. The plant is rarely over an inch or so tall as it creeps along the surface of the soil. It will grow in very poor gravelly soil.

ERICA—Heath. Usually evergreen, they are low shrubs of the heath family largely from the Mediterranean region and South Africa. Not as hardy as the heathers. In mild regions they are attractive for outdoor groupings and used in rock gardens. Grown by florists as pot plants for Christmas and Easter. Heaths have numerous, very small, needle-like or very narrow leaves usually in whorls and spread apart. Persistent flowers are small and urn-shaped. Heaths require a lime-free sandy soil with some leaf mold or peat and no excess of moisture. They should be pruned from time to time to encourage new growth and prevent bareness at the base of the plant. Full sun or partial shade and a mulch of pine needles all help. They are best planted in groups, many of the species are grown on the Pacific coast, a few can be grown in the East.

E. australis—Spanish Heath. This shrub from Spain and Portugal is hardy from zone 5 southward on the Pacific coast only. An upright open branched shrub 5 to 8 ft. tall.

E. carnea—Spring Heath, from southern Europe, is mostly prostrate, 12 in. high, with leaves in fours and tiny red flowers in early spring. Hardy up to zone 3. 'Alba' has white flowers and 'Rosea' is rose colored. Useful for the rock garden.

E. tetralix—Cross-Leaved Heath is native to Europe and hardy up to zone 3, naturalized in Massachusetts. Not over 2 ft. tall, grayish leaves in fours and rosy-red flowers in dense terminal clusters from June till October.

E. vagans—Cornish Heath is from western Europe, spreading but not prostrate, grows to 1 ft. tall or more with leaves in fours or fives and purplish-pink flowers in late summer. Hardy from zone 4 southward.

EUONYMUS. Deciduous or evergreen shrubs, vines and small trees of the bittersweet family. Most are of upright habit, a few prostrate, and they do well in sun or partial shade and are not fussy about soil. Inconspicuous flowers appear in May and June followed by colorful attractive fruits and bright autumn coloring. Most of the deciduous and a few of the evergreen kinds are hardy North. They make good hedges and thrive under trying city and seaside conditions.

E. alatus—Hardy from zone 3 southward and of interest for its horizontal branches and scarlet autumn coloring. Grows to around 8 to 9 ft. Var. *compactus* has brilliant red fall coloring, seldom over 4 ft. tall, an excellent low hedge plant requiring little clipping.

75. Winterberry euonymus *(Euoñymus bungeanus)*, hardy from Washington, D.C. south, may be used trimmed or untrimmed, it is drought-tolerant and will thrive under trying conditions. Grown here on the Southern Plains it reaches a height of 10 feet and a spread of 14 feet.

U. S. D. A. Photo

E. americanus—Strawberry Bush. A deciduous, sparsely branched shrub growing 5 to 8 ft. in height and hardy from zone 4 southward. Showy in the fall with pink warty fruit and scarlet covered seeds. Native from New York to Florida and Oklahoma.

E. bungeanus—Winterberry Euonymus. Hardy from Washington, D. C. south. A rapid grower to a height of 10 to 12 ft. with light green foliage and yellowish flowers. It is drought-resistant and will stand shearing. May be used as an untrimmed or trimmed hedge.

E. europaeus—Spindle Tree. This is a European deciduous shrub or tree growing from 20 to 25 ft., sometimes an escape in the United States. Very showy in the fall with pinkish-red fruits. Hardy from zone 3 southward. There are fruits of varying colors, from white to crimson.

'Alba' has white fruit, 'Intermedia' bright red and 'Nana' is a dwarf up-right form from 3 to 4 ft. The plants need no special attention except to check for scale. Use a dormant oil spray for control.

E. fortunei—Wintercreeper. See Vines.

E. japonicus—Evergreen Euonymus. Not hardy north of Philadelphia. A slow growing, arching shrub from 5 to 8 ft. tall or may be pushed to 15 ft. Adapts to extremes in heat, frost, smog or exposures on the ocean. Develops dark green glossy leaves and brilliant crimson berries when unpruned. Makes a good hedge or shelter plant on coastal sands. Sometimes used as a tub plant. Develops a dense fibrous root system. Widely grown throughout the South for its fine foliage. There are numerous forms with white and yellow variegated leaves.

'Albo-marginatus' is popular with narrow margins of white along the leaves becoming silvery, var. *compactus* is almost ball-like in its compact habit and its leaves turn a striking red in the fall and var. *erectus* is more erect and dense than the type, the foliage a brighter green. In 'Aureo-marginatus' the leaves have a golden yellow at the center forming an irregular pattern against the dull dark green of the margin, 'Microphyllus' *(E. pulchellus)* is of a dwarf compact habit with smaller leaves of a bright shining green, excellent as a low hedge but not in the shade unless grown very dry. A satisfactory substitute for box as an edging plant.

E. obovatus—Running Euonymus. This is a prostrate, deciduous shrub native to eastern North America, hardy from zone 2 southward. Of value only as a ground cover, its brilliant crimson coloring in the fall is an asset.

FIRE THORN—See *Pyracantha.*

FIVE-LEAVED ARALIA—See *Acanthopanax sieboldianus.*

FLOWERING or JAPANESE QUINCE—See *Chaenomeles lagenaria.*

FORSYTHIA—Golden Bell. Deciduous shrubs from Asia belonging to the olive family and prized for their wealth of brilliant yellow flowers produced before the leaves appear. Among the showiest of spring-flowering shrubs and some of the first to flower. All are hardy up to zone 2. Of easy culture, not particular as to soil or site, but should have some sun and plenty of room. Best used as specimen or accent plants because of their size and spreading upright or arching habit, many growing 7 to 9 ft. tall with a spread as wide. Prune just after flowering for best blossoms and to keep the plant in good shape. Comparatively pest and disease free. Easily propagated by stem cuttings or uprooting the plentiful supply of suckers to supply new plants.

F. intermedia is a hybrid growing to 9 ft. tall with arching or spreading branches, perhaps the best of the golden bells and including several useful forms. 'Primulina' has pale yellow flowers more numerous toward the ends of the branches. 'Spectabilis' is a strong grower with the largest and showiest flowers in the group.

F. ovata is a Korean species, the hardiest and earliest to bloom with amber-yellow flowers borne singly. Not as outstanding as the above.

F. suspensa, the weeping golden bell grows to 8 ft. or more. Its slender branches often bend to the ground, rooting at the tips. In flower it forms a golden yellow mound. Var. *sieboldi* has more slender leaves, very effective trailing over a rock or wall. Var. *fortunei* is an upright grower with arching branches.

F. viridissima is conspicuous with its bright green stems and is the only forsythia of any value for autumn coloring, its leaves turn dark purple in the autumn. Rather stiff in habit it is more tender than most and later to bloom. Its flower buds are often killed during severe winters.

FOUNTAIN RED CEDAR—See *Juniperus virginiana tripartita.*

GAULTHERIA SHALLON—Salal. Belongs to the heath family and is native from Alaska to California, in the western part of the United States. This evergreen, more or less spreading shrub, seldom grows over 1½ ft. tall. It has rather large heart-shaped leaves, panicles of pinkish-white flowers and dark purple fruits. Hardy from zone 4 southward and used as an under shrub, for rock gardens or as a ground cover growing best in sandy, peaty soil in partial shade. Takes moisture but also is quite drought-resistant. Plant potted specimens as they transplant readily.

GAYLUSSACIA—Huckleberry. Ornamental North American berry-bearing shrubs of the heath family valuable for both their attractive foliage and fruit. In some localities they are confused with *Vaccinium corymbosum,* the high-bush blueberry. The fruit of the huckleberry is distinguished by the 10 large, bony seeds which crack loudly between the teeth when eaten, fruit of inferior quality. Blueberry seeds are very small, scarcely noticeable. Huckleberries like partial shade and like blueberries must have an acid soil. They will grow in dry, hot areas. The florists' huckleberry, sold for its foliage, is not a huckleberry but *Vaccinium ovatum.*

G. *baccata*—Black or High-Bush Huckleberry. This is a shrub not over 3 ft. tall, native in eastern North America and hardy from zone 2 southward. Sometimes called G. *resinosa.* It has decorative foliage and black shining fruit.

G. *brachycera*—Box-Huckleberry, Juniper-Berry. Native from Delaware to Tennessee, it is hardy from zone 3 southward. A nearly prostrate evergreen shrub it is not over 18 in. tall forming a small rounded mass with leaves 1 in. long and blue berries effective in August. Valuable as a ground cover in shady, peaty places, also useful in the rock garden.

GENISTA. Deciduous or half-evergreen low, ornamental shrubs of the pea family found in Europe, Asia and Africa. Not quite hardy North but one or two species may survive in favored positions with winter protection. Valued for their showy yellow or white flowers and the fact they thrive in hot, dry sandy soils in mild climates. Attractive on sunny banks. Do not transplant easily. Propagate by seeds, cuttings and layers. Closely related to Cytisus, the common genista grown by florists for Easter which is *Cytisus canariensis* or *C. racemosus.*

G. *germanica* is an upright spiny little shrub about 18 in. high with rather small flowers, hardy from zone 4 southward.

G. *hispanica*—Spanish Gorse or Broom. A densely branched, spiny and prickly, often leafless shrub usually not over 18 in. tall with clusters of golden-yellow flowers in May and June. Hardy from zone 4 southward. Var. *nana,* half as high, is often used to cover sloping banks.

G. *tinctoria*—Woadwaxen, Dyer's Greenwood. This is the best known and hardiest of the genistas. Of upright and slender growth to 3 ft. and with striped branches it has many yellow flowered terminal clusters during the summer. Hardy from zone 3 southward. There are many horticultural forms. 'Plena' has double flowers.

GERMANDER—See *Teucrium.*

GORSE—See *Ulex.*

HALIMODENDRON HALODENDRON—Siberian Salt-Tree. An ornamental deciduous shrub that grows to 6 ft. or less, from central Asia, belonging to the pea family. It does well in light sandy soil and is a good subject for seaside gardens. Upright, and spreading with slender branches it has fine gray-green foliage, is silky-silvery and graceful in appearance, and covered with lilac pea-like flowers in summer. Drought-resistant, it tolerates alkaline soil and suckers profusely. Hardy from zone 4 southward. Happy on very sandy soils or by the sea.

HAMAMELIS — Witch-Hazel, Winter-Bloom. Deciduous shrubs or small trees native to North America and Asia they bloom from late fall to early spring while the twigs are bare. They do well in sandy loam, are vigorous and bushy with good foliage which turns yellow and orange in the autumn. Fragrant flowers are borne in clusters. They prefer moist sites but will also thrive in dry areas.

H. mollis is an Asiatic shrub or small tree 10 to 25 ft. tall, hardy from zone 3 southward, the showiest of the witch-hazels. The leaves are grayish-white beneath and the flowers, which appear in February and March, have golden-yellow petals from a purplish red calyx.

H. vernalis is native to the southern part of the country, central United States to Louisiana, hardy from zone 4 southward, from Philadelphia south. A shrub with many stems usually less than 6 ft. high.

H. virginiana is the common witch-hazel, a coarse large shrub growing to 15 ft. tall or more, native to eastern North America from Canada to Florida and hardy from zone 2 southward. Light yellow flowers appear in October while the leaves are falling.

HEATH—See *Erica.*

HEATHER—See *Calluna.*

HELIANTHEMUM — Sun-Rose, Frostweed. Prostrate or sprawling woody plants of the rock-rose family suitable for the rock garden, border planting or used as a ground cover. They thrive in a dry, limestone soil and full sun bearing fleeting white, yellow, rose or purple rose-like flowers from July to September on plantings mostly low growing from 6 to 24 in. high. They need winter protection in the North. Propagate by seed sown in the spring, greenwood cuttings or division of the roots.

H. nummularium—Sun-Rose. The most common species grown in the North, about 1 ft. tall, with yellow flowers 1 in. across. A native in the Mediterranean region often offered in the trade as *H. chamaecistus* and *H. vulgare*. Popular as a rock garden plant and ground cover it has many horticultural varieties. Var. *albo-plenum* is a double white, var. *aureum* deep yellow, var. *cupreum* copper variegated with yellow, var. *macranthum* white with yellow blotches, var. *mutabile* has pale rose flowers that change to lilac or nearly white and var. *roseum* is pale rose, there is also a double form.

HIPPOPHAE RHAMNOIDES—Sea Buckthorn. A deciduous hardy shrub, sometimes tree-like, from 8 to 25 ft., with spiny branches and belonging to the oleaster family, native to Europe and Asia. It has a rounded, open habit, often with the lower trunk devoid of branches. Grown chiefly for its attractive foliage and profuse bright orange or orange-yellow fleshy berries borne in large clusters in the fall. Its narrow willow-like leaves are grayish-green on the upper surface and silvery-green beneath. Does well in seashore plantings, also in inland areas, is well equipped to bind sand dunes and mass plantings are decorative. Once established it makes an ornamental fall display. Not particular as to soil it is hardy to the limits of zone 2. Male and female plants are necessary for a crop of the showy orange colored berries. Propagated by seeds, cuttings or layers. Suckers freely.

HONEYSUCKLE—See *Lonicera*.

HUCKLEBERRY—See *Gaylussacia*.

HUDSONIA—Beach Heather. These are hardy heath-like plants comprising 3 similar native species of very low, evergreen, mat-forming shrubs with needle-like leaves, and bearing numerous very small bright yellow flowers. They do well in dry sandy sites or near the beach. Not often cultivated because they are short-lived. Propagated by seeds or cuttings.

H. ericoides is native far to the west in dry, sandy sections.

H. montana grows in the mountains of North Carolina.

H. tomentosa is found growing on sandy shores and dunes near the Atlantic coast from New Brunswick southward to North Carolina.

HYPERICUM—St. John's-Wort. Perenial herbs and low shrubs from the north temperate zone, some weedy; popular for use in naturalistic plantings, the border, rock garden or as a ground cover. Decorative, they usually have bright yellow flowers with profuse stamens and often evergreen foliage. Most thrive in dry, sandy soils in open situations. Their blooming period is prolonged if given semi-shade. The creeping species are increased by division and suckers, the shrubby sorts by greenwood cuttings.

H. calycinum—Aaron's-Beard, Rose-Of-Sharon. This is a low shrub not over 12 in. high that can become a menace because of its spreading tendencies by means of suckers. Valuable as a ground cover where little else will grow. Prune back old growth in early spring and the young fresh foliage will then make a fine background for the large, golden flowers 2 in. wide that bloom in mid and late summer. Hardy from zone 4 southward, farther north if given protection. One of the most attractive. Propagate by division.

H. kalmianum—Kalm St. John's-Wort is an evergreen under-shrub native from Quebec to Illinois growing to 3 ft. in height and doing well in dry sandy soil and windy sites. Golden-yellow flowers are less profuse than in some species and the plant is of a more straggly habit.

H. moserianum—Gold Flower is an under-shrub. Low spreading, it has short, arching branches, not over 2 ft. high, with reddish stems. Its golden-yellow flowers are abundant all through late summer. A good ground cover. 'Tricolor' has white variegated leaves edged with red. Hardy from Washington, D. C. south, from zone 5 southward.

H. patulum is an evergreen shrub from Japan, 2 to 3 ft. tall, of dense and bushy habit, with a profusion of large, golden saucer-like flowers in late summer that make it a very worthwhile garden shrub. Hardy from zone 5 southward. Var. *henryi* is more vigorous with larger flowers, hardy up to zone 4, possibly 3.

H. prolificum—Bush Broom, Shrubby St. John's-Wort. This is native from New York to Iowa and southward to Georgia. A dense, evergreen shrub it grows 4 to 5 ft. in height, has small, narrow leaves and small flowers in flat-topped clusters over many weeks of the summer.

HYSSOPUS OFFICINALIS—Hyssop. A small evergreen Eurasian under-shrub of the mint family widely grown as an ornamental and as a culinary and medicinal herb. It is somewhat woody and grows to 18 in. in height, a row making a low hedge of rich green foliage and abundant spikes of purplish-blue from June on. The plant likes a sunny site on well-drained limy, sandy soil and pruning each spring. Propagate from seed or cuttings or by division. 'Albus' has white flowers, 'Ruber' red and 'Grandiflorus' has larger flowers.

ILEX—Holly. A genus of evergreen and deciduous glossy leaved trees and shrubs highly ornamental and noted for their brilliantly colored berries. They range from hardy to quite tender. Some can be grown in poor dry soil.

I. cornuta—The Chinese or horned holly is a handsome erect Chinese relative of the English holly, growing to 9 ft. in height and of a rigid bushy growth. One of the best hollies for dry and hot localities, hardy from zone 4 southward. Some hybrids and strains are hardy as far north as southern New York state. The evergreen leaves are very dark and shining, the bright red berries are comparatively large, though not very freely produced, but effective in the fall and winter. An excellent holly. 'Burfordi' has wedge-shaped leaves that have only a few spines at the tip of the leaf and drooping branches. 'Rotunda' is a dwarf form.

I. glabra—The inkberry is native to eastern North America with willowy growth, hardy from zone 3 southward, evergreen southward but only half evergreen northward, turning a rusty green in late fall. It grows 3 to 4 ft. tall, sometimes taller and is found in swampy areas but also grows on poor dry sandy soil.

I. opaca—The American holly is not as handsome as the English holly but it is hardier, native from Massachusetts to Florida and west

76. *Hypericum calycinum,* low growing and semi-evergreen, is a useful low shrub or ground cover for dry areas. It's deep yellow flowers appear through mid-summer.
McFarland Photo

to Missouri and Texas. Plentiful on the North Carolina sand hills where it is a massive, spreading tree up to 40 ft. in height, difficult to transplant.

I. vomitoria—The true yaupon is a weed along the Carolina Coast, native from Virginia to Florida and Texas. It is an evergreen shrub or tree growing 15 to 25 ft. high.

JAPANESE LAUREL—See *Aucuba japonica*.

JUNEBERRY—See *Amelanchier alnifolia*.

JUNIPERUS—Juniper. This member of the pine family includes many valuable garden shrubs both prostrate and the shrubby kinds, excellent in contemporary layouts and good as ground covers. Their small leaves are mostly grayish-green and the berry-like fruits are blue or reddish. They are invaluable for plantings in dry, exposed areas. Nearly all are aromatic and they are distinguished from other coniferous evergreens by their small, dry, berry-like fruits. Also see *Juniperus* under Trees.

J. chinensis—Chinese Juniper. An Asiatic evergreen sometimes treelike, 40 to 60 ft., but usually shrubby and especially so in its horticultural forms found in the nurseries and in wide garden use. Among the most useful are the following: 'Aurea' is an upright form 3 to 5 ft. tall, the young branchlets a golden yellow. 'Globosa' is dwarf and compact in form, rather round in outline with mostly scale-like leaves. In 'Globosa Alba' the branchlets are marked with white while 'Globosa Aurea' is marked with yellow. Var. *japonica* makes a dense shrub with low spreading branches and needle-like leaves, whorled. 'Pfitzeriana' is one of the most popular evergreens. Of partly upright form it will take city conditions and its spreading, sometimes horizontal branches, make a hollow in the center of the plant. It may grow 4 to 6 ft. in height and 5 to 8 ft. wide, is dark dull green in color. 'Pyramidalis' is a narrow, pyramidal shrub with upright branches and glaucous, linear bluish-green leaves. 'Variegata' is a slow grower, exceedingly compact, the ends of the branchlets white-tipped.

J. communis—Common Juniper. An upright tree or shrub usually growing 6 to 12 ft., sometimes up to 40 ft. Hardy from zone 1 southward, south to Pennsylvania and Illinois and in the mountains of New Mexico and northern California. The needle-like leaves have a broad white band above, are sharply pointed, spreading and in whorls. The bluish-black fruits ¼ in. in diameter are used to flavor gin. The species is quite variable and has many interesting varieties. Var. *depressa* is a wide spreading, low-growing prostrate juniper that rarely exceeds 3 to 4 ft. It does exceedingly well in dry, rocky soil. Among the best for the small garden. In var. *depressa* 'Aurea' the young growth is often yellow. Var. *hibernica*—Irish Juniper—is a good accent plant with its narrow, columnar form and upright branches and dark green leaves. It may need support. Var. *oblonga pendula* is a graceful, columnar form with narrow leaves and upright branches, tips are pendulous. Var. *suecica*—Swedish Juniper—has a columnar shape and bluish-green leaves, the tips of the branches are drooping.

J. conferta—Shore juniper is a prostrate low shrub suited to sandy soils, good for planting on sand dunes and near the shore, hardy from zone 5 southward.

J. horizontalis—Creeping Juniper. Grows well in sandy, rocky soil. Hardy from zone 1 southward, Nova Scotia to British Columbia, south to New Jersey, Minnesota and Montana. A prostrate shrub with long spreading branches. Needle-like leaves are bluish-green or grayish-blue. Var. *douglasi*—Waukegan Juniper—is a trailing form with blue-gray leaves that turn grayish-purple in the fall. Var. *glauca* is glaucous, having a whitish or grayish bloom. Var. *glomerata* is a very low dwarf form with short compact branches. Var. *plumosa*—Andorra Juniper—is low with horizontal branches forming a flattened top, foliage more plumelike or feathery.

J. procumbens—Considered by some as a variety of *J. horizontalis*. A slow, prostrate juniper frequently planted as a ground cover. Branches ascend to 20 to 30 in. in height.

J. sabina—Savin. Shrubby with ascending or spreading branches generally 4 to 5 ft. all but will sometimes grow to 10 ft., a handsome dwarf evergreen. Hardy from zone 3 southward. Will take city condition and likes limey soil. Plant has a slightly disagreeable odor. Var. *cupressifolia* is a low almost prostrate form and var. *tamariscifolia* is another low form with ascending branches usually not over 2 ft.

J. virginiana 'Tripartita'—Fountain Red Cedar is low and shrubby, to 5 ft., with spreading branches and mostly dark green needle-like leaves. Native to eastern and central North America, hardy most everywhere, from zone 2. Also see Trees.

77. Among the most useful evergreen ground covers for dry gardens are the junipers, such as deep green *Juniperus sabina tamariscifolia*, which spreads indefinitely and often roots where the branches touch the soil. This habit makes it possible for the gardener to detach these layered sections and plant them elsewhere. Junipers make their best growth in sunny parts of the garden.

U. S. D. A. Photo

KERRIA JAPONICA (Sometimes listed under *Corchorus*). A Chinese deciduous shrub with slender green branches and of the rose family growing 4 to 6 ft. and nearly as wide. Its light green twiggy stems hold their color and are decorative all winter long. Hardy from zone 3 southward, young growth is often winter killed but the injury is usually not serious. Thin out the old stems every few years. Not fussy as to soil except that it be well-drained and a sheltered position is helpful, must have sun or only slight shade. Abundant single yellow flowers appear in late spring and sometimes there is a scattering throughout the season. Propagation is by division and cuttings. 'Pleniflora' has double, ball-like flowers nearly 2 in. in diameter, it usually grows taller and may be trained aginst a wall or to a porch. It is more showy and vigorous than the typical form. Called the Japanese Rose. There are also varieties with white-and yellow-variegated leaves.

KINNIKINNICK—See *Arctostaphylos uva-ursi.*

KOLKWITZIA AMABILIS—Beauty Bush. A deciduous Chinese, upright shrub of twiggy and graceful habit with arching branches belonging to the honeysuckle family. Hardy as far north as Boston, from zone 3 southward. It is of easy culture, flowers best in poor soil, tolerates dryness and enjoys an exposed situation, wants sun. It grows 4 to 6 ft. tall and 3 to 4 ft. wide. Prune to prevent legginess. Its gray-green foliage

78. One of E. H. Wilson's introductions to horticulture, the beauty bush (*Kolkwitzia amabilis*) is noted for its late spring profusion of pink flowers, recalling those of the weigela, though smaller. The shrub not only endures but appears to flower rather better on dry slopes, and its only shortcoming is that its 8 foot height and width is hard to tolerate in a small garden, particularly when it offers neither colorful fall fruit nor foliage.

Genereux Photo

79. *Leiophyllum buxifolium* — The sand myrtle makes a useful ground cover in sandy, peaty soils in full sun, studded with small white or pinkish flowers in late spring, native from New Jersey to South Carolina and Kentucky.

McFarland Photo

turns a yellowish-tan in the fall and is attractive throughout the summer months. Grown primarily for its showy masses of fragrant, bell-shaped, shell-pink flowers with yellow throats, reminding one of weigelia. Flowers are abundantly produced in terminal clusters in May and June. Propagate by cuttings of green wood in late summer.

LAVANDULA — Lavender. Fragrant herbs and shrubs of the mint family. No sandy soil is too hot or dry for these sun-loving plants. They enjoy a perfectly drained limy soil. Lavenders are not long-lived but live longer on dryish sterile or rocky soils. They need clipping each year after they have flowered to keep them shapely. Or take wood with the flowers as they are cut during the summer for indoor decoration to allow light to penetrate deep within the bush as they like sun and light.

L. spica (formerly *L. officinalis*, sometimes known as *L. vera*)—English or True Lavender. This Mediterranean evergreen subshrub grows from 1 to 3 ft. tall and is popular in the milder climates of the Pacific Coast and in the South where they make beautiful hedges. Narrow, lance-shaped, felty-whitish-gray green leaves make a useful garden feature. Small fragrant lavender flowers are used in sachets and perfumes. It grows as far north as Philadelphia with protection. Good dwarf kinds as 'Munstead,' 'Hidcote' and others are often preferred for edging; easily increased by cuttings, a good pot plant.

LAVENDER-COTTON—See *Santolina chamaecyparissus*.

LEAD PLANT—See *Amorpha canescens*.

LEIOPHYLLUM BUXIFOLIUM — Sand Myrtle. A low, compact, twiggy evergreen shrub of the heath family, growing 1½ to 2 ft. tall and about half as wide. Native from New Jersey to South Carolina and Kentucky, found in highly acid soils and suited to open garden sites having sandy peaty soils. Hardy from most of zone 3 southward. Likes full sun, will take some shade. An excellent ground cover. Attractive in late spring when studded with small white or pinkish flowers. Useful in the rock garden and for edging evergreen plantings. Set out young plants from pots, planting several in a clump rather than singly. Propagated by seeds or layers. *L. lyoni* is more densely branched and more prostrate in habit. May be a variety of *L. buxifolium*.

LIGUSTRUM—Privet. These are diciduous and evergreen shrubs native in Europe, Asia and Australia, a member of the olive family. Practical and very useful shrubs they are well able to care for themselves in almost any soil, under nearly any exposure and in more than ordinary drought. Their use in hedges has perhaps been over emphasized. The natural form of the plant is pleasing as used in the shrubbery or alone. The white heads of flowers and close-clustered blue berries are more than worth the small effort they demand. Prune any time after the berries have dropped late in summer to induce foliage growth. Little trouble with pests or diseases.

L. amurense—Amur Privet. From northern China this species is the hardiest of the privets, hardy from zone 3 southward, useful in the North and often sheared as a hedge plant. It will grow 10 to 15 ft. high and about half as wide. The branches are erect and densely foliaged, half-evergreen, the light green leaves held late. Resembles the California privet.

L. japonicum—Japanese or Wax Privet. A handsome bushy, evergreen shrub that grows from 10 to 15 ft. with large durable leaves and fragrant flowers from July to September, the new growth reddish. It makes an excellent large clipped hedge in a very hot situation or will endure considerable cold where it becomes deciduous. This is the best one to grow under arid conditions from zone 5 southward. 'Rotundifolium' (sometimes offered as *L. coriaceum*) is a lower more compact shrub of extremely slow growth, much smaller, with leathery dark round leaves. It is desirable anywhere restricted growth is a consideration. Milky-white flowers appear in May and June in tight little heads. It does better in shade in either a tub or in the ground.

L. lucidum—An evergreen shrub or small tree up to as much as 30 ft. Suitable for a narrow parking in the street or screening, it also makes an excellent tall hedge, sheared or untrimmed. Large dark shining leaves and waxy, white, sweet smelling flower clusters make it a valuable plant from zone 5 southward. It will take the salt wind and is planted in central and northern Florida, in Texas and California.

L. ovalifolium—California Privet. This half evergreen, large, erect Japanese shrub is of a compact rather stiff habit, of rapid growth it grows from 5 to 20 ft., if not clipped, the most widely used hedge plant in the United States. It has handsome thick glossy leaves and large

80. A curved hedge of Swedish privet, a strain of *Ligustrum vulgare* introduced from Sweden and hardier than the common strain, pictured here on a farm in the central Great Plains. Maintenance would be easier and the hedge more in keeping with the surroundings if left to grow natural.

U. S. D. A. Photo

panicles of creamy-white flowers. Used less in California for hedges than in the East, hardy from zone 4 southward. In zone 3 it is sometimes killed to the ground or outright in severe winters. It withstands salt spray, wind, smoke and dust in almost any degree. 'Aureo-marginatum', Golden Privet, is less vigorous and needs good soil in a sunny position to do its best. There are many variations in leaf color, none as good a hedge plant as the typical form.

L. quihoui—Quihoui Privet. A Chinese privet 4 to 6 ft. tall with spreading branches, somewhat rigid, with extremely strong wood.

Creamy-white flower spikes appear in branched clusters, 5 to 8 in. long, during August and September. Hardy from zone 6 southward. Drought-resistant, will survive on an annual rainfall of 15 in.

L. sinense—A Chinese shrub with spreading branches, much planted in the South, only half evergreen in the northern part of its hardiness range which is from zone 6 southward. It grows 7 to 12 ft. high and nearly as wide, makes a showy specimen when in flower in the summer with profuse small white branching clusters 3 to 5 inches long.

L. vulgare—Common Privet. A native of Europe this privet grows to 15 ft. tall with slender spreading branches, hardy from zone 3 southward, the safest privet to use north of zone 4. That is one reason it has been used so much. It has many variations mostly in the color of the leaves, golden or white margined or variegated, though these are not superior to the typical plant. 'Xanthocarpum' has yellow berries.

LILAC—See *Syringa.*

LONICERA—Honeysuckle. This is a large genus including shrubs and woody climbers or trailers valued for their showy, often fragrant flowers and decorative fruits. Mostly hardy North, of easy cultivation, not fussy as to soil, they thrive in almost any place. Most prefer open sunny situations. The shrub forms are useful in mixed shrub plantings or for screening or hedge purposes. Although a reasonable amount of moisture is desirable some are quite drought-resistant. They will take heavy pruning to keep them from becoming leggy. Propagation is by seeds or cuttings.

L. maacki—Amur Honeysuckle. A vigorous, upright Asiatic shrub with wide spreading branches, hardy from zone 3 southward. One of the best for fall display. Useful either untrimmed or sheared as a hedge or for a screen planting. It grows 10 to 15 ft. tall and as wide or even wider, grows fast when young. It has large dark green leaves that stay on the plant late in the season, fragrant white flowers changing to yellowish, in late May and June, and profuse bright red berries effective in the fall and they remain late. Drought-resistant, it is among one of the handsomest and tallest growing of the honeysuckles. Var. *podocarpa* is much like the type, but with broader leaves and of a more spreading habit.

L. tartarica—Tartarian Honeysuckle. One of the best known of the bush honeysuckles and one of the best hardy ornamental shrubs. An upright, vigorous shrub of pleasing habit, it grows 8 to 10 ft. tall and is hardy from zone 2 southward, from Russia and Siberia. It bears a profusion of pink or white flowers in late May followed by dark red berries effective in June and July. Will grow in almost any soil and is not bothered by pests or diseases.

It is variable, some of the best forms being 'Alba', white flowers; 'Angustifolia', pale pink flowers; 'Lutea', pink flowers and yellow fruit; 'Nana', habit dwarf to 3 ft. high and pink flowers; 'Parvifolia', one of the best with white flowers; 'Pulcherrima', deep pink to red flowers, considered better than 'Rosea'; 'Sibirica', the deepest pink of the bush honeysuckles and 'Virginalis', the largest flowers of any *L. tatarica* variety, rose-pink in color.

LYONIA MARIANA—Staggerbush. A deciduous member of the heath family found growing from Rhode Island to Florida and Texas, hardy from zone 3 southward. Sometimes sold as *Pieris mariana*. A bushy shrub that grows 4 to 6 ft. tall with small white or pinkish flowers freely borne in dense nodding clusters during May and June. It prefers an acid sandy soil, enjoys a permanent mulch of dried leaves and dislikes any root disturbance. Although it likes a reasonable amount of moisture and some shade it will adapt to considerable dryness. Shrubs for the informal border and suitable for massing. Increase by cuttings.

MAHONIA. Handsome evergreen, thornless, low-growing shrubs found in North and Central America, Europe and Asia belonging to the barberry family. A few are hardy North where they appreciate a sheltered position from the wind and hot sun. Some of the western species do well as far north as Canada where they are protected by a heavy covering of snow all winter. Excellent for massing, for the shrubbery border, foundation planting and used as a ground covering.

M. aquifolium—Oregon Holly-Grape. This native from British Columbit to Oregon is hardy from zone 3 southward and popular on both the west and east coasts. It thrives under adverse conditions. Its lustrous dark green, leathery leaves turn bronze to purplish in autumn. It grows to 3 ft. in height, rarely 6 ft. Fragrant yellow flowers in dense-erect terminal clusters appear in early May followed by bluish black grape-like fruits in summer. Perhaps the most popular of the Pacific northwest plants grown in the East. It can be kept low by pruning and increases rapidly by means of underground stolons which makes it effective as a ground cover of some height.

M. repens—Creeping mahonia is smaller in size than the above, only 10 in. tall, and it spreads rapidly making a good ground cover, but its foliage is not as attractive as that of *M. aquifolium*.

MOCK ORANGE—See *Philadelphus*.

MYRICA—Bayberry, Wax-Myrtle. Shrubs or trees belonging to the bayberry family, grown for their attractive and aromatic foliage and decorative fruits. Two species are admirable shrubs for very dry sandy lime-free soils, both native to such areas and both comonmly called bayberry. The true baybery is *Pimenta acris*. Sexes are on separate plants.

M. californica—California Bayberry. A slender, upright tall shrub or small tree to 35 ft. in height, native from Washington to California, grown on the Pacific coast for its lustrous evergreen, bronzy colored leaves to 4 in. long and its purple berries, effective in fall and winter.

M. cerifera—Wax Myrtle. A tall shrub or small tree, to 35 ft. tall, the southern form of *M. pensylvanica*, native from New Jersey to Florida and Arkansas, with evergreen 3 in. long leaves and small gray berries. Hardy from zone 4 southward.

M. pensylvanica—Bayberry. A deciduous shrub 3 to 9 ft. tall, native from Newfoundland to western New York and Maryland along the east coast seashore. Dull green, semi-evergreen foliage and waxy grayish-white berries are effective in fall and winter. They persist far into the winter unless the birds get them. The waxy little fruits are used in the famous New England bayberry candles. The bayberry lends itself to a wide variety of effects either by itself or in combination with *Prunus maritima* (Beach Plum). It is useful for dry hillsides or as a sand binder for seaside gardens. Hardy from zone 2 southward. Sometimes listed as *M. carolinensis*.

NEW JERSEY TEA—See *Ceanothus americanus*.

NINEBARK—See *Physocarpus*.

OREGON HOLLY-GRAPE—See *Mahonia aquifolium*.

81. Bayberry *(Myrica pensylvanica)* is a native found growing in dry sandy soil along the coast of eastern North America. The grayish-waxy, very aromatic fruit is used in making bayberry candles.

Genereux Photo

PEA-SHRUB or TREE—See *Caragana*.

PEROVSKIA ATRIPLICIFOLIA—Afghan Sage. A handsome little soft-wooded shrub 3 to 4 ft. tall with slender silvery-gray stems, small oval silvery green leaves and spikes of soft violet-blue flowers in late summer. When brushed against the plant gives off a sage-like odor. It needs a well-drained soil, likes limy sand, and a sunny location. Needs to be cut back severely in the spring. In the North it behaves like a herbaceous perennial. Propagate by seeds and cuttings.

PHILADELPHUS—Mock-Orange. A member of the saxifrage family; graceful, free-flowering, shrubs, mostly of medium size and valued for their showy display of white or creamy fragrant flowers in late spring and early summer. They are of the easiest culture and not particular as to soil provided it is well-drained. They can take shade better than most flowering shrubs. Prune immediately after flowering for they flower from wood of the previous year.

   P. coronarius—Sweet Mock Orange. Hardy from zone 2 southward, the most widely cultivated of the mock-oranges, and especially good for planting in dry situations. A shrub to 10 ft. tall. Creamy-white, very fragrant, flowers in terminal clusters in early June. 'Aureus' has bright yellow leaves in youth, 'Dianthiflorus' and 'Flore-plenus' have double flowers, 'Pumilus' is a dwarf form with smaller leaves and 'Variegatus' has white bordered leaves.

PHOTINIA. These are handsome ornamental shrubs of the rose family, from northern Asia, with striking evergreen leaves and very small white flowers in profuse flat-topped clusters followed by red berries. Easy to grow they like a sunny place in well-drained soil, are quite drought-resistant.

   P. glabra is an evergreen shrub from Japan hardy from zone 5 southward, growing 8 to 10 ft. tall, with lustrous foliage, and a summer bloom of small white flowers arranged in clusters followed by rather persistent red pea-sized berries.

   P. serrulata—Chinese Photinia. A vigorus evergreen shrub, or sometimes a tree to 35 ft., from China, hardy from zone 5 southward. A handsome shrub with dark lustrous evergreen leaves to 8 in. long. New foliage is a reddish bronze and flat heads 6 in. across of small white flowers appear in mid-May, followed by bright red berries in fall and early winter. Prune to prevent legginess and to force new shoots and the bright colorful new foliage growth. Needs well-drained soil and not too much moisture.

P. villosa—Oriental Photinia. A large deciduous shrub or small tree, with somewhat spreading branches 8 to 15 ft. tall from Japan, China and Korea, hardy from zone 3 southward. Its foliage turns red in the fall and clusters of hawthorn-like white flowers appear in early spring followed by bright red berries persistent into the winter.

PHYSOCARPUS—Ninebark. Attractive hardy, deciduous, white-flowered spirea-like shrubs native in North America and belonging to the rose family. Of spreading habit, its bark peels off in long strips, its leaves are more or less lobed, the whitish flowers, though small, are attractive because of the profusion of their clusters in June. Of easy culture in any ordinary garden soil and full sun. Quite drought-resistant. Propagated by seeds or cuttings.

P. intermedius parvifolius—Dwarf Illinois Ninebark. A dense, upright growing shrub with foliage much like that of the Alpine currant, of a dark green, fine texture. A reliable foliage plant suitable for hedges or any low-barrier planting.

P. opulifolius—Eastern Ninebark. Native to eastern North America it is hardy from zone 2 southward. The plant does well in almost any soil, grows vigorously and quickly, making a show in a short period of time. Erect or with arching branches it grows 5 to 8 ft. tall, resembles a coarse spirea. Useful in the background or as a filler. A dependable shrub but too coarse for a small planting. 'Luteus' has yellowish foliage turning bronzy. 'Nanus' is a dwarf form with small dark green leaves.

PICEA—Spruce. An important group of useful ornamental conifers, trees and some shrubby kinds, of the pine family, many species native to North America. Whorled branches, narrow, needle-like leaves and drooping cones distinguish them from the firs which bear upright cones. They will grow in almost any kind of soil if there is good drainage. They have shallow root systems and enjoy moisture but will adapt to considerable drought. Dense close foliage with strong branches make them excellent wind breaks, some will endure severe pruning and make good hedge plants. Hardy from zone 1 and 2 southward.

P. abies—Norway Spruce. The some 50 dwarf varieties are shrubs used as specimen plants in the small garden or for the rockery. Slow of growth it takes years to get sizable plants. One of the commonest of cultivated evergreens. 'Argentea' has green and white variegated foliage, 'Aurea' golden yellow, 'Clanbrasiliana' is a wide-spreading rounded form not growing over 2½ ft. tall, 'Maxwelli' is low and moundlike and twice as broad as high, 'Microsperma' is dense and pyramidal growing to 10 ft. high and equally as wide, 'Procumbens' is one of the lowest forms no more than 3 to 4 ft. but it may reach a diameter of 15 ft., and 'Pumila' and 'Pygmaea' are dwarf varieties suitable for the rock garden and not exceeding 2 ft.

P. glauca densata—Black Hills Spruce. A slow growing variety from South Dakota it is extremely hardy to cold, moderately drought-resist-ant, and tolerant of soil alkalinity. Makes a dense growth. *P. glauca* is really a tree. The Cheyenne Horticultural Field Station, Cheyenne, Wyoming, conducting experiments with hedges for the central Great Plains found some of the coniferous evergreens especially well adapted as hedges, furnishing shelter and having an attractive appearance during the winter months. Hardy from zone 1 southward. At various times called *P. alba* and *P. canadensia*.

P. pungens 'Engelm'—Colorado Blue Spruce is another hardy, drought-resistant tree, extremely tolerant of soil alkalinity. The Chey-enne experiments found it makes an excellent tall screen or windbreak in their area. When planted close together and sheared they can be developed into an excellent formal hedge 5 ft. high and 3 ft. wide. Hardy from zone 1 southward.

PINK LOCUST—See *Robinia hispida.*

PINUS—Pine. Pines grow well in rather poor well-drained sandy loams in which they develop long tap-roots which serve to anchor them and make the most of any available moisture in the soil. They are light-loving and become unsightly shaded. See *Pinus* under Trees.

P. aristata 'Engelm'—Bristle-Cone Pine. It is native to the Rocky Mountains, hardy and moderately tolerant of alkaline soil, quite drought-resistant. Planted 2 ft. apart it can be developed into an

82. Many of the spruces such as the Black Hill spruce, *Picea glauca densata* make good drought-resistant hedges (more so than the familiar hemlock), but they require regular shearing to be kept under control.

U. S. D. A. Photo

attractive sheared hedge 6 or 7 ft. high and about 4 ft. wide. See Trees.

P. mugo—Mugo or Swiss Mountain Pine. Usually shrubby in growth with bright green leaves 2 in a bundle, about 2 in. long, cones are 2½ in. It makes an excellent informal hedge 6 ft. high and as wide. An excellent specimen plant. The var. *mughus* (Mugho Pine) is a shrubby almost prostrate form, very popular. Var. *compacta* is a dense rounded form, var. *prostrata* a tree to 80 ft. Mugo pine grows in southern Europe high up in the Alps. It is hardy from zone 2 southward.

83. A shrubby, much-branched, dwarf form of *Pinus aristata*, the bristle-cone pine is a native of the Rocky Mountains and Southwest, and does well in well-drained sandy loam with ample light.

Lewis Photo

POTENTILLA—Cinquefoil. These are mostly sturdy, hardy perennials or subshrubs, natives of the northern hemisphere belonging to the rose family. The stems are creeping or erect, the creeping species rooting at the joints. The strawberry-like flowers are usually yellow, sometimes white although shades of orange, red, crimson and pink are to be found in the newer hybrid forms which are both single and double. Exceptionally good for the small garden and enjoyed for their long period of bloom, flowering all summer, and attractive tiny leaves. A grouping of 3 plants is effective. They grow and flower well in the

84. The many cultivated varieties of potentilla are useful where drought-tolerant, 2 to 3 foot tall, flowering shrubs are desired. Various shades of yellow potentillas are available, as well as a white. All look best when massed and as the shrub may be divided almost as early as an herbaceous plant (preferably in the spring), it is easy to build up a stock of many specimens in a short time. Early summer is the main blooming time, and although flowers appear sporadically thereafter, the first burst of color is the most important.

Genereux Photo

sun in ordinary garden soil or on even poor stony or sandy soils. Excellent for beds and borders, rock work and bare banks. Hardy from zone 2 southward. The leaves are persistent in warmer areas. Readily increased by seed or division of the roots.

P. *fruticosa*—Bush cinquefoil is a small, much branched shrub that grows from 1 to 4 ft. tall and tolerates a limy soil. Many varieties of this species have been found over a wide area. Var. *grandiflora* has single deep yellow flowers 1¼ in. in diameter, var. *parvifolia* also has single deep yellow flowers but only ½ in. wide, var. *purdomi* has smaller leaflets, is less hairy and has pale yellow flowers and in var. *veitchi* the leaflets are not hairy, the flowers are creamy-white, single and 1 in. in diameter.

PRINSEPIA SINENSIS—Cherry Prinsepia. A deciduous spiny, upright, shrub with slender arching branches native to Manchuria, belonging to the rose family, and grown for its bloom and fruit. It grows 8 to 10 ft. in height and 7 to 8 ft. wide, thrives in a sunny site in well-drained soil, very drought-resistant. It is about the first shrub to come into leaf with light green foliage. Small bright yellow flowers appear in clusters followed by cherry-like fruits. Hardy from zone 3 southward. Useful as an untrimmed or clipped hedge, shears well. Propagated by seeds, cuttings and layers.

PRIVET. See *Ligustrum*.

PRUNUS—The Stone Fruits. A large and important group of bushy shrubs and small twiggy trees belonging to the rose family with showy flowers early in the spring. All are sun loving and thrive best in a medium weight soil, heavy enough to retain moisture, yet well-drained, short-lived in clay, they grow well in sand with enough moisture. Those listed below are drought-resistant.

P. *besseyi*—Western Sand Cherry, Hansen Bush Cherry. This is a dwarf low shrub, with often prostrate stems, native to central North America, from Wyoming and Manitoba south to Kansas; hardy from zone 1 southward. Valued on the Plains for its sweet fruit. Used for grafting stock to increase hardiness or for dwarfing. Well suited to dry hot climates.

P. *maritima*—Beach Plum. A native American, sometimes thorny, shrub found chiefly along the eastern coastal area from New Bruns-

85. Among the most appealing native dryland plants is the beach plum, *Prunus maritima*, whose masses of white flowers are showy in early spring. The purple fruit makes good jelly. Varying from 3 to 6 feet in height (and often twice as wide), depending upon exposure, beach plum is well worth growing, but nursery-grown, small plants are preferred, as the roots of wild specimens are far-ranging.

Taloumis Photo

wick to Delaware and well suited to seashore plantings, hardy from zone 3 southward. A deciduous shrub that grows from 3 to 6 ft. in height, delights in a sandy soil. Numerous dainty, white single or double flowers appear in early May followed by red to dull purplish fruits in late summer. One form has yellow fruits.

PYRACANTHA COCCINEA—Scarlet Firethorn or Firebush. An Asiatic, thorny shrub of the rose family, pyracantha is closely related to the cotoneaster and grown for its fine foliage and ornamental fruit. Masses of white flowers in June are followed by many brilliant bright red berries in fall and winter. They are beautiful shrubs when grown as climbers, trained against a wall, or as a hedge or in the shrub border, excellent on a slope. They enjoy a sunny situation and well-drained soil, are fairly drought-resistant. Plants grow 6 ft. as a bush or 20 ft. against a wall. Hardy from zone 4 southward, in protected spots as far north as Boston. Deciduous in the North, evergreen in the South. 'Aurea' has yellow fruit, 'Lalandi' with orange-red berries is hardier and more vigorous than the typical form.

RED OSIER—See *Cornus stolonifera*.

RHAMNUS—Buckthorn. Shrubs and trees of the buckthorn family which are grown for their handsome foliage and attractive fruits, mostly in hot arid climates and under extreme drought. Very tolerant of soils and sites.

   R. davurica—Dahurian Buckthorn. A vigorous stout, hardy shrub with somewhat spiny twigs from North China, Manchuria and Korea growing 8 to 20 ft. with lustrous foliage and small shiny black berries in the fall. Hardy from zone 2 southward.

   R. frangula—Alder Buckthorn. This vigorous, hardy shrub growing not over 18 ft. has been widely distributed by birds. Valued for its lustrous dark green foliage that turns bright yellow in autumn, its dense habit of growth and abundant small berries changing from red to dark purple to black in the fall. Easily grown in almost any soil. Hardy anywhere. Used for clipped or informal hedges and as screen plantings. 'Asplenifolia' has much narrower and wavy-margined leaves, the foliage hence feathery.

86. *Rhamnus frangula* 'Tallhedge' is one of the few fastigiate trees which have received much publicity from the nursery trade. It makes a reliable informal hedge in dry soil and is a more desirable plant than the overly-used privet.

Lewis Photo

RHUS—Sumac. Deciduous or evergreen shrubs or small trees belonging to the cashew family and native over a wide area of North America and a familiar part of the roadside picture. Grown chiefly for their handsome foliage which takes on brilliant coloring in the fall. Their bright red spike-like fruits add fall interest too. The native deciduous kinds are hardy North, the evergreen kinds require a warm climate. Useful for massing for naturalistic effects, for use in the shrub border and they do extremely well on dry sandy banks or on rocky hillsides.

This genus includes both poison ivy and poison sumac but none of the cultivated species are poisonous to the touch. Many sumacs spread rapidly so great care must be taken in placing them.

They vary in height from fragrant sumac, 3 ft. tall, to the tall growing staghorn sumac which may reach a height of 30 ft. Some plants have both sexes on one plant, in others the sexes are on separate plants. In buying from a nursery be certain which you are getting if you want your plant to bear fruit. Propagate by root cuttings or layers.

R. aromatica—Fragrant Sumac. Also known as *R. canadensis*. A low spreading or sprawling shrub 18 to 36 in. high, a good cover plant for dry rocky slopes and can be used in front of taller plants. It has highly aromatic 3-part leaves, short spikes of small greenish-yellow flowers in spring, and small red hairy fruit in summer. The dense foliage turns yellow and scarlet in the fall. It is native to eastern North America and hardy from zone 2 southward.

R. copallina—Shining or Flame-Leaf Sumac. Native to eastern United States it grows to 30 ft. and is one of the most ornamental of the sumacs, conspicuous with its dark green glossy leaves and scarlet autumn coloring. A good specimen plant for dry soil. Sexes are separate.

R. glabra—Smooth Sumac. This is a good shrub for mass planting, very handsome in the fall with bright red foliage and showy, hairy scarlet fruit. Sexes are separate. Native to eastern United States it grows from 8 to 20 ft. and is hardy from zone 2 southward. 'Flavescens' has yellow fruit and the leaves turn yellow in the fall. In 'Laciniata' the leaflets are deeply divided.

R. typhina—Staghorn Sumac. Sometimes called *R. hirta*. This large shrub or small tree grows from 10 to 30 ft. high with branches densely covered with velvety hairs, the fuzzy twigs reminding one of the antlers of the young deer. The foliage is fern-like and handsome, red and especially colorful in the fall. Native to eastern United States and hardy from zone 3 southward. Sexes are separate. Not suitable for the small garden but good for massing where it will do well on very dry soils, attractive in the fall and all winter long with its colorful crimson pyramidal fruit clusters. 'Laciniata' has deeply divided leaflets and in 'Dissecta' the leaflets are even more deeply cut.

RIBES ALPINUM—Mountain Currant, Alpine Currant. An ornamental shrub belonging to the saxifrage family, it grows 5 to 8 ft. tall and is hardy from zone 5 southward. A good shrub for dry, sandy soils. It makes a densely compact, upright plant, excellent as a hedge, its dark green, fine textured leaves appearing very early in the season. Scarlet berries are effective in late summer. Sexes are on separate plants. Unfortunately it is listed by the U. S. D. A. as an alternate host for the white pine blister rust, a destructive disease of 5-needled pines so consult your county agent before considering it.

ROBINIA—Locust. One of the most beautiful of shrubs or small trees in flower and foliage, especially suited to hot, dry soils where its growth is less lush than on heavier soils and its brittle shoots more wiry, yet giving a very satisfying account of itself. Give it some shelter from the cold winds. See *Robina* under Trees.

R. *hispida*—Rose Acacia, Pink Locust. A handsome spreading shrub 3 to 4 ft. tall, the brittle branches are covered with red bristles, the leaves compound with 7 to 13 oval leaflets and pendulous and pinkish-rose colored flowers appear in May or June. Native from Virginia to Alabama it is hardy from zone 3 southward. Suckers freely.

R. *kelseyi*—Another handsome shrub or small tree that grows to 10 ft. in height. It has oval 9 to 11 leaflets and pendulous pinkish-rose colored flowers in May or June. Native to North Carolina it is hardy from zone 3 southward.

ROSA—Shrub Roses. Also see *Rosa* under Vines. Included here are the native species, the old-fashioned types, loved and cultivated for centuries, and very drought-tolerant. Use in the border, shrubbery plantings and the landscape scheme but with discretion in view of their vigorous growth and crowding tendencies. Use them freely and naturally in the outlying shrubbery or to cover over waste ground. The colors cover as wide a range as the bedding type rose or climbers and flowers are both single and double. They are hardy, will want sun, take considerable heat and dryness and are quite free of pests. There are many hybrids and varieties too numerous to list.

R. *carolina*—Carolina or Pasture Rose. Native to eastern United States from Maine to Florida and west to Wisconsin, Kansas and Texas. Hardy from zone 3 southward it is one of the best of our native roses, good for the shrub border, growing 3 ft. tall. It increases by underground stems forming dense thickets. Single rose-pink colored flowers about 2 in. wide in late June and July are followed by red fruit in very early fall.

R. foetida—Austrian Brier, Austrian Yellow. A lovely erect or arching shrub growing 7 to 10 ft. with single clear bright yellow flowers, 2 to 3 in. wide, blooming in late spring. Var. *persiana* (Persian Yellow) is double flowering and var. *bicolor*—Austrian Copper Brier—is a single coppery red. All are vividly colored, blooming in early June, with a rather unpleasant odor. Red berries are effective in the fall.

R. harisoni—Harison's Yellow Rose. An erect or arching hybrid growing to 6 ft. tall, a reliable favorite. Conspicuous yellow double flowers, 2 in. wide, appear in early June and last for several weeks. Fruits are not ornamental. Descended from *R. spinosissima*. Often miscalled Persian yellow.

R. hugonis—Father Hugo Rose. A handsome, free-flowering shrub from China that grows 6 to 8 ft. tall, branches are somewhat drooping with flattened straight prickles and bristles. Free-flowering single, canary-yellow blooms 2 in. in diameter appear in late May, one of the best single yellow species.

R. rugosa—Rugosa Rose, Salt Spray Rose. A native of Japan and China, hardy from zone 3 southward, a common escape near the seacoast in eastern United States. A stiffly upright bush, it grows 4 to 6 ft. tall or more and ultimately may make a patch 10 to 20 ft. in diameter. It has spiny or thorny stems, rough, wrinkled dark green foliage that turns a gorgeous orange in the fall. Generally fragrant red or pinkish to white flowers, usually solitary, to 3½ in. wide, in July and August are followed by large conspicuous brick red fruits. There are many horticultural varieties, some with double flowers. Vigorous and hardy they endure much cold, heat, dryness and even poor soil and the salt spray of the seaside. They will take shearing. A serviceable and excellent rose for general planting purposes, for rustic use and naturalizing or as a clipped hedge.

Var. *alba* has white single flowers, var. *alba-plena* white double flowers, var. *plena* double fuchsia-purple blooms and in var. *rosea* the single flowers are rose.

R. setigera—Prairie Rose. Often 15 ft. high, found native in eastern and central United States as far west as Nebraska and Texas, hardy from zone 3 southward. Needs plenty of room with its wide arching habit since it looks best growing naturally and it is a vigorous grower. One of the latest to bloom, with single rose-colored flowers 2 in. wide appearing early in June. The leaves turn reddish in the fall along with the red fruits.

R. spinosissima—Scotch Rose, Burnet Rose. A very spiny erect Eurasian shrub with small leaves and of generally dwarf stature, rarely over 3 ft., extremely hardy, the stems densely covered with straight prickles and bristles. Numerous solitary pink, white or yellow 1 to 2 in. wide flowers appear in early June. The fruit is not ornamental. There are many varieties and forms of this long cultivated shrub. Var. *alba plena* has double white flowers; var. *altaica* has 3 in. wide pale yellow, almost white flowers, more vigorous and less prickly than the species; var. *lutea*—Yellow Scotch Rose—is easy to grow and var. *lutea plena* has double yellow blooms.

R. virginiana—Virginia Rose. Sometimes offered as *R. lucida*. Native to eastern North America, from Newfoundland to Virginia. Alabama and Missouri, hardy from zone 2 southward. It is a vigorous grower often spreading by underground stems. Of interest the year round it has single magenta to pink flowers appearing in mid-June, glossy dark green foliage attractive throughout the summer. Leaves turn a brilliant scarlet to orange in autumn and colorful red twigs and red berries add winter interest. Useful and effective as an informal hedge kept 3 to 4 ft. tall or grown as a barrier. If it becomes too rank cut it back to the ground, it will quickly grow back. Var. *alba* has white flowers and var. *lamprophylla*—Glossy Virginia Rose—is smaller than the species, 3 ft. with lustrous green leaves.

R. wichuraiana—Memorial Rose. A prostrate or trailing rose with strong hooked prickles. White fragrant 2 in. flowers in clusters appear from July to October. Hardy from zone 3 southward. One of the parents of many old time and modern favorites, used for covering walls and dry banks, among them the universally known Dorothy Perkins and Dr. Walter Van Fleet.

ROSE-ACACIA—See *Robinia hispida*.

ROSMARINUS OFFICINALIS—Rosemary. A hardy, evergreen subshrub of upright habit and much-branched, from the Mediterranean region, and of the mint family. Plants grow to a height of 6 ft. They prefer dry, well-drained soil and sun. In the Pacific coast states where soil is dry and rocky they are planted as hedges, also in the southern states. The aromatic lustrous dark green, needle-like foliage is white and woolly on the underside. Small light violet-blue flowers in spikes are borne in April and May over a long period. In the northern states they require sheltered positions, best treated as a pot plant and wintered inside. Practically ever-blooming in warm places near the sea, it should be grown slowly in the sun for good form and close texture, pinch back from time to time. Remove any dead or dying wood. It will serve better in poor soils and should be starved for the gnarled irregular stem that is so picturesque. Clippings may be used in cookery or will scent the house pleasantly as they dry out.

Var. *prostratus,* growing flat to the ground, is an excellent cover in the right place, rerooting or hanging down the face of a low wall. The plant will lie more or less flat against the ground but breaks any monotony with interesting risings.

RUTA GRAVEOLENS—Rue. This is an undershrub or woody herb of the rue or citrus family, growing to 3 ft. in height, with much divided, aromatic, bluish-green leaves and dull yellowish flowers in terminal clusters.

SALIX TRISTIS—Dwarf Gray Willow. A native low shrub growing in dry, sandy places in eastern United States from Maine south to Florida and west to Minnesota; hardy from zone 2 southward. It is scarcely 2 ft. high, the leaves white underneath giving the overall effect of gray foliage. Excellent for a sand garden, poor soil on a bank or in the rock garden. The best dry-land willow species.

SALT SPRAY ROSE—See *Rosa rugosa.*

SAND MYRTLE—See *Leiophyllum buxifolium.*

SANTOLINA CHAMAECYPARISSUS — Lavender — Cotton. A native of the Mediterranean region belonging to the composite family, this stiff, broadly branching, subshrub grows to 2 ft. tall. Dense, aromatic silvery-gray woolly foliage is of a fine pleasing texture and remains throughout the winter. The buttony yellow flower heads are of less importance than the foliage. Easily cultivated in a sunny location, it will grow in poor sandy or gravelly dry soil and will also take salt-laden winds. It will spread out fitting nicely to a dry wall or sunny slope, or shear up into the straight lines of a hedge. Prune after flowering to keep the plants presentable or cut back almost to the base of the previous year's growth each spring. Best accepted as a short-lived plant and replaced as it becomes less attractive with age. Hardy up to zone 5 and above as far as Boston with a mulch. Sometimes offered as *S. incana.*

SAVIN—See *Juniperus sabina.*

SEA BUCKTHORN—See *Hippophae rhamnoides.*

SERVICEBERRY—See *Amelanchier alnifolia.*

SHEPHERDIA — Buffalo-Berry. Spreading shrubs or small trees of North America belonging to the oleaster family able to withstand extreme cold and dry, windswept sites, seashore and stony soils, planted for hedges where no other hedge plant will survive.

S. *argentea*—Silver Buffalo-Berry, Wild Oleaster, Silverleaf. A tall thorny shrub with coarse-textured silvery leaves and red oval fruit, sour, but used for jellies and jams. The plants grow 10 to 18 ft. tall and to 16 ft. wide. Excellent used as a shelter belt, hedgerow or trimmed hedge.

S. *canadensis*—Russet Buffalo-Berry. Not over 8 ft. tall. Useful for dry, rocky banks or alkaline areas in the Midwest and Prairie States. Tends to grow open and straggly so not very ornamental.

SHRUB ROSE—See *Rosa.*

SILVERBERRY—See *Elaeagnus commutata.*

SMOKE TREE—See *Cotinus.*

SNOWBERRY—See *Symphoricarpos albus.*

SPANISH GORSE or BROOM—See *Genista hispanica.*

SPARTIUM JUNCEUM—Spanish Broom, Weaver's-Broom. Not really a broom, this ornamental South European shrub of the pea family is grown for its racemes of fragrant large golden-yellow pea-like flowers in early summer. It is essentially leafless with quill-like green stems or branches. It grows upright to 10 ft. with slender rush-like branches, handsome in bloom. Hardy as far north as Philadelphia, from zone 6 southward, zone 5 with protection. Much planted in the western states on hot, dry, rocky banks where it blooms almost the year round, all year in California. Excellent for naturalizing. Face off with lower shrubs. It needs severe pruning to keep it neat and under control. Like the brooms it is hard to transplant. Resists all drought, takes any exposure in the sun, may be grown in a light soil if drainage is good. It lasts indefinitely by reseeding when grown dry and is less subject then to aphis and genista worm. Remove any dead wood. Propagated by seeds or cuttings of green wood. Var. *nanum* is an identical form that reaches only 3 to 5 ft. in height.

SPINDLE TREE—See *Euonymus europaea.*

SPIRAEA—Spirea. Spirea is planted for its white or red flowers borne in flat clusters; also for its gracefully arching branches. Not particular as to soil or situation, they will grow in sun or shade but will flower much better in sunshine and respond to and need annual pruning. Those that bloom on the previous year's wood as S. *vanhouttei* should be pruned just after flowering, those blooming on the current year's wood early in spring before growth starts. If necessary all can be cut to within a few inches of the ground and they will recover rather quickly.

S. *vanhouttei*—Bridal Wreath, Vanhoutte Spirea. This is the best of the many, many species and varieties. A slender shrub with beautifully arching branches it grows to 6 ft. in height. Its vigorous growth, general dependability, graceful habit, with many slender branches coming from the base of the plant, and abundant white flower clusters in late May make it a valuable shrub. It will also take city smoke and other adverse conditions better than most. It makes a good tall flowering shrub or specimen plant. Hardy from zone 3 southward. Cut branches are a good subject for forcing indoors early in the season for decoration.

SPRUCE—See *Picea.*

ST. JOHN'S-WORT—See *Hypericum.*

STRAWBERRY BUSH—See *Euonymus americana.*

SUMAC—See *Rhus*.

SUMMER LILAC—See *Buddleia*.

SWEET FERN—See *Comptonia peregrina*.

SYMPHORICARPOS. These are ornamental deciduous shrubs of the honeysuckle family native to North America and excellent for partly shady places or for the open. Smoke-resistant, so a good city shrub, and they thrive in a wide variety of soils and exposures, sun or shade. Easily propagated by seeds, cuttings or by division or detach some of the numerous suckers.

S. *albus*—Snowberry, Waxberry. This shrub is hardy from zone 2 southward, found throughout northern North America. It grows not over 3 ft. tall with slender, upright spreading branches, is deciduous with inconspicuous pinkish flowers and clusters of pure white berries that persist into the winter, their chief attraction. Well suited for the front of the border or for under planting. Liked by the bees. Enjoyed by flower arrangers. Var. *laevigatus* is nearly twice as tall and has larger leaves. This is the form most commonly grown and usually listed under the'name S. *racemosus*.

S. *orbiculatus* — Coralberry, Indian Currant. A shrub with erect branches that grows 5 to 7 ft. tall, native from Pennsylvania to Georgia and westward to South Dakota and Texas, hardy from zone 3 southward. It is attractive in the fall from the abundance of reddish-purple fruit and the persistent crimson foliage. Often sold as S. *vulgaris*. There is a variegated leaf form.

SYRINGA—Lilac. The lilac is a popular old-fashioned, flowering shrub of the olive family brought to America from Europe by the early settlers. Valued primarily for its free-flowering and ornamental bloom produced in the spring. Usually fragrant, the single or double flowers are borne in large panicles and range in color from pure white to deep crimson, through many shades of lilac, with some near pink and blue. Of vigorous habit they make good screen plantings and high hedges. Not fussy as to soil although they do better with lime than acid and like a well-drained soil in an open situation. Susceptible to lilac scale which must be controlled by spraying with a miscible oil while plants are dormant. Sending out new suckers from the base each year causes the plant to get wider and wider and flowers become smaller and less numerous as time goes on unless a good pruning job is done. Cut out some of the older, dead, or weakened wood leaving the more vigorous shoots to eventually replace the old. Plants can be renovated by cutting back almost to the ground in early spring. They quickly recover from any severe pruning. Too rich a soil will cause lush foliage growth at the expense of flowers.

S. *amurensis*—Amur Lilac. A shrub or small tree that grows 5 to 15 ft. tall with whitish-yellow or creamy flowers in large pyramidal heads in mid-June. Hardy from zone 3 southward. Var. *japonica*—Japanese Tree Lilac—has larger, hairy leaves and may become a tree up to 30 ft. The shiny cherry-like bark has winter interest. Outstanding as either a specimen plant or planted as a windbreak or screen. It is more tree-like in habit than the species, taller and slightly later to flower.

S. *chinensis*—Chinese Lilac. A hybrid shrub which is usually densely branched, seldom over 10 to 12 ft. tall and as wide, requiring considerable space but it will stand some clipping. It has compact, small leaves and is free-flowering with fragrant lilac-purple flowers in loose clusters. The most drought-resistant of the lilacs. Hardy from southern New England or zone 4 southward. It makes a good screen or hedge.

S. *oblata dilatata*—Korean Early Lilac. Upright and compact, it resembles the common lilac in habit, growing 10 to 12 ft. tall and as wide. The foliage turns a wine-red in the fall, the flowers are a pale pink-lilac. Hardy from zone 3 southward and drought-resistant.

S. *persica*—Persian Lilac. A compact shrub with slender arching branches it grows about 5 to 6 ft. tall, its flowers are pale lilac and it is hardy from zone 3 southward.

S. *vulgaris*—Common Lilac. This is one of the best loved lilacs, often found in the countryside marking the site of a former dwelling, although of European descent, it has escaped cultivation and appears native in some places. There are several hundred forms of this old-favorite, all of which flower in the spring. A large shrub up to 20 ft. in height, of a stiff upright habit, it usually has lilac colored flowers. However in many horticultural forms there are white, pink and purple flowers. Hardy from zone 2 southward. Many of the so-called "French" hybrids are of this species.

TAMARIX—Tamarisk. Deciduous shrubs or trees native to Europe and Asia of graceful habit and unusual appearance, they have long slender branches and heath-like leaves. The twigs which are completely covered by the small, scale-like leaves are shed with the leaves in the fall. Freely borne small pinkish-rose flowers in loose racemes give the plants a feathery appearnce. With age ungainly wood develops at the base so use lower growth in front or cut to the ground every few years to entirely renew. They are good plants for windswept places, to grow in drought and in alkali ground or under salt spray along the ocean, standing anywhere in pure sand, even with roots in tainted water. Plants are not so well adapted to regions of high rainfall. A few are hardy as far north as Massachusetts. Propagated by seed and cuttings which root readily.

T. odessana—Odessa Tamarix. A shrub 4 to 6 ft. tall with upright slender branches and minute pink flowers in midsummer, from July to September, blooming on current year's growth, with almost scale-like leaves. One of the lowest so one of the best for small gardens and the easiest to keep pruned. Hardy from zone 3 southward.

T. parviflora—Small-Flowered Tamarix—One of the three hardiest species with reddish bark and pink flowers in April and May. Flowers on previous year's growth so prune immediately after flowering. Similar to *T. odessana* but it blooms earlier. Hardy from zone 4 southward.

T. pentandra—Five Stamen Tamarix. This is the hardiest of the species, from zone 3 southward. A strong grower with purple branches and foliage and large panicles of pink or rose-pink flowers in late summer, August and September. Prune heavily to keep it a good size. Scale-like leaves give it a light airy texture. Blooms on current year's growth so prune in early spring when still dormant.

TAXUS—Yew. These evergreen shrubs or trees are of slow growth and variable forms with broad, flat leaves (needles), native throughout the northern hemisphere. The low growing forms are among the most useful evergreens for the small garden. Their rich, dark green foliage remains uniform in coloring throughout the year. Of dense habit, they will take clipping, make good hedge plants, screens and excellent specimens and are used for topiary work. While they like moisture they will grow well in many kinds of soil, liking plenty of humus and they do well in either sun or shade. The juice of the foliage is poisonous.

T. baccata 'Repandens'—Spreading English Yew. Its low growing, spreading, almost prostrate habit and luxuriant dark bluish-green foliage, coupled with its ability to grow in heavy shade, make it a valuable plant for landscape purposes. The hardiest of all the varieties of the English Yew. It does not enjoy long hot summers and grows best in light sandy loam and partial shade. Hardy from zone 4 southward.

T. cuspidata—The Japanese yew is generally used as a shrub but it will grow up to 50 ft. at maturity. One of the best for ornamental purposes and the best for hedges. Somewhat similar to *T. baccata* but with darker evergreen needle-like leaves and it is far more hardy and faster growing. Hardy from zone 3 and probably zone 2 southward. Sometimes sold as *T. sieboldi*. The widely advertised var. *capitata* is perhaps a seedling form of *T. cuspidata.*

'Nana', often offered as *T. brevifolia,* is a good shrubby form of slow growth with short needles, very dense and compact when young, later becoming more wide spreading, often with a picturesque habit. Will take clipping. Makes an excellent specimen plant. 'Densa' is a compact form scarcely over 3 ft. high, as broad as it is tall (smaller than 'Nana'), very handsome.

TEUCRIUM—Germander. These shrubby plants belonging to the mint family are not particular as to soil, but a well-drained light sandy soil seems to suit them best. Grown for ornament or fragrance they are well suited to rock gardens and flower border use. Propagate by root division, by seeds or cuttings.

T. chamaedrys—Wall germander is a prostrate or procumbent subshrub with stems about 1 ft. high and loose spikes of reddish-purple or rose flowers. A good bedding or edging plant it blooms in late summer. Not generally hardy north of zone 6 although with protection they may be grown farther north.

T. fruticans—Tree or Shrubby Germander. This evergreen, woolly, brushy subshrub grows 2 to 5 ft. tall with very light gray foliage and pale blue flowers in some moderation over the year, mostly summer, it has silvered stems. Dry, rocky or gravelly well-drained soil, in the sun, with the least fuss is where it survives and where the best color in leaf and flower will be found. A good filler in the right place. They

87. Two good plants for use between steps or other dry areas are at the left above the stone, glossy-leaved germander *(Teucrium chamaedrys)*, and low-growing creeping thyme *(Thymus serpyllum.)*

McFarland Photo

thrive along the Gulf Coast and in California, in the rock garden or very dry border, hardy from zone 7 southward. Grow in the cool greenhouse North. Propagate by seeds or division of rhizomes.

TRAILING ARBUTUS—See *Epigaea repens.*

ULEX—Furze, Gorse. These are much branched twiggy shrubs with rigid, dark green spiny branches native in Europe belonging to the pea family. Not entirely hardy North but may survive with protection.

88. *Teucrium fruticans* — Shrubby germander has very light gray foliage, pale blue flowers and silvered stems. It does well in dry rocky or gravelly well-drained soils, in the sun. An excellent filler in the right place. Hardy from zone 7 southward.

Marten Photo

Only 2 are much cultivated. They are low and almost leafless. Not easy to transplant so sow where they are to grow or make cuttings. They prefer a sandy, slightly acid soil. Good plants for sandy banks to bind earth on embankments or for open wastes.

U. europaeus grows to 3 ft. or more, doing well in sandy or gravelly soil in a sunny location. An excellent seaside plant. Showy, fragrant yellow flowers are produced almost continuously in mild climates as in California. Hardy from zone 4 southward. 'Plenus' has double flowers.

VACCINIUM—Blueberry. Blueberries belong to the heath family and are used in landscaping primarily for the beauty of their colored leaves in the fall. They must have lime-free soil and thrive best in sandy, peaty earth. Some are drought-resistant. Not susceptible to any serious insect pests or diseases. Although frequently found growing in the wild in moist or wet places they do well on poor sandy soils. Useful where the area to be planted can be treated in a naturalistic, informal manner. The berries attract the birds.

V. angustifolium laevifolium—Lowbush Blueberry. Deciduous and a native over nearly half the country, it grows low to a height of only 1 to 1½ ft., excellent as a woody ground cover in acid soil plantings. Fertilize to increase the fruit production which ripens in late summer. Foliage turns scarlet in the fall. Stands heat and dryness and is hardy from zone 2 southward. Formerly known as *V. pensylvanicum*.

V. pallidum—Dryland Blueberry. A good blueberry for planting in dry soil growing to 3 ft. in height. Native to eastern United States. The foliage turns scarlet in the autumn.

VIBURNUMS. Useful sturdy shrubs or small trees easily grown and maintained for ornamental purposes and belonging to the honeysuckle family. Mostly compact and bushy plants with attractive foliage which in many cases takes on good coloring, most have showy flowers followed by decorative fruits. All benefit with some pruning. A few will withstand drought.

V. lantana—Wayfaring Tree. This is a vigorous stout, upright, tree-like shrub up to 15 ft. with light gray-green wrinkled leaves, white beneath, turning deep red in the fall. White flowers in flat clusters appear in mid-May followed by clusters of red berries which change to black, a source of bird food. It will thrive in drier places than most viburnums, is naturalized in eastern United States, hardy from zone 3 southward.

V. laurustinus tinus—A handsome native of the Mediterranean area, this is the most useful of the evergreen species where hardy. A bushy grower from 7 to 10 ft. or more it has luxuriant masses of dark, glossy green leaves. In mild climates the clusters of pinkish-white flowers open during the winter. It makes an excellent hedge and is hardy from protected parts of zone 6 southward. It is grown on the West Coast and in the Gulf States where it does not like too much water; susceptible to mildew then. A good evergreen accent shrub. May be grown in the cool greenhouse in pots for winter flowering. Also known in several horticultural forms, one with variegated leaves.

V. lentago—Nannyberry, Sheepberry. A native vigorous shrub, often more tree-like, it grows 20 to 30 ft. tall and is hardy from zone 2 southward. The large lustrous green leaves take on a purplish-red fall coloring. Flat clusters of creamy-white flowers are followed by juicy black berries enjoyed by the birds in fall and winter. Useful as a background or screen and effective planted at the edge of a woodland.

VITEX. A diverse group of woody plants, evergreen and deciduous, tropical to sub-tropical, some surviving far north into much colder climates, others adapting as well in arid places as in humid climates. In common they have foliage of striking and unusual character with no pests or serious diseases. They are more rugged and perservering than appearances would indicate. Fairly drought-resistant.

V. agnus-castus—Chaste Tree. This is a deciduous exotic looking shrub or small tree rather erect and slender, growing 8 to 10 ft. high, with gray aromatic foliage. Fragrant flowers are a pale lilac-blue in dense showy terminal spikes appearing in late summer when few other shrubs are in bloom. It takes heat and poor or dry soils in the sun, is better performing there than with a surplus of the good things. Must have good drainage. A good specimen plant. In the North the stems are often winter-killed but the roots send up new shoots which flower the same year. It is usually better to cut the stems back to stubs permitting new growth to develop each year. Var. *latifolia* is somewhat hardier than the species. It does not winter kill from zone 5 southward. Propagation is chiefly by cuttings. Var. *alba* is white while var. *macrophylla* (*V. agnus-castus latifolia*) is somewhat hardier than the species, has larger leaves and deep colored-flowers, one of the best.

WAX-MYRTLE—See *Myrica cerifera*.

WEAVER'S-BROOM—See *Spartium junceum*.

WILD OLEASTER—See *Shepherdia argentea*.

WITCH-HAZEL—See *Hamamelis*.

WOADWAXEN—See *Genista*.

YEW—See *Taxus*.

89. *Vitex agnus-castus* — One of the less well-known late summer-flowering shrubs, the chaste tree is notable for its profusion of lavender blossoms. It is seldom reliably hardy much north of Boston, although it can be expected to grow back from the base even if the tops are cut down by winter cold. Like most half-hardy shrubs, its chances for survival are best on well-drained soil.

U. S. D. A. Photo

GROUND COVERS WITHSTANDING DRY SOILS

Both woody and herbaceous ground covers are being used more and more by home gardeners and landscape architects to reduce maintenance. They have long been used in shaded areas beneath trees and on banks or hillsides where maintaining grass in good condition is an expensive chore, but the possibilities of their extensive use in creating pleasant garden scenes in combination with outdoor living areas is a new trend. There are ground covers for every location and the high cost and scarcity of garden labor is responsible for their increased use.

Designers are now creating amazing and pleasing effects with these plants and thereby reducing upkeep noticeably. In addition to an attractive appearance, ground covers have the practical benefits of preventing soil erosion, retaining soil moisture and serving as a decorative mulch. There is quite a long list of ground covers for hot, dry situations and sandy soils, plants that withstand considerable dryness without damage. Some of the vines listed later are also equally useful as ground covers, in the right location.

DROUGHT-TOLERANT WOODY GROUND COVERS

These plants are all described and listed alphabetically under Shrubs, a few are described under Vines, as indicated.

Arctostaphylos uva-ursi—Bearberry.

Calluna vulgaris—Scotch Heather.

Ceanothus americanus—New Jersey Tea.

Celastrus scandens—Bittersweet. See Vines.

Chaenomeles japonica alpina—Alpine Flowering Quince.

Comptonia peregrina—Sweet-Fern.

Corema conradi—Broom Crowberry.

Cotoneaster species.

Cytisus species—Broom.

Diervilla lonicera—Dwarf Bush Honeysuckle.

Erica species—Heath.

Euonymus fortunei—Wintercreeper. See Vines.

Euonymus obovata—Running Euonymus.

Forsythia suspensa sieboldi—Weeping Forsythia.

Gaultheria shallon—Salal.

Helianthemum nummularium—Sun-Rose.
Hypericum species—St. John's-Wort.
Juniperus species—Juniper.
Lavandula spica—English or True Lavender.
Leiophyllum buxifolium—Sand Myrtle.
Lonicera japonica 'Halliana'—Hall's Honeysuckle. See Vines.
Mahonia aquifolium—Oregon Holly-Grape.
Mahonia repens—Creeping Mahonia.
Myrica pensylvanica—Bayberry.
Pinus mugo mughus—Mugho Pine.
Potentilla fruticosa—Bush Cinquefoil.
Rhus aromatica—Fragrant Sumac.
Robinia hispida—Rose Acacia, Pink Locust.
Rosa rugosa—Rugosa Rose.
Rosa virginiana—Virginia Rose.
Rosmarinus officinalis prostratus—Dwarf Rosemary.
Salix tristis—Dwarf Gray Willow
Santolina chamaecyparissus—Lavender-Cotton.
Symphoricarpos orbiculatus—Coralberry, Indian Currant.
Vaccinium angustifolium laevifolium—Lowbush Blueberry.

DROUGHT-TOLERANT HERBACEOUS GROUND COVERS

The ground covers mentioned below are mostly perennials.
Achillea millefolium roseum—Pink Yarrow.
Achillea tomentosa—Woolly Yarrow.
Aegopodium podagraria variegatum—Variegated Goutweed.
Aethionema coridifolium warleyense 'Warley Rose'—Stone-Cress.
Alyssum saxatile—Gold Dust, Basket-Of-Gold.
Antennaria dioica rosea—Pussytoes.
Arabis species—Rock-Cress.
Arenaria verna caespitosa—Moss Sandwort.
Armeria maritima—Thrift.
Artemisia schmidtiana nana—'Silver Mound' Artemisia.
Artemisia stelleriana—Beach Wormwood.
Campanula carpatica—Carpathian Bellflower .
Cerastium tomentosum—Snow-In-Summer.

Convolvulus mauritanicus—Ground Morning Glory.
Coronilla varia—Crown Vetch.
Dianthus species—Pinks.
Festuca ovina glauca—Blue Fescue. Grass, Perenial
Galium vernum—Yellow Bedstraw.
Gazania—Annual.
Gypsophila repens—Creeping Gypsophila.
Hedysarum coronarium—French Honeysuckle.
Hemerocallis fulva 'Kwanso'—Tawny Daylily.
Lotus corniculatis—Bird's-Foot Trefoil, Ground Honeysuckle.
Matricaria tchihatchewi—Turfing Daisy.
Mesembryanthemum species—Succulent.
Ophiopogon japonicus—Japan Grass, Lily-Turf. Grasses, Perennial.
Pachysandra terminalis—Japanese Pachysandra.
Pelargonium peltatum—Ivy Geranium.
Phalaris arundinacea picta—Ribbon Grass. Grasses, Perennial.
Phlox amoena (P. procumbens)—Trailing Phlox.
Phlox subulata—Ground Phlox, Moss Pink.
Portulaca grandiflora—Rose Moss. Annual.
Potentilla tridentata—Three Toothed Cinquefoil.
Saponaria ocymoides—Rock Soapwort.
Sedum species—Stonecrop. Succulent
Sempervivum species and vars.—Houseleek, Hen-and-Chickens.
Stachys lanata—Lamb's-Ears.
Thymus species—Thyme.
Verbena bipinnatifida—Annual.
Vinca minor—Periwinkle.
Viola pedata—Bird's-Foot Violet.
Waldsteinia fragarioides—Barren or Dry Strawberry.

VINES WITHSTANDING DRY SOILS

Where poor soil conditions are a problem do everything possible to improve the situation. Add humus to the soil and use a mulch in order that every bit of moisture be conserved. This will increase the list of vines that can be used. Where little can be done about the soil and rainfall and artificial watering are inadequate study drought-resistant vines listed below and make the best choice for your situation. Many act as die-back shrubs depending upon the exposure.

Many vines are so rampant in growth the pruning they require to keep them under control would discourage their use. If they are put on buildings they must be kept out of windows and off roof tops necessitating even more work. It is an art to thin them out, so they form attractive traceries on masonry and not just a mass of foliage.

There are both shrubby and herbaceous vines that will take dry soil conditions. The type you select should be determined by its intended use, the site and the available moisture. Many of the vines also make good ground covers, are quite inexpensive and give quick returns.

AKEBIA. Twining shrubby vines, leaves almost evergreen, from China and Japan. Of light and graceful growth to about 12 ft. Useful for shade and for sprawling over rocks, clothing old stumps, arbors or pergolas. Dark colored flowers appear in early spring followed by attractive grayish-purple, sausage shaped fruits which often do not develop. Hardy from zone 4 southward. Like sun and a well-drained soil. Propagation by seeds, root division and by cuttings.

AMPELOPSIS. Woody, tender, tendril-climbing vines belonging to the grape family. Easily grown, not fussy as to soil or situation doing well in dry soils. Will grow on walls but should be tied at first as they lack sucking-disks. Useful to cover walls, arbors or for trellis work and to ramble over rocks. Propagate by seeds, cutting or layers.

A. aconitifolia—A tall growing, slender vine with dissected leaves from China. Fruit first bluish then turning to yellow or orange. Hardy from zone 4 southward, possibly from zone 3.

ARISTOLOCHIA DURIOR—Dutchman's-Pipe, Pipe-Vine. A tall, high climbing, hardy, woody vine of the wild ginger family native to eastern United States and cultivated for its fine foliage, making an excellent screen plant for porches and arbors. Its roundish or kidney-shaped leaves are 6 to 14 in. wide. The common name comes from the pipe or U-shaped tubular yellowish-green flowers which have a wide flared mouth. Long known as *A. macrophylla* and *A. sipho*. Propagate by seed.

AUSTRALIAN PEA—See *Dolichos lignosus*

BALLOON VINE—See *Cardiospermum halicacabum.*

BALSAM-APPLE, WILD—See *Echinocystis lobata.*

BIGNONIA CAPREOLATA—Cross-Vine, Trumpet-Flower. A beautiful evergreen, woody tendril climbing vine found wild from Maryland and southern Illinois to Florida and Louisiana but will grow considerably farther north as a trailing plant or creeper. Reliably hardy from zone 6 southward. Funnel-shaped reddish-orange flowers about 2 in. long are pale within and grouped in clusters, appearing in late May. Foliage turns a reddish green in autumn. Will do well in any soil and is excellent as a screen or for shade. Also called *Anisostichus capreolatus.*

BITTERSWEET—See *Celastrus* and *Solanum dulcamara.*

BLACK-EYED SUSAN—See *Thunbergia alata.*

BOUSSINGAULTIA BASELLOIDES — Madeira Vine, Mignonette Vine. A tropical herbaceous twining vine of the American tropics, an escape in Florida and Texas, grown outdoors in the South, with some winter covering it will survive up to zone 6. North of this lift the roots and store in a cool, frost free place for the winter. The slender winding stems are regularly spaced with the attractive heart-shapd shining leaves which mingle evenly with the long spikes of small fragrant white flowers in late summer. Tuberous roots develop to a good size in rich, sandy soils for a long-lived and permanent plant. Tiny tubercles form along the stem. Grows quickly when established to as much as 20 ft. in one year. Goes wild in moist soils and gets out of control. This tall creeper is often used to clothe a porch, trellis or arbor. Easily propagated by seeds, sown in the spring, by root division or plant the small tubercles that develop along the stems in the leaf axils.

BUTTERFLY PEA—See *Centrosema virginianum.*

CALIFORNIA ROSE—See *Convolvulus japonicus.*

CALONYCTION ACULEATUM—Moonflower. A twining, perennial, tropical American vine of the morning glory family closely related to the morning glory but the moonflower blooms at night. The large trumpet-shaped white flowers with a broad flat rim give the vine its common name. It has a milky juice and somewhat prickly stems with three-lobed, broadly oval leaves 6 to 8 in. long. Perennial only in zones 8 and 9, grown as an annual northward where they will bloom the first year from seed. Grown as a porch climber over much of the United States.

CAMPSIS — Trumpet-Creeper. Handsome woody, vigorous growing vines climbing by aerial rootlets, with attractive deciduous compound foliage and showy trumpet-shaped flowers from mid-July on. Adapted to covering banks and rambling over rocky formations. Excellent as screens or for use on walls and arbors, presenting a bold, tropical appearance. May do damage on wooden buildings by loosening shingles. They prefer fertile soil and a sunny site but will grow readily in most any soil and take considerable drought. Rather thick cigar-like fruit pods on the bright tan stems add winter interest. Propagated readily by seed, layers or by cuttings.

C. grandiflora—Chinese Trumpet-Creeper. Sometimes called *C. chinensis*. Not as high climbing as *C. radicans* and produces fewer aerial roots but has larger and more brilliant trumpet-shaped scarlet flowers 3 to 5 in. across at the bell end. Good foliage with 7 to 9 leaflets. Not as hardy as the native variety, only from zone 5 southward. Long known as *Tecoma grandiflora* and *Bignonia grandiflora*.

C. hybrida is a hybrid between the two, more hardy than *C. grandiflora*, with flowers almost as showy.

C. radicans—Trumpet Creeper or Vine. This is a native species growing from Pennsylvania southward and westward to Missouri, Florida and Texas. Often climbs to 30 ft. or more with numerous aerial roots. It is the hardiest and can be grown from zone 3 southward. An excellent city vine as well as for the country. Nearly as showy as the Chinese vine with its orange-scarlet flowers 2 in. wide, the tube 3 times as long as the expanded part. Attractive dark green leaves have 9 to 11 leaflets. It suckers badly and is invasive, hard to eradicate. Used on fence posts and to attract humming birds through the long hot weeks of summer. Formerly known as *Tecoma radicans* and *Bignonia radicans*.

C. tagliabuana is a hybrid between *C. grandiflora* and *C. radicans* and more handsome and hardier than either. Mostly offered under the varietal name of 'Mme. Galen.' Tawny-orange flowers nearly 1 in. long in loose clusters from mid-July until October.

90. Trumpet vine *(Campsis radicans)* grows rapidly and produces striking orange blossoms, but it is a problem to keep it from getting under clapboards and over windows. An ideal vine to admire on somebody else's house.

Hubbard Photo

CARDIOSPERMUM HALICACABUM–Balloon Vine, Heartseed. A tropical herbaceous vine, perennial in the south, planted as an annual in the north, of the soapberry family. It is used in warm regions and is naturalized in southeastern United States. Climbs by means of tendrils and is excellent for covering wire fences or trellises, with support will grow 10 to 12 ft. Quick growing and graceful with deeply cut leaves and small white 4-petaled flowers. The seed pods are inflated like balloons, each black seed is marked with a white, heart-shaped spot. Seed should be sown where the plants are to grow or started early indoors. In mild regions may self-sow. Enjoys a light well-drained soil in a sheltered location.

CELASTRUS–Bittersweet, Staff-Tree. Deciduous woody vines of twining habit, vigorous growers and deep rooting, useful for walls, fences, arbors and trellises and grown for their brilliant autumn fruit. Like holly the sexes are on separate plants so must have a male and a femle plant for berries. Will grow in most any soil or situation, in sun or shade and in dry areas. Root easily and may be propagated by cuttings or by suckers.

   C. orbiculatus–Oriental Bittersweet. A 30 ft. handsome vine from western China with good foliage, bright orange-yellow berries that persist after the leaves drop. Flowering and fruiting clusters mostly in leaf axils so often partially hidden. Hardy in protected areas from zone 4 and southward. Often sold as *C. articulatus*.

   C. scandens–Bittersweet. A native, rampant, shrubby, not tall growing, woody vine much used for covering low wall tops, to clamber up through old trees or ramble in rocky places and over rough banks. Of value late in the season when the leaves turn yellow and the yellow fruits open to reveal crimson-coated seeds. Flowering and fruiting clusters mostly terminal so not hidden by the foliage. The fruiting branches make attractive indoor decoration for winter use. Keep within bounds by frequent and heavy pruning. Hardy from zone 2 southward.

CENTROSEMA VIRGINIANUM–Butterfly Pea. A perennial twining low vine of the pea family found from New Jersey south, with white to purplish pea-like flowers, blooming the first year from seed. Hardy as far north as Philadelphia. Likes sun and any soil. Useful for the fence or trellis.

CLEMATIS. Attractive woody climbing plants of the buttercup family widely distributed in the temperate region. They thrive in enriched, light loamy soil slightly on the limy side. The four listed below will take considerable drought.

C. *apifolia*—October Clematis. A woody vine from Japan growing 5 to 9 ft. tall and hardy from zone 1 southward. Dull white flowers ½ to 1 in. wide in loose clusters bloom in September and October furnishing a creamy mass of bloom.

C. *paniculata*—Sweet Autumn Clematis, Japanese Clematis. Somewhat like Virgin's Bower although superior to it in all respects. Easiest to grow of the clematis group. Flowers in September and October and has loose panicles of small white pleasantly fragrant florets followed by plumy seed pods typical of all kinds of clematis, many of which are quite decorative. Can be used with other flowers to make interesting bouquets. Semi-evergreen foliage of this species is dark green and glossy, the best foliage to be found in the entire group. Hardy from zone 2 southward. Also known as C. *dioscoreifolia robusta*.

C. *texensis*—Scarlet Clematis. A slightly woody vine native to Texas and hardy from zone 3 southward growing 4 to 6 ft. tall, the vine eventually will cover an area 6 to 10 ft. square. Sometimes called C. *coccinea*. Has handsome bell or jug-shaped flowers of bright rose-pink or scarlet from July to September followed by lovely feathery seed heads. It needs full sun and apparently grows better in the naturally sweet soils of the midwest than it does in the acid New England soils. If grown in a sheltered spot it will bloom early in summer and continue until frost. May die to ground in winter but sprouts quickly from the base in the spring. Blooms on the current year's growth. The hybrid 'Dutchess of Albany' is a good grower and will push its way to the top of a garden house with slender shoots and deep pink flowers.

C. *virginiana*—Virgin's Bower, Love-Vine, Old Man's-Beard. Male and female flowers on separate plants. Not showy in flower and scarcely noticed until fall when its very plumy, feathery seed pods are seen along the roadsides. Native to eastern North America and hardy everywhere climbing to 18 ft. or often sprawling in the wild.

CLOCK VINE—See *Thunbergia alata*.

91. *Clematis texensis* — Scarlet clematis, one of the less commonly seen clematis species, provides inch-long urn-shaped flowers during mid-summer. Though less showy than the large-flowered hybrid clematis, despite its bright coloring, this species is appreciated by gardners who enjoy growing less common plants. It does well in dry gardens.

McFarland Photo

COBAEA SCANDENS—Cup-and-Saucer Vine. Although a vigorous tendril-bearing woody perennial vine in the tropics and deep South in the North it is grown as an annual because of its quick growth. It is attractive and unusually graceful for such a rampant climber. Showy, large cup or bell-shaped flowers rest in a saucer and range in color from pink to purple followed by plum-shaped fruits. It grows up to 20 ft. in length. Start the seeds indoors 5 to 6 weeks before outdoor planting is safe, one seed to a pot. Notch the side of the seed with a knife and press edgewise into moist soil, barely covering it. Seeds should sprout in 10 to 14 days, plants do well in sun or part shade.

CONVOLVULUS JAPONICUS—California Rose. Sometimes known as *Calystegia pubescens*. A twining, perennial climber of the morning glory family from eastern Asia growing up to 20 ft. with narrow arrow-shaped leaves. Bright pink morning glory flowers 2 in. wide, bloom in the day time throughout the summer. Of easy culture growing in any soil, self-seeding so must be watched, likely to become a nuisance. Hardy everywhere. In the eastern states there is a double-flowered form which is a troublesome weed, usually prostrate.

CROSS VINE—See *Bignonia capreolata*.

DOLICHOS. Tropical, perennial twining vines of the pea family with compound 3-part leaves and showy pea-like flowers. Grown as an annual vine in the United States and most successful from zone 7 southward as they like heat. Not fussy as to soil and easily grown from seed.

D. *lablab*—Hyacinth Bean. Grown as an annual in the north. A rapid grower it reaches a height of from 15 to 30 ft. Seed can be sown out-doors or started inside in pots. They should be planted where they are to stand. Stiff spikes of reddish-purple pea-like flowers are followed by flat pods. Var. *giganteus* has white flowers and is of larger growth. Excellent as a quick cover in heat along the Gulf Coast and California.

D. *lignosus*—Australian Pea. A low somewhat woody vine that will rapidly cover a low wall or fence with a loose blanket of persistent foliage although the leaves will drop in any frost. Abundant white or rose-purple flowers bloom over a long period of time.

DUTCHMAN'S-PIPE—See *Aristolochia durior*.

ECHINOCYSTIS LOBATA—Wild Balsam-Apple, Wild or Mock Cucumber. A herbaceous quick growing tendril-bearing vine of the cucumber family, widely distributed in eastern North America. A fast growing annual it often reaches 20 ft. Useful for a quick covering or as a temporary screen to hide unsightly objects. It has deeply lobed oval or heart-shaped leaves and clusters of small white or greenish flowers in branched racemes. Fruit is a puffy, rather papery, egg-shaped, prickly pod about 2 in. long. Easily grown from seed.

ELAEAGNUS PUNGENS REFLEXA—See Shrubs.

EUONYMUS FORTUNEI—Wintercreeper. Also known as *E. radicans*. A trailing or climbing evergreen from eastern Asia that can climb to 20 ft. or more on a rough surface by means of stem rootlets. Hardy from zone 4, with protection from zone 2 southward. They like sun or half shade and are not fussy as to soil. One of the finest small vines in some of its varieties. Effective as a ground cover against a boulder or well placed in the rock garden, excellent on retaining walls and viewed close up as in a patio or entrance. Attractive glossy small, thick leaves and round pinkish-orange fruit. '*Acutus*' is an especially good climber or ground cover with smaller pointed leaves, '*Argenteo-marginatus*' has silvery margined leaves, '*Carrierei*' is a low shrubby form with showy fruit used for bedding, in '*Coloratus*' the leaves turn reddish-purple in the autumn and '*Minimus*' (sometimes sold a *E. kewensis*) has very tiny dark green leaves, marked white along the veins, useful in the rock garden. Var. *vegetus* is a somewhat shrubby form.

FLEECE VINE—See *Polygonum auberti*.

HEDERA HELIX—English Ivy. A woody creeping evergreen or if allowed to climb it may reach 80 to 90 ft. in length, completely covering walls in favorable situations. Much grown in the United States for landscaping, as house plants and use in window boxes. Easily propagated from cuttings or layers. There are many horticultural varieties with varying degrees of hardiness as well as leaf form. Northerners must select clones for their climate, one of the best is called 238th Street. It holds its color all winter and makes new growth very early in the spring. The English ivy wants some shade. Although it enjoys moisture it will grow in most any kind of soil.

92. Evergreen winter creeper *(Euonymus fortunei vegetus)*, a useful dry bank ground cover, is effective on a slightly shaded slope.

Genereux Photo

93. English ivy *(Hedera helix)* is a satisfactory ground cover in moderately dry locations. Here it is perhaps well-watered with birds splashing ample water on it.

Taloumis Photo

HONEYSUCKLE—See *Lonicera*.

HUMULUS JAPONICUS—Japanese Hop Vine. A rapid, vigorous, annual climber from China and Japan of the mulberry family attaining a height of 12 to 20 ft. with slender, twining stems. The leaves are divided into several lobes and toothed along the margins. The luxuriant foliage makes a dense ornamental covering for fences, unsightly buildings, verandas or trellis-work arbors. Not bothered by insects, heat or drought. Var. *variegatus* has leaves splashed with white and in var. *lutescens* leaves are bronzed or golden.

HYACINTH BEAN—See *Dolichos lablab*.

HYDRANGEA PETIOLARIS—Climbing Hydrangea. Hardy from zone 3 southward. This ornamental woody vine climbs by means of aerial rootlets and may reach a height of 40 ft. or more. Sometimes sold as *H. scandens* or *H. volubilis*. Also known as *H. anomala*. Broadly oval or rounded or heart-shaped leaves are 2 to 4 in. long. Loose white flower clusters 6 to 12 in. wide are conspicuous in July and August. Without support it is a straggling prostrate bush but clings firmly to walls and tree trunks and makes a good cover for a rocky slope or stone wall. Slow to get started but once established hardy and drought-resistant.

IPOMOEA PURPUREA *(I. major)*—Morning-Glory. Twining tender annual vine, a native of tropical America, and a favorite for covering trellises, fences and walls. Their large dark green, heart-shaped leaves make an excellent screen. The showy trumpet-shaped flowers in purple, pink or blue are borne in profusion and there are double forms and also white ones. Flowers remain open on cloudy days but soon wilt if the sun strikes them but another day and there is a full new crop. The quickest and showiest of the annual vines they are best sown where they are to grow or start seed early indoors. Will grow readily in most any soil. Do not fertilize as rich soil will produce leaves in place of flowers. Place in full sun or light shade. Self-sown plants will result in smaller-flowering vines and poorer colors. In buying seeds specify what color you want and whether you want large or small flowering kinds.

JAPANESE HOP VINE—See *Humulus japonicus*.

LACE VINE—See *Polygonum auberti*.

94. Although the climbing hydrangea *(Hydrangea petiolaris)* is usually slow to start growing, it is fast to develop once established, even in a dry soil. As the plant will grow over 40 feet tall it will require hand pruning to be restricted to the location shown here.

Taloumis Photo

LANTANA—Annual.

LATHYRUS LATIFOLIUS—Everlasting Pea, Perennial Pea. Of the pea family, a perennial that climbs by tendrils up to 9 ft. or more. Not fragrant but excellent for general garden use as it can be trained on pillars, an old fence or stump, to fill in any gap. Abundant rose-pink flowers in long-stalked clusters in midsummer. Available in various colors but so rampant a grower it must be controlled or it will become a nuisance. Var. *albus* has white flowers and var. *rosea* is a clear pink. Will grow in any soil. Increase by seed or division.

LEADWORT—See *Plumbago capensis.*

LONICERA—Honeysuckle. Climbing species are included here. Also see *Lonicera* under Shrubs.

L. heckrotti—Everblooming Honeysuckle. Probably a hybrid. An attractive low shrub with spreading, sometimes twining branches, hardy from zone 3 southward. The flowers which are purple on the outside and yellow within the slender tube are 1½ in. long, start to bloom in June and continue over a long period, one of the most free flowering of the climbing kinds. Leaves are oblong to oval, 1 to 2½ in. long and whitish beneath.

L. japonica—Japanese Honeysuckle. A vigorous, rampant, half-evergreen climber growing 15 to 30 ft., naturalized in eastern United States where it can get out of control and smother all other vegetation. Hardy from zone 3 southward. Fragrant white flowers tinged purple, fading to yellow in June. It is a good porch vine and an excellent ground cover. 'Aureo-reticulata' has smaller and lighter green leaves veined with yellow and 'Chinensis' has 2 in. long flowers reddish on the outside, the new wood reddish, the foliage with ruddy tones. In 'Halliana' (Hall's Honeysuckle) the flowers are pure white fading to yellow and not tinged purple. Requires a sturdy, heavy support. Prune in winter to lighten the weighty mass. Evergreen south but drops leaves quickly in frost.

L. sempervirens—Trumpet or Coral Honeysuckle. A twining vine, evergreen in mild climates, native from Massachusetts to Florida, Texas and Nebraska, hardy from zone 3 southward. Trumpet-shaped flowers about 2 in. long in terminal clusters, bright orange or red outside with yellow throats and no fragrance, appear from mid-June to August followed by red berries in the fall. The end pair of leaves are joined together so that the stem appears to pierce the leaf. Aphids are a troublesome pest often causing the leaves to roll, making it difficult to control by spraying. May reach a height of 30 ft. but never forms a dense plant.

MADEIRA VINE—See *Boussingaultia baselloides.*

MENISPERMUM CANADENSE — Canada Moonseed. A twining, woody vine, climbing to 12 ft. with attractive foliage, the round-oval leaves 4 to 8 in. long. Native from Quebec to Georgia and Arkansas. Easily grown from seed or cuttings of ripened wood. Suitable for covering arbors and trellises.

MIGNONETTE VINE—See *Boussingaultia baselloides.*

MOCK CUCUMBER—See *Echinocystis lobata.*

MOONFLOWER—See *Calonyction aculeatum.*

MORNING GLORY—See *Ipomoea purpurea.*

NASTURTIUM—See *Tropaeolum majus.*

PERIPLOCA GRAECA—Silk Vine. A milky juiced, woody, stem-climbing, twining vine of the milkweed family, hardy to Philadelphia, from zone 5 southward. It may climb from 25 to 40 ft. Deciduous leaves are 2 to 4½ in. long, glossy dark green above, paler beneath. Greenish-brown flowers 1 in. wide in long-stalked terminal clusters. Easily propagated by seeds or by layering, inclined to be invasive. Likes the sun and a well drained soil.

PLUMBAGO CAPENSIS — Leadwort. A tender vine-like shrub of rampant, straggling habit growing to 8 ft. or more. Azure-blue phlox-like flowers in terminal clusters or spikes on slender stems. Grown outdoors in the Gulf States and California where it is evergreen to cover a trellis or as a tub plant. Likes a sandy loam. In the north it is used in the garden during the summer months and taken indoors as a cool greenhouse or house plant for the winter. Cut back to 1 in. in the spring. Excellent as a pot or tub plant. Var. *alba* is a white form. Propagated by seeds or cuttings.

POLYGONUM AUBERTI—Fleece Vine, Chinese Fleece Vine, Lace Vine, Silver Lace Vine. A fast growing, hardy, twining, woody perennial from western China and Tibet growing to 20 ft. or more in length and of the buckwheat family. The vine has slender stems, deciduous, dense, lance-shaped, bright green foliage and small greenish-white flowers produced in large masses from June or July on. Useful for the pergola or trellis and will grow nearly anywhere filling a need where choicer plants will not grow. Requires severe pruning each winter or the mass of stems will get out of hand.

95. Chinese fleece vine *(Polygonum auberti)*, a fast-growing, drought-tolerant vine, is much admired for its abundance of white late summer blooms.

Hubbard Photo

ROSA SPECIES—Rambler and Climbing Kinds. Since roses are one of the best known and best loved of all flowers if you are in a dry area inquire around to find out which ramblers and climbers are the hardiest in your section. Success with this group depends largely upon their hardiness. Once established they will thrive with no extra watering and are long lived. Not true vines they always need to be tied. Prune immediately after flowering cutting out some old canes to permit the vigorous young new growth ample room, they will bloom the next year. There are hundreds of varieties available in varying heights and colors, both in singles and doubles. Visit a rose garden or nursery in June if you are interested in acquiring new rose plants. No catalog can take the place of actually seeing the rambler or climber while in flower.

Ramblers are the more rank climbers with small flowers in clusters descendents from *R. multiflora*, *R. setigera* and *R. wichuraiana*. Their wood is willowy so they can easily be trained on arches or trellises and the slender, trailing varieties will creep over the ground rooting as they run. Useful to cover steep banks, to train over fences or walls or cover unsightly places. Generally hardy throughout the rose growing section. In very severe winters they may be damaged somewhat in unprotected areas but they generally renew themselves quickly. On the island of Nantucket they are hardy often covering the roof of a small cottage. Dorothy Perkins is a familiar rambler.

The climbers are sports, seedlings or mutations of the hybrid teas and perpetuals, those with the large flowers. Well known examples are Paul's Scarlet (red), Dr. W. Van Fleet (pink) and American Pillar (rose and white).

SILK VINE—See *Periploca graeca*.

SMILAX—Greenbrier. A genus of woody tendril climbing vines, usually prickly, belonging to the lily family. (Do not confuse with *Asparagus asparagoides*, commonly called smilax and widely used by the florist in decoration.) They grow in all sorts of soils, often in sandy poor ones and are of the easiest culture. Unsurpassed for making an impenetrable prickly thicket but can become a real nuisance. Propagated by seeds and division.

S. *herbacea*—Carrion Flower. Native to eastern North America. Less rampant than the following species, it is not thorny and usually dies back in winter. Makes a good screen.

S. *laurifolia*—False China-Brier. A high climbing very prickly vine. Thick, leathery evergreen leaves 2½ to 5 in. long, 3-veined, dark green above, paler beneath. Native from New Jersey to Florida and westward, hardy from zone 4 southward. Similar to but more hardy than S. *lanceolata*.

SOLANUM DULCAMARA — Climbing Nightshade, Bittersweet. A scrambling shrubby vine of the nightshade family growing to 8. ft., more often prostrate or nearly so, and naturalized throughout North America. An attractive climber for the wild garden. A hardy perennial that will grow in any soil. Violet potato-like flowers in loose clusters are followed by scarlet poisonous berries. The juice of its wilted leaves

96. Of all the ramblers, none is better known than double-pink Dorothy Perkins, although scentless, prone to mildew attack and flowering only once, in June, this highly drought-tolerant rose serves a useful purpose where quick cover is wanted on a banking or hot wall. It would take a great deal of work to keep it tied to the porch trellis here shown and would need constant pruning so as not to interfere with passers-by on the concrete walk. Flanked on either side with the aggressive Englemann Virginia creeper continual trimming is necessary to keep it from taking over.

U. S. D. A. Photo

is also poisonous so best not to grow where children are. *Celastrus scandens* is the plant generally known in America as bittersweet.

THUNBERGIA ALATA—Black-Eyed Susan Vine, Clock Vine. Tender climbing plants from tropical Africa, grown as a twining perennial in the south, as an annual in the north where it blooms in late summer and autumn although a slight frost cuts their tops to the ground. This dainty, twining climber has perky black-eyed flowers 1½ in. across in colors of orange, yellow, cream and white. Easy to grow but wanting a long growing season. Its tendency to trail makes it highly effective in rock or wall work where it cascades effectively. Useful as a ground cover or it can be trained to a low trellis or fence. Tying at intervals will keep the vine in place. Useful and highly effective in hanging baskets or draping the front of a window or porch box. Var. *alba* has white flowers and var. *aurantiaca* has orange flowers with the characteristic black "eye". Propagated by seeds, cuttings and layers.

TROPAEOLUM MAJUS—Nasturtium. The trailing types are a tall climbing, twining, half hardy annual from Peru that needs a wire or trellis support, fast growing to 8 or 10 ft. Colorful and easy to grow they give quick and effective results blooming rapidly from seed. Flowers come single, semi-double and double and although typically orange-yellow or yellow-red they may be had in pale primrose-yellow, creamy-white, geranium scarlet, sulphur blotched red, deep garnet and vermilion. The leaves are roundish in outline and borne in abundance. Unexcelled for verandas, trellises, to cover old stumps, fences, rough ground or unsightly objects. Can be grown on a wire mesh frame in a container on the patio. A real eye catcher and will attract the humming birds.

Of easy culture, wanting full sun but giving good returns on dry, gravelly banks in poor soil. Rich soil and shade produce more foliage than flowers. Watch for aphids. With any sign of infestation spray with a good insecticide. In warm climates they seed themselves and may live over like perennials. In the North pull them out with autumn's first frost.

TRUMPET-CREEPER—See *Campsis*.

TRUMPET-FLOWER—See *Bignonia capreolata*.

WINTERCREEPER—See *Euonymus fortunei*.

VI Drought-Resistant Annuals and Perennials

The terms annual, biennial and perennial are used for convenience since many flowers treated as annuals in the North often behave in the South as short-lived perennials. Also many perennials and most biennials will bloom the first year if given an early start and sown indoors before outdoor sowing is possible. In many gardens the self-sowing nicotiana will prove more enduring than a delphinium or chrysanthemum. A gaillardia could be called an annual, biennal or perennial depending on the parentage and location where it is grown.

The drought-resistant biennials and short-lived perennials best grown as annuals have been listed in this chapter under annuals. The list of herbaceous plants that can be planted where water is a problem could be extended considerably if poor soil is improved to make it more moisture-retentive and by the use of mulches that conserve water. It must be remembered that all plants need to be watered until they become well established. The amount of moisture in the soil will not be sufficient to take care of the transplant's needs until it has become secure and acclimated in its new environment. The drought-resistant plants must have good drainage and sufficient nourishment and moisture for their needs but in general they require little care and maintenance by comparison with more demanding plants.

Since their roots do not go as deep, annuals and perennials will show the lack of water, during dry spells, much quicker than well established shrubs and trees and may require spot watering for satisfactory results or even for survival. It is the nature of many annuals, as a defense against late summer drought, to come into flower rapidly, and in abundance, set seed in great quantity and then subside when heat and dryness arrive. As far as perennials are concerned, you can be fairly sure that those with deep, fleshy roots (such as gypsophila, hollyhocks, and eryngium) can endure any amount of drought. As a gardener's awareness of the means of plant adaptation increases, he will find it easier to select species that are reliable.

Some of the more unusual and odd things not generally available in this country, as *Anagallis linifolia*, are worth importing from Thompson and Morgan, Ipswich, England, or Suttons and Sons, Reading, England. While a U.S. Department of Agriculture import permit is needed to bring in plants, flower seeds are simple to import without any red tape. Thompson and Morgan list a good many of the rare varieties not available through the usual sources.

DROUGHT-TOLERANT ANNUALS

Easy to grow, inexpensive, and quick to produce, annuals are invaluable and unequalled for supplying a maximum of flowers and color in the garden and for cutting purposes. To promote good branching, pinch out the terminal buds or shoots of most of the young plants in order to develop bushier specimens, reduce the ultimate height and cause more abundant flowering. Cut all you want for indoor decoration since the plants will bloom more profusely and over a longer period of time if they are kept cut. If faded flowers are not removed and the plants are allowed to ripen seeds, they will stop blooming. For a description of drought-tolerant annuals listed below see our earlier book *The Picture Book of Annuals*, published by Hearthside Press Inc.

Abronia umbellata—Sand Verbena.

Amaranthus—Amaranth.

Ammobium alatum grandiflorum—Winged Everlasting.

Arctotis stoechadifolia (A. grandis)—African or Blue-Eyed Daisy.

Anagallis linifolia—Pimpernel.

Argemone grandiflora—Mexican Poppy, Prickly Poppy.

Artemisia sacrorum viridis—Summer Fir, Russian Wormwood.

Aster amellus (A. annuus)—Italian Aster, Starwort.

Brachycome iberidifolia—Swan River Daisy.

Calandrinia grandiflora—Rock Purslane.

Calendula officinalis—Pot Marigold.

Callirhoe pedata—Poppy Mallow.

Centaurea cyanus—Bachelor's Button, Cornflower.

Chrysanthemum, Annual.

Cladanthus arabicus (C. proliferus).

Cleome spinosa—Spider Flower.

Coreopsis tinctoria—Calliopsis, Annual Coreopsis.

Corydalis lutea—Yellow Corydalis.

Cosmos bipinnatus hybrids—Cosmos.

Cynoglossum amabile—Chinese Forget-Me-Not

Dianthus chinensis (D. sinensis, D. seguieri)—China or Annual Pink.

Diascia barberae—Twin Spur.

Dimorphotheca aurantiaca—Cape Marigold, African Daisy.

Echium plantagineum excelsum—Viper's Bugloss.

Eschscholzia californica—California Poppy.

Euphorbia heterophylla—Annual Poinsettia.

Euphorbia marginata (E. variegata)—Snow-On-The-Mountain.

Everlastings—*Ammobium, Gomphrena, Helichrysum, Helipterum,* and *Xeranthemum.*

Gazania longiscapa—African Daisy.

Gomphrena globosa—Globe Amaranth.

Grasses, Ornamental

   Agrostis nebulosa—Cloud Grass.

   Avena sterilis—Animated Oat.

   Briza maxima—Quaking Grass.

Bromus brizaeformis—Quake Grass.

Hordeum jubatum—Squirrel-Tail Grass.

Lagurus ovatus—Hare's- or Rabbit's-Tail Grass.

Zea mays japonica—Ornamental Maize, Rainbow Corn.

Gypsophila elegans—Annual Baby's-Breath.

Hedeoma pulegoides—American Pennyroyal.

Helichrysum bracteatum—Strawflower.

Helipterum manglesi—Swan River Everlasting.

Ipomoea purpurea—See Vines.

Lantana camara—Lantana, Red or Yellow Sage.

Lantana montevidensis—Weeping or Trailing Lantana.

Layia elegans—Tidy Tips.

Limonium sinuatum—Sea Lavender.

Lobularia maritima—Annual Sweet Alyssum.

Machaeranthera tanacetifolia—Tahoka Daisy.

Mentzelia lindleyi—Blazing Star, Bartonia.

Mirabillis jalapa—Four O'Clock.

Nicotiana alata—Flowering or Ornamental Tobacco.

Nolana atripicifolia—Chilean Bellflower.

Oxypetalum caeruleum—Southern Star.

Pelargonium hortorum—Geranium.

Pelargonium peltatum—Ivy-Leaved Geranium.

Perilla frutenscens—Perilla.

Petunia Hybrids. These half-hardy annuals are quite adaptable, but must have sun to bloom. The varieties that have a particularly vigorous growth and more fleshy leaves will often outlast other petunias in general adverse climatic conditions.

Phlox drummondi—Annual Phlox.

Polypteris hookeriana.

Portulaca grandiflora—Rose Moss.

Rudbeckia bicolor—Annual Coneflower.

Rudbeckia hirta Selections—Gloriosa Daisy.

Sanvitalia procumbens—Creeping Zinnia, Trailing Sanvitalia.

Saponaria calabrica—Soapwort.

Senecio cineraria—Dusty Miller.

Tagetes—Marigold. They have medium tolerance to dry conditions, although their flowering becomes less prolific and size smaller in drought.

Tithonia rotundifolia—Mexican Sunflower.

Tropaeolum Hybrids—Nasturtium.

Ursinia anethoides—Ursinia.

Venidio-Arctotis.

Verbascum—Mullein.

Verbena bipinnatifida.

Verbena (hortensis) hybrida—Garden Verbena.

Vinca rosea—Madagascar Periwinkle.

Xanthisma texanum—Star of Texas.

Xeranthemum annuum—Immortelle.

Zinnia Hybrids. *Z. angustifolia* and *Z. linearis* show the most drought-resistance.

DROUGHT-TOLERANT PERENNIALS

It is not necessary to select prima donnas if water and upkeep are a problem. You can find hardy, trouble-free perennials if you take your time and are discriminating, choosing carefully. There are many which

97. One of the dusty millers, *Senecio cineraria,* grown for its distinctive white-felty foliage, the leaves cut into narrow, interesting lobes.

Genereux Photo

do not need frequent division and transplanting and are quite tolerant of dry soils. In just the right location, some seem to defy time and destruction so select only those plants that will be happy and are suitable in the location where you want them. For a description of the drought-tolerant perennials listed below see our *The Picture Book of Perennials*, published by Hearthside Press Inc.

Achillea-millefolium—Common Yarrow; *A. tomentosa*-Wooly Yarrow; *Aegopodium podagraria*—Goutweed; *Aethionema coridifolium*—Lebanon Stone-Cress; *Aethionema grandiflorum*—Persian Stone-Cress; *Ajuga genevensis*—Bugle-weed; *Ajuga reptans*—Carpet Bugle; *Althaea rosea*—Hollyhock; *Alyssum; Anaphalis margaritacea*—Pearly Everlasting; *Anemone pulsatilla*—Pasque-Flower; *Antennaria*—Pussytoes; *Anthemis tinctoria*—Golden Marguerite, Yellow Camomile; *Anthyllis vulneraria*—Sand Clover, Kidney Vetch; *Antirrhinum asarina; Arabis*—Rock-Cress; *Aralia nudicaulis*—Wild Sarsaparilla; *Arenaria*—Sandwort; *Armeria*—Thrift, Sea Pink; *Artemisia*—Wormwood; *Asclepias tuberosa*—Butterfly-Weed, Orange Milkweed; *Aster novae-angliae*—New England Aster; *Aster novi-belgi*—New York Aster; *Aubrieta deltoidea*—Purple Rock-Cress.

Baptisia—False or Wild Indigo.

Callirhoe—Poppy Mallow; *Campanula*—Bellflower; *Centaurea cineraria* —Dusty Miller; *Centaurea gymnocarpa*—Dusty Miller; *Centranthus*

98. Here is a case where a perennial plant ordinarily considered practically a weed proves effective in a dry area under a maple. In a garden, goutweed (*Aegopodium podagraria variegatum*) could be a nuisance, running in among other plants, but here the plant is neatly contained by the turf.

Genereux Photo

99. Thrift or sea pink, *Armeria maritima*, available in both pink and rose-red flowers, is one of the best perennials for the dry garden. The blossoms appear for several weeks during early summer.

Taloumis Photo

ruber—Red Valerian; *Cerastium tomentosum*—Snow-in-Summer; *Cerastostigma plumbaginoides*—Leadwort; *Chrysopsis*—Golden Aster; *Convolvulus mauritanicus*—Ground Morning Glory; *Coreopsis*—Tickseed; *Coronilla varia*—Crown Vetch.

Desmodium canadense—Bush Trefoil; *Dianthus*—Pink; *Dicentra*—Bleeding-Heart; *Dictamus albus (D. fraxinella)*—Gas Plant.

Echinacea—Coneflower; *Echinops ritro*—Globe-Thistle; *Epimedium*—Barrenwort; *Erigeron*—Fleabane; *Eryngium*—Sea-Holly; *Eupatorium*—Boneset, Thoroughwort; *Euphorbia corollata*—Flowering Spurge; *Euphorbia cyparissias*—Cypress Spurge; *Euphorbia epithymoides*—Cushion Spurge; *Euphorbia myrsinites*.

FERNS: *Cystopteris bulbifera*—Common Bladder-Fern; *Nephrolepis exaltata*—Sword Fern; *Pellaea atropurpurea*—Purple Cliff Brake; *Polypodium virginianum*—Wall Fern; *Pteridium aquilinum*—Bracken; *Woodsia ilvensis*—Rusty Woodsia; *Woodsia obtusa*—Blunt-Lobe Cliff Fern or Common Woodsia.

Filipendula hexapetala—Dropwort.

Gaillardia aristata—Blanket Flower; *Galium mollugo*—White Bedstraw, False Baby's-Breath.

GRASSES, PERENNIAL: *Ammophila*—Beach Grass; *Arrhenatherum elatus tuberosum (A. bulbosum)*—Meadow Oat; *Axonopus furcatus*—Carpet Grass; *Cortaderia selloana (C. argentea)*—Pampas Grass; *Cynodon dactylon*—Bermuda or Bahama Grass; *Dactylis glomerata variegata* —Orchard Grass; *Elymus arenarius*—Sea Lyme Grass, Dune Grass; *Eremochloa ophiuroides*—Centipede Grass; *Erianthus ravennae*— Plume Grass; *Festuca ovina*—Sheep's Fescue; *Miscanthus sacchariflorus; Miscanthus sinensis (Eulalia japonica)*—Eulalia; *Ophiopogon japonicus*—Japan Grass, Lily-Turf; *Panicum virgatum*—Switch Grass. *Pennisetum alopecuroides (P. japonicum)*—Fountain Grass; *Phalaris arundinacea picta*—Ribbon Grass, Gardener's Garters; *Stenotaphrum secundatum*—St. Augustine Grass; *Stipa pennata*—Spear, Feather, or Needle Grass; *Zoysia*.

Gypsophila—Baby's-Breath.

Hedysarum coronarium—French Honeysuckle; *Helenium autumnale*— Sneezeweed; *Helianthemum nummularium*—Sun Rose; *Helianthus*— Sunflower; *Hemerocallis*—Daylily. Grown with a minimum of water their hardiness, longevity and heavy root systems do give them a drought-tolerance. Although wanting moisture, they will take dryness making less growth with fewer and smaller flowers.
Heuchera sanguinea—Coral Bells; *Hieracium villosum*.

Iberis sempervirens—Perennial Candytuft. *Iris.* The hardy and dependable beared iris will undoubtedly take the most abuse and show the least distress from lack of water, requiring moisture only in growth and in bloom. Their handsome flowers come early, during May, before disastrous summer droughts.

Kniphofia uvaria—Torch Lily, Red Hot Poker.

Lamium maculatum—Dead Nettle; *Lathyrus littoralis*—Beach Pea; *Lathyrus maritimus*—Beach Pea; *Liatris*—Button Snakeroot; *Lilium*— Lily. Select early varieties, acting on the premise that at least there should be some water during the winter and early spring to give them a good start.

100. *Helianthemum atriplicifolium* — One of the sun-roses grown on the west coast showing it in full bloom, with golden-yellow flowers. Of spreading habit it thrives in dry limestone soil and full sun.

Marten Photo

Limonium latifolium — Sea-Lavender, *Sea-Pink; Linum* — Ornametal Flax; *Lotus corniculatis*—Bird's-Foot Trefoil, Ground Honeysuckle; *Lychnis chalcedonica* — Maltese Cross; *Lychnis coronaria* — Mullein Pink.

Macleaya cordata—Plume-Poppy; *Malva*—Mallow; *Matricaria tchihatchewi*—Turfing Daisy; *Myrrhis odorata*—Myrrh, Sweet Cicely.

Nepeta mussini—Catnip, Catmint.

Oenothera fruticosa — Sundrops; *Oenothera missouriensis* — Missouri

101. *Iris cristata* — Crested iris is an attractive little native used for spring effect in the wild garden, with narrow, graceful leaves a bit taller than the light blue blossoms. Will withstand just about anything in the way of exposure and drought and is easily increased by the division of its countless surface creeping rootstocks every 2 or 3 years.

Genereux Photo

102. The 'Golden Chalice' hybrid lily will do extremely well in the dry garden.

Wall Photo

Primrose; *Opuntia compressa*—Prickly-Pear.

Pachysandra procumbens—Allegheny Spurge; *Pachysandra terminalis*—Japanese Spurge; *Papaver orientale*—Oriental Poppy; *Penstemon*—Beard-Tongue; *Phlox amoena*—Trailing Phlox; *Phlox divaricata*—Wild Sweet William, Blue Phlox; *Phlox subulata*—Ground Phlox, Ground or Moss Pink; *Platycodon grandiflorum* — Balloon-Flower; *Polemonium caeruleum* — Jacobs Ladder, Greek Valerian; *Potentilla tridentata* — Three-Toothed Cinquefoil.

Rosa—Rose. Climbing roses do well even in dry seasons. Also see under Vines and Shrubs.

Rudbeckia hirta selections—Black-Eyed, Susan, Gloriosa Daisy; *Rudbeckia lacinata hortensia*—Golden Glow.

Sagina subulata—Pearlwort; *Salvia*—Sage; *Saponaria*—Soapwort; *Saxifraga; Sedum*—Stonecrop; *Sempervivum*—Houseleek, Hen-and-Chickens; *Solidago*—Goldenrod; *Sphaeralcea coccinea (Malvastrum coccinea)* —Prairie Mallow; *Stachys*—Betony; *Stellaria holostea; Stokesia laevis*—Stokes-Aster.

Tephrosia virginiana—Goat's-Rue, Wild Sweet Pea; *Thermopsis caroliniana*—Aaron's-Rod; *Thymus*—Thyme; *Tunica saxifraga*—Saxifrage Pink, Tunic-Flower; *Tussilago farfara*—Coltsfoot.

Valeriana officinalis—Garden Heliotrope; *Verbascum*—Mullein; *Vinca minor*—Periwinkle, Creeping Myrtle; *Viola pedata*—Bird's-Foot Violet.

Waldsteinia fragarioides—Barren or Dry Strawberry.

Yucca smalliana—Spanish Bayonet—Adam's-Needle; *Zauschneria californica*—California Fuchsia.

103. Several species of the prickly pear (Opuntia) are useful for dry gardens, mainly in warmer parts of the country. In colder areas, as far north as Massachusetts, yellow flowered *O. compressa* is hardy in well-drained locations. When using opuntias, it is good to place them around rocks, where little weeding (hence fewer spines in the fingers) need be endured.   McFarland Photo

VII Desert Flora,
Including Cacti and Succulents

Desert vegetation varies greatly from one section of the Southwest to another, both in growth form and species. It is unlike vegetation in any other section of the United States. Small desert trees such as the palo-verde, desert ironwood, Joshua tree and crucifixion thorns (all listed below) are somehow able to give the landscape an appearance of woodland.

DESERT TREES

ACACIA, GREEN BARKED—See *Cercidium torreyanum*.

ADAM'S NEEDLE—See *Yucca smalliana*.

BEAR GRASS — See *Yucca glauca*.

BURSERA—Elephant Tree. Shrubs or small trees with reddish brown twigs and massive papery-barked trunks. The small trees grow 6 to 15 ft., sometimes up to 30 ft. high and are characteristic of extremely arid regions. The reddish-brown twigs on older branches become light-colored and papery in the outer thin layer. The enlarged trunk and stems take up and store quantities of water during the brief rainy periods which the tree then utilizes during prolonged periods of dryness. It is called the elephant tree because of its swollen trunk and branches.

CANOTIA HOLACANTHA—Crucifixion Thorn. A small tree, 6 to 18 ft. tall, resembling the palo-verde *(Cercidium torreyanum)*, with ascending yellowish-green branches and trunk, the branches are leafless and thorny. The principal value of the plant is for erosion control. With other crucifixion thorns (*Holacantha emoryi* and *Koeberlinia spinosa*), it has adapted to the desert climate by the complete elimination of leaves.

CERCIDIUM TORREYANUM — Palo-Verde, Green-Barked Acacia. Palo-Verde means "green stick" in Spanish which refers to the color of the bark. It is a desert tree or large shrub of the pea family that grows wild in the Southwest usually found alongside desert washes. It is cultivated some for its masses of golden blossoms in April and May. Green-barked, spiny and leafless for much of the year the green bark of the trunk and branches take over in place of leaves. Its showy yellow flowers are not pea-like but nearly regular, about ¾ in. wide. In *C. floridum*, blue palo-verde, the stems and leaves are blue-green and in *C. microphyllum* the stems and leaves are yellow-green.

CRUCIFIXION THORN—See *Canotia holacantha*.

DALEA SPINOSA—Smoke Tree. A small tree, sometimes shrubby, distinguished by its smoky to silvery appearance and its compact mass of leafless branches, all ending in sharp spines. The ashy gray branches make it appear like a cloud of smoke in the distance. It is conspicuous in early summer for its profusion of bright purple or indigo flowers and used as an ornamental in frost free areas.

DESERT IRONWOOD—See *Olneya tesota*.

ELEPHANT TREE—See *Bursera*.

FAN PALM—See *Washingtonia filifera*.

HESPERALOE PARVIFLORA. Closely related to the yuccas these stemless Texas desert plants are members of the lily family with rush-like rosettes of drooping leaves. Many plants in this group have curling white threads along the sides of sword-like leaves. The plants send up and outward gracefully curved, arching day-blooming flower stalks with rose-colored, nodding flowers. Var. *engelmanni* has bell-shaped and smaller flowers.

HESPEROYUCCA WHIPPLEI—See *Yucca whipplei*.

JOSHUA-TREE—See *Yucca brevifolia*.

MESQUITE—See *Prosopis juliflora.*

OLNEYA TESOTA—Desert Ironwood. Among the largest and most outstanding of desert trees, it belongs to the pea family. Found growing on gravelly or sandy mesas or rocky foothills of the desert and along sandy washes in company with mesquites *(Prosopis juliflora)* and palo-verdes *(Cercidium torreyanum).* A lovely sight in May and June laden with lavender, wisteria-like flowers. The tree grows 10 to 30 ft. in height. It is easily recognized by its ever-blue-green, leaves. The bark is gray with a tendency to be stringy, this development on all but the smaller branches enables one to readily distinguish it from the blue palo-verde which also has blue-green foliage and is also restricted to similar areas.

PALO-VERDE—See *Cercidium torreyanum.*

PROSOPIS JULIFLORA — Mesquite — Screw Bean. These spiny or thorny trees or large shrubs of the pea family give a unique character to the desert and are among the most significant and dominant plants of the Southwest. The roots have been found to penetrate a 50 to 60 ft. depth to tap sources of ground water.

They may grow only a few feet high in the wild where they are found bordering desert washes, often forming dense thickets. Under cultivation they grow 10 to 25 ft. tall, are many-branched

104. A grove of wide-spreading native mesquite trees (*Prosopis juliflora*) which casts a dapple shade over the patio and planting of cacti and other succulents. A practical and effective planting for this section of the country.   Bool Photo

with twice-compounded leaves and many pairs of leaflets close together, not toothed. It flowers from late April to June. The flowers are not pea-like, but small and greenish in roundish spikes, growing from the axils of the leaves. The very narrow, leathery, straight pods do not split open.

Var. *glandulosa,* the honey mesquite is the most common one, smooth without hairs, having rigid, narrow leaflets. The flowers furnish honey bees with nectar. Var. *torreyana,* the western honey mesquite, is very similar with smaller leaflets. Var. *velutina,* the velvet mesquite, has dense, short hairs over practically the entire plant, including the seed pods.

P. pubescens—The scrub bean has tightly coiled pods and the spines are attached to the stalks of the compound leaves.

SMOKE TREE—See *Dalea spinosa.*

SOAP TREE—See *Yucca.*

SPANISH BAYONET—See *Yucca.*

WASHINGTONIA—Fan Palm. Two species are native in California, northern Mexico and southwest Arizona and widely planted there, less commonly along the Gulf Coast and in Florida. Easily distinguished by the arrangement of their grayish-green leaf blades which are nearly circular in outline and arranged like the fingers of a hand. The division extends only ½ or ⅔ of the way to the base.

Much planted in California as avenue trees, where they are statuesque yet solemn, the spent or withered leaves hang naturally and indefinitely as a drab ash-colored mantle. The densely thatched tall trunks provide a deep shade welcomed in hot, dry climates. Individual flower clusters suggest a corn tassel. Not hardy above zone 7.

W. filifera—This species is superior in the dry soils of Florida, less planted in California.

W. robusta—The California or Mexican fan palm is taller than *W. filifera,* the trunk is more slender, and usually clothed above with a dense, shaggy, fibrous network, the trunk naked toward the base. The fan-shaped leaves are only at the top of the trunk, drooping off the stem at maturity. It is used a great deal in plantings of the south California coast.

In the commonly cultivated date palms *(Phoenix dactylifera),* the blade is greatly elongated and divided all the way to the midrib with the separate leaflets arranged like the segments of a feather. While the date palm needs an intensely dry, hot atmosphere it also needs some moisture at its roots, but not too much.

YUCCA—Spanish Bayonet. Bold, striking, tree-like plants, chiefly Mexican, belonging to the lily family, they are typical of the arid subtropical flora in the Southwest, perhaps the plant most frequently associated with the desert scene. Plants are effective grouped or used singly as accents adding a tropical note. The sharp, narrow, spear-like leaves are set in dense clumps at the ground although some have distinct trunks. Their conspicuous flower clusters are truly magnificent, the waxy pure white, creamy or greenish bells of the massive flower heads are more or less closed by day and open at night, usually fragrant. The height of the flowering season is in May but some species flower in June and others in April. Yuccas thrive best in hot dry situations.

The many species are in two groups, the narrow-leaf and the wide-leaf. Narrow-leaf soap-trees produce dry, capsular fruits, wide-leaf yuccas bear fleshy fruits.

Y. aloifolia – Spanish Bayonet or Dagger. Produces a simple or branched trunk growing 10 to 25 ft. tall and is found in southwestern United States to Mexico and in the West Indies. It is grown in Florida and along the Gulf Coast. The stiff leaves are 2½ ft. long and 2 in. wide, prolonged into a very sharp point. White or purple-tinged flowers are nearly 4 in. wide, the showy cluster often 2 ft. long, valued for its late flowering.

Y. brevifolia—Joshua-Tree. The largest of the genus and of the narrow-leaf group, found from California to Utah. A grotesquely branching, fantastic desert plant often reaching 30 to 40 ft. in height, the leaves are in dense terminal rosettes, known as the old man of the desert. The blossoms, which do not open as wide as those of other species, grow in tight clusters at the tips of the branches, appearing in March and April. They do not blossom every year, the intervals between blossoming depending upon rainfall and temperature. Useful in dry barren places, thriving in the same situations as desert cacti.

Y. elata—Soap-Tree Yucca. The state flower of New Mexico and common throughout the Southwest. It never grows over 30 ft. in height.

The spectacular plant is found blooming in May and June on the desert grasslands.

Y. glauca — Bear Grass, Great Plains Yucca. An attractive plant, found growing in New Mexico, northward to Iowa and South Dakota, it is one of the hardiest of the yuccas. The leaves are about 3 ft. long, only about ½ in. wide, white margined and finely thready on the margin. The flowers are greenish-white.

Y. recurvifolia has recurving 2 in. wide leaves. It is native from Georgia to Mississippi and grows to 6 ft., the trunk branching.

Y. smalliana syn. *filamentosa*—Adam's Needle. Hardy over much of the United States as far North as zone 3 if protected from too much winter moisture. The commonest yucca in cultivation in the East, native from Delaware to Florida and Mississippi. Practically stemless, the stalk of the flower cluster may be 8 to 12 ft. high, bearing clusters

105. A garden in Claremont, California, without lawn, using bare earth and gravel for ground surfacing and native boulders for steps. Spanish bayonet or dagger *(Yucca aloifolia)*, with its long stiff very sharp pointed leaves, is native to the area and effective here.

Cornell Photo

of waxy white or creamy-white bell-shaped flowers 2 in. long. It does best in the sun in light sandy or gritty soil and is salt resistant. Propagate by seeds or offsets.

Y. torreyi—Torrey Yucca. The stiff, fleshy, long leaves have needle-sharp tips. It is this type leaf that gives the plants the name Spanish bayonet. Torrey yuccas bloom in April. *Y. schotti* and *Y. schidigera* are quite similar.

Y. whipplei. Chaparral yucca now known as *Hesperoyucca whipplei*. A single California desert plant grown on dry rocky slopes, steep hillsides or in the wildflower garden. Almost stemless, the leaves are 12 to 20 in. long, the white flowering stalks 10 to 12 ft. high and the cluster at the end is branched.

DESERT SHRUBS

ACACIA. Many species of acacia are grown in the Southwest as shade or ornamental trees and as shrubs. Spines or prickles are present except in *A. angustissima*.

A. angustissima hirta—Fern Acacia. Low shrubs or bushes, sometimes scarcely woody, recognized by the absence of spines or prickles and their compact heads (about ½ in. in diameter) of white flowers tinged with pink or lavender.

A. constricta—White-Thorn. This pretty spreading shrub is armed with long, slender, straight white spines and is abundant over dry slopes and mesas from Texas to Arizona and Mexico. It is frequently used in landscape work. The ball-like yellow flowers are fragrant and sometimes continue to bloom from May till August, occasionally again in November. *A. farnesiana* is very similar to *A. constricta* but the plant is much larger.

A. greggi—Catclaw Acacia. It is recognized by its dark brown or gray prickles, similar to the claws of a cat, scattered irregularly along the branches. A very thorny large shrub or small slender tree, forming thickets on the rocky hillsides and bordering desert washes. Fragrant pale yellow flowers in dense, cylindrical spikes bloom in May and attract the bees. The string-bean like fruits turn red in late summer making a spectacular display.

A. millefolia—The Santa Rita acacia has finely divided bright green foliage and white flower clusters that make it highly desirable for ornamental plantings.

ARTEMISIA TRIDENTATA—Sagebrush. A much branched shrub, widely distributed in arid parts of the west where little else will grow. Plants grow 4 to 8 ft. and have silvery-gray, aromatic foliage. Not very ornamental.

BACCHARIS SAROTHROIDES—Desert Broom or Mexican Broom. An erect, coarse evergreen shrub of the composite family growing 3 to 6 ft. tall. It greens up quickly following rains. Inconspicuous flowers bloom from September to February. The fruits of the female plants develop as masses of spectacular cottony threads, giving the shrub an attractive snow-covered appearance. It is common, growing wild along desert washes and roadsides in sandy alkaline soil. Easily propagated by cuttings or the plants may be dug in the wild. During autumn the abundant masses of white, cottony "seeds" contrast sharply with the green branches. The attractive shrub is frequently planted as an ornamental.

BRITTLE BUSH—See *Encelia farinosa.*

CALLIANDRA ERIOPHYLLA—False-Mesquite, Fairy Duster. A low, bushy shrub, somewhat straggly, that grows from a few inches to 3 ft. in height. It is Japanese in appearance, with mimosa-like leaves and long-stamened pink or reddish-purple flowers appearing in clusters from February to May. Very similar and closely related to the acacia. During periods of drought the leaves enter a state of continued wilt but revive promptly as rains come. The plant spreads rapidly by means of underground sprouts.

CHILOPSIS LINEARIS—Desert or Flowering Willow. A tall shrub or small tree of the bignonia family, it seldom grows over 12 ft. and has a short, crooked, black-barked trunk, spreading branches and willow-like leaves. Violet-scented flowers in short terminal clusters appear from April until August, often after the start of the summer rains. Long, slender persistent seed pods dangle from the branches for months. The desert willows have been used widely as ornamentals, prized for their graceful habit and large, attractive, sweet-scented orchid-like flowers.

DALEA FREMONTI—Fremont Dalea, Indigo-Bush, Pea-Bush. This low shrub of the pea family is less than 3 ft. tall with odd zigzag branches. It is noted for its royal purple flowers which bloom from April to June. There are many other Dalea species in the desert, all with deep blue to indigo and rose-violet pea-like flowers. All are commonly referred to as indigo-bush or pea-bush. There are many varieties of *D. fremonti* available.

DESERT BROOM—See *Baccharis sarothroides.*

DESERT MALLEE—See *Eucalyptus macrocarpa.*

ENCELIA FARINOSA—Incienso, Brittle Bush. A showy desert shrubby-like plant of the composite family that grows from 3 to 5 ft. tall ranging from western North America to Chile. Grown in California and the Southwest for their showy heads of yellow flowers in branched clusters, handsome when in bloom.

EPHEDRA—Mormon Tea. A scraggly desert shrub rarely more than 4 to 5 ft. tall, forming an intricate network of brittle, almost leafless green, yellow-green or blue-green branches. In the spring the male plant is a beautiful mass of yellow clusters of anthers and the green seeds are a feature of the female plant although less conspicuous. Years back a palatable drink was brewed from the dried stems. Ephedras are easily propagated by division of the clumps.

  E. trifurca. The longleaf ephedra grows 3 to 4 ft. in height or even much taller with yellow-green, stringy branches and tiny, scale-like leaves. Dense clusters of small, fragrant yellow flowers appear in the spring.

EUCALYPTUS MACROCARPA — Desert Mallee. This is a heavy stemmed sprawling shrub that may be trained into a gangling tree. It has mealy-white leaves, thick and rigid in ranks along the newer wood. A spectacle when in bloom with 3 in. flowers, scarlet to crimson. Takes heat and drought but must have perfect drainage. Not for the orderly, trim garden, nor heavy or wet soils.

FOUQUIERIA SPLENDENS—Ocotillo. One of the most distinctive shrubs of the southwestern deserts, adding a distinctive character to the region. The shrub normally grows to about 10 ft. in height. It has many long, spreading green-barked beautifully wrought stems, thickly set with hooked spines. These cones bear at their tips in irregular clusters brilliant scarlet flowers from April to June, sparingly after the summer rains. Following rains the stems cover themselves with clusters of bright green leaves and when drought comes the leaves are shed to be renewed again after another rain. Used to fence yards, the thorny branches form an impenetrable enclosure. Grown as a greenhouse plant in the North. The odd plant is decorative, lending a distinct atmosphere to Spanish grounds. The full-sized stems are planted as cuttings.

LARREA TRIDENTATA—Creosot Bush. Most adaptable, its natural range extends over the Southwest and into adjoining Mexico. The much-branched shrubs cover thousands of square miles, often in pure sand. They grow 5 to 8 ft. tall, have waxy leaves and yellow flowers through much of the year but they bloom most profusely in April and May. Fuzzy, white globular fruits almost as spectacular as the flowers. Can endure long periods of drought. Following rains its foliage gives off a musty, resinous odor suggestive of creosote.

LEUCOPHYLLUM TEXANUM — Texas Silverleaf, Barometer Bush. Also known as *L. frutescens*. A loose-growing, attractive spreading desert plant native to Texas and New Mexico and belonging to the figwort family, it grows from 3 to 6 ft., or more. Small, abundant silvery-gray leaves give it a distinguished appearance throughout the year. When it bursts into bloom it is a beautiful sight, with showy bell-shaped violet-purple flowers. Sensitive to moisture it will blossom within a few hours after a soaking rain. Frequently used as a hedge.

MIMOSA—Cat-Claw, Sensitive Plant. An immense genus of mostly tropical plants of the pea family. The small flowers are not pea-like but form in dense, ball-like clusters, the leaves are arranged feather-fashion and sensitive. The shrubs found growing in the Southwest are differentiated from the mesquites by the presence of rose-type prickles instead of spines and by the presence of more than 2-pair of primary leaflets in each compound leaf. Of limited value except for *M. pudica*, the sensitive plant is grown in the United States as a curiosity in the greenhouse. Some offer food and shelter to wild life, others are palatable to domestic livestock.

M. dysocarpa wrighti — Velvet-Pod Mimosa. Its showy spikes of purple flowers about 1 in. long and ½ in. in diameter make it a desirable species for ornamental plantings. The pods are smooth without prickles or almost so.

OCOTILLO—See *Fouquieria splendens.*

POINCIANA GILLIESI—Paradise Poinciana, Bird-Of-Paradise Bush. This striking shrub or small tree, 3 to 10 ft. high, of the pea family, is not a southwestern desert native but was introduced from South America. It has escaped from cultivation and established itself in parts of the desert where conditions are suitable. Popular as an ornamental, its yellow blossoms with bright red stamens protruding 4 to 5 inches are very showy, although ill-smelling. Appreciated for the long blooming period which may last from April to September. The branches are straggling and sticky-hair , the foliage graceful and feathery with its numerous, small leaflets. Although not as spectacular as the royal poinciana *(Delonix regia)*, they are handsome shrubs.

SAGEBRUSH—See *Artemisia tridentata.*

STENOLOBIUM STANS — Yellow Elder, Yellow-Trumpet Flower. Sometimes listed as *Bignonia* or *Tecoma stans.* A glossy-leafed erect shrub of the bignonia family found growing on dry, rocky hillsides. It bears golden trumpet-shaped flowers from May till October. The attractive yellow flowers and bright green leaves make the plant desirable as an ornamental in southern parts of the United States and in Mexico.

WHITE THORN—See *Acacia constricta.*

CACTI

Most of these weirdly decorative, always interesting plants are native to the arid sections of the American continents. All are succulents, capable of storing sufficient moisture to enable them to withstand arid conditions. The stored moisture is mucilaginous in nature which helps retard evaporation. Many will recover from weeks or months during which their roots have been bone dry.

The species vary widely in shape and size from small, flat, rounded kinds to tree-like growths and from slender vines to huge columnar, branched or unbranched forms. Leaves except in rare cases are absent; when present they soon fall. All are perennials, the seedlings having 2 seed-leaves. The showy blossoms are generally large with many petals and numerous stamens, the petals and sepals frequently intergrade. The berried fruits, often edible, are one-celled with no partitions between the seed.

The flowers are generally gaudy in coloring and often larger than the plants on which they bloom, shades of yellow and red are most common but colors range from creamy-white or pale-pink to bright scarlet or cerise. Some last for a very brief period after they open in the desert, opening at dawn and wilting with the rising sun. Most of the brief blooming varieties are strongly fragrant. Those that last longer often are more delicately scented. The flowers are produced in the desert during the rainy season. Indoors they bloom mostly in winter or early spring. It depends to some extent on the temperature of the indoor window sill in winter.

The distinguishing characteristic of a cactus is the areole, a center of growth, often a slight depression and usually bearing fine short hairs, bristles or spines, or long hair or wool. From this point of growth spring spines, leaves when present, new joints, branches and flowers. This specialized organ is found in no other plants. The position and number of areoles are factors in differentiating species.

Cacti are adapted to outdoor culture in regions where climatic conditions approximate those of their native habitat, as found in southwestern United States and adjacent Mexico, with extremely warm summer temperatures and low rainfall, where slush, fog and other types of moisture are lacking in winter. In the Southwest the tree-like saguaro *(Carnegiea gigantea)*, is a striking and familiar feature of the desert landscape.

Many cacti are fully as slow in growth as forest trees and as difficult to move successfully. Specimen may be dug only to die, as very few transplant easily, however many are easily propagated by seed, cuttings or from offshoots treated as cuttings and by grafting. Most desert cacti like an alkaline soil and open dry air. They require more water during the blooming and growing periods than at other times but should have a decided rest period after this time has passed. It is safer to underwater than overwater.

Scientists tell us cacti were originally bog plants which have resourcefully adapted themselves to the most adverse conditions. There is a group of cacti native to the tropical jungles, semi-epiphytic in their habits, found climbing over the trunks of dead trees and blooming along with orchids. Examples are the beautiful orchid cactus *(Epiphyllum)* ... and the Christmas or crab cactus *(Zygocactus truncatus)* ... which require more shade, more fertile soil and more atmospheric moisture. But here we are only interested in those drought-tolerant kinds which originate in the arid desert.

The cactus family includes some 125 genera and over 1200 species, with many hybrids and named varieties, and there have been many changes in nomenclature over the years. The popularity of these plants is so great and growing them so highly specialized that there are now many cactus societies throughout the country, and many fine collections. Botanists have made 3 great subdivisions of garden types.

1—*Cereus* and its allies which include the cacti with stems, sometimes thick, branched and tree-like, or vine-like or prostrate forms. All bear spines. It is from this group that the grotesque desert forms come. Some genera supply the close, spiny hedge plants so useful in the Southwest.
2—Globular or low-growing plants that do not have elongated stems. Here are found the small button-like, ball-like and cylindric types, often half-hidden in the ground, some have a large plant body. This type is often used in dish gardens North.
3—*Echinocatus* and its allies which include those plants with a single, usually unbranched, plant body that is stout, cylindrical or barrel-shaped, usually too large for pot culture but used effectively outdoors in frost-free areas. The plant body is generally prominently ribbed or grooved and very spiny.

It is possible to have an outdoor cactus garden in the North if you select hardy kinds, as some cacti are found native in most states of the union. Provide adequate drainage with sufficient protection from winter slush and moisture. Protection from too much moisture is a chief requirement.

Of course a window sill or indoor cactus garden is possible anywhere. Well-drained porous soil, a limited water supply and a warm dry, atmosphere, so typical of many of our homes, furnish ideal growing conditions. Handle the plants with thick gloves or wooden forceps and visit a cacti specialist to learn about the many miniatures available for indoor gardens. Below we list some of the more familiar desert cacti one sees in the landscape and several that make good greenhouse or house plants in the North.

ARIZONA ORGAN-PIPE CACTUS—See *Lemaireocereus thurberi*

ASTROPHYTUM MYRIOSTIGMA—Bishop's-Cap. A very low and slow growing Mexican cactus, the globose plant body suggesting a

106. The tall plant is *Cereus peruvianus*, tree-like, and much branched with a columnar plant body, deeply angled or ribbed and spiny. The smaller plants are golden barrels *(Echinocactus grusoni)*.

Bool Photo

107. A wide variety of cacti and succulents are native to colder regions and with proper soil preparation and good drainage may be grown in the colder areas. This garden of Joseph Vilchek in Brooklyn, New York, contains a dozen *Sedum* species; *Coryphantha vivipara; Echinocereus viridiflorus; Neobesseya missouriensis* and *N. wismanni; Opuntia compressa* (only native cactus growing in this area) plus *Opuntia* species *aurea, fragilis, humifusa, nemoralis, polyacantha, rhodantha* and *rutila;* and *Yucca filamentosa, Y. glauca* and *Y. gloriosa.* In very hot and dry weather, a little watering will do no harm but rapid drainage is essential.

Brooklyn Botanic Garden Photo

bishop's hood. Mostly 5 ribbed and lacking spines. The 2 in. long flowers are orange-yellow, the petals brown-tipped, and borne at the top of the plant.

BARREL CACTUS—See *Echinocactus* and *Ferocactus.*

BERGEROCACTUS EMORYI. Useful for the desert garden as a part of a collection or for color over dry rocky ground. The plant is found in small colonies in southern and lower California where it has the habit of making large patches. It is usually of low growth up to 2 ft., although sometimes forming erect thickets much taller. Day-blooming greenish-yellow flowers appear along the side of the stems. It is difficult to transplant so best started from seed sown where plants are to grow.

CARNEGIEA GIGANTEA—Giant Cactus, Saguaro. This is the largest cactus in the world and found growing in southeastern California, southern Arizona and neighboring Mexico. A full-grown plant may be 250 years old and weigh as much as 6 tons or more. The huge erect plant is often 2 ft. thick and although rarely exceeding 30 ft. specimens may grow to 50 ft. in height, with many ribs and stout, strong spines. Old specimens are apt to have 3 or 4 huge candelabra-like branches curving upward. The white blossoms form as huge bud clusters at the branch tips, opening a few at a time each night, generally in May, and staying open until mid-afternoon of the following day. It is the state flower of Arizona. The red edible fruits, the size and shape of an egg, are used for sweetmeats. The giant cactus does not take kindly to cultivation but is a picturesque part of the dessert landscape.

CEREUS

Mostly tall, even tree-like, plants with a spiny, columnar body, without hairs or very small ones,deeply angled or ribbed. They generally have large white, funnel-shaped, night-blooming flowers. However the plants do not flower before maturity which may mean 6 ft. or more, a matter of maybe 20 years, but the young plants are rather attractive even without their flowers.

C. hildmannianus, the Argentine cereus is tall and columnar, to 15 ft.; often much branched, with 5 or 6 ribs, the young joints dark blue. The foot-long white flowers are green on the outside, the ovary purplish.

C. peruvianus, from southeastern South America, is much-branched and tree-like, sometimes growing to 40 ft. It has bluish-green branches with 4 to 8 ribs and long, slender, needle-like spines. The white flowers are reddish on the outside and about 6 in. long. Likes a chalky soil but will survive most anything.

CHOLLA—See *Opuntia*

CLEISTOCACTUS STRAUSSI—Silver Torch

From Bolivia. This tall, erect plant is very elegantly covered with fine white spines. The green stem is hardly seen in well-grown plants. Slightly branching from the base, the erect and slender stems, generally under 3 ft., have many shallow ribs and numerous bristle-like very sharp spines. Red flowers about 4 in. long appear on the sides of the stems. It is fairly quick growing in warmth and sunshine. Offshoots develop at the base. It makes a good greenhouse and house plant.

ECHINOCACTUS. These cylindrical or barrel-shaped, ribbed cacti are very spiny. Grown outdoors in frost-free areas, they are generally too large for pot culture. Flowers bloom on the extreme top of the plant.

E. grusoni—Golden Barrel Cactus. The best known and possibly the most handsome species, a native of Mexico. A dense wool clothes the top of the orange-shaped cactus (16 to 30 in. in diameter) with many ribs and numerous golden-yellow spines. Red and yellow day-blooming flowers are borne at the summit of the plant.

E. ingens. The giant barrel cactus of Mexico is nearly 5 ft. tall and 4 ft. thick, woolly at the top. Brownish spines are in clusters of 8, with a single spine in the center. Yellow flowers measure about ¾ in. long.

ECHINOCEREUS—Hedgehog Cactus, Strawberry Cactus, Calico Cactus. There are many species and varieties, some develop into cushion-like mounds composed of several hundred oblong stems huddled together, others grow in loose clusters of cylindrical stems making a spectacular display when in flower. Grown for ornament or interest in desert regions or in the greenhouse or as house plants North. They usually grow in open clumps 6 to 18 in. high, resembling spine-covered cucumbers standing on end. The hedgehog cactus is the first one to bloom in the spring. Solitary day-blooming, bell-shaped flowers are borne on the sides but toward the top of the branches. The fruits are a dark mahogany red, juicy and rich in sugar and eaten like strawberries. Some of the best known and more ornamental are listed below.

E. dasyacanthus—Texas Golden Rainbow. Similar in appearance to *E. rigidissimus,* the rainbow echinocereus, except for the color of its blossoms. The stubby, upright stems usually grow singly but sometimes occur in small clusters.

E. engelmanni—Engelmann Echinocereus. One of the more common species of hedgehog cacti. It grows as 2 to 12 or more robust, cylindrical stems to 12 in. in height, often found growing with the creosote bush *(Larrea tridentata).* Flowers, which bloom from March to May, close at night and reopen the following morning. The blossoms vary in color from shell-pink and rose to purple and lavender, and the spines are variable too, from gray and yellow to dark brown. It is sometimes called the calico cactus because of its many-colored spines.

E. rigidissimus—The Rainbow-Cactus. So called because of alternating horizontal bands of red and white spines that encircle the single, sturdy stem marking the growth of different seasons and years. Not common, but among the more beautiful of the hedgehogs. Growing in rocky situations it blooms from June till August. The large flowers, from one to four, crowded around the crown, are often larger than the plant itself. The spines are small and lie densely flat over the somewhat fluted stem, which is from 3 to 14 in. high.

E. triglochidiatus—Claret-Cup Echinocereus. There are several varieties of this species from New Mexico. They sometimes flower in cushion-like mounds composed of several hundred oblong stems as wide as 4 ft. and 1 ft. high, huddled together, with a foothold in crevices among the rocks or on rocky slopes, often with over 50 claret blooms on one plant. This makes them much in demand for planting out in Arizona cactus gardens.

ECHINOPSIS—Sea Urchin Cactus. Native to South America, this genus comprises some 20 or more species, not including varieties and the many hybrids. The white or pale pink flowers are long and trumpet-shaped, often sweet-scented. The low, ridged or fluted barrel-shaped body sometimes grows to 9 in. in height. They produce offsets freely which girdle the main body. They can stand cold in winter if kept dry. Once they start flowering they throw off less offshoots.

108. This picture taken at the Huntington Botanic Garden shows a sea urchin cactus (*Echinopsis*) in flower. A *Kleinia* species and *Graptopetalum paraguayensis* are planted in the rear. Other succulents shown include the *Echeveria* 'Doris Taylor', some houseleeks and another sea urchin cactus.

Cornell Photo

E. eyriesi is one of the most commonly cultivated. The flowers shoot out from the sides in odd-looking tubes which develop into pale green and then into lily-white flowers.

E. multiplex from southern Brazil has showy rose-red flowers and is a good window sill or dish garden plant.

ELEPHANT CACTUS—See *Pachycereus pringlei*.

FEROCACTUS—Barrel-Cactus, Compass Cactus. Desert cacti often mistaken for young saguaros. Some are quite small, others tall, they grow from 2 to 8 ft. in height. Massive, heavy-bodied and cylindrical they are covered with clusters of stout spines. The majority produce clusters of orange-yellow to red flowers around the crowns of the plant in late summer. However the yellow-flowered California barrel-cactus blossoms in the spring. Their tendency to lean toward the light gives them the common name of compass cactus. The pale yellow fruits are not spiny. *F. wislizeni,* an Arizona native reaches 6 ft. in height at maturity. Its orange-yellow flowers are 2 to 3 in. long and it blossoms from July until September. *F. acanthodes,* a California native, has yellow flowers in March to May.

FISH-HOOK CACTUS—See *Mammillaria.*

HEDGEHOG CACTUS—See *Echinocereus.*

LEMAIREOCEREUS. Although restricted to a very limited area the organ-pipe cacti are spectacular and always attract attention. Tall and tree-like the ribbed cacti have clumps of erect, column-like branches or stems covered with many stout spines and growing up to 15 ft. White, pinkish to lavender or reddish bell or funnel shaped-flowers are not very large and may be either day or night blooming.

L. marginatus *(Pachycereus marginatus)*—Organ-Pipe Cactus. This spiny tree-like native of Mexico grows 15 to 20 ft. tall and is popular because of the neat white margins along its deeply ribbed stems. Day-blooming funnel-shaped, brownish-purple flowers are about 1½ in. in length, not very showy. This is a commonly planted hedge in Mexico.

L. *thurberi*—Organ-Pipe Cactus. Ribbed columnar cactus that grows in clumps and is very distinctive with dark red-purple spine-covered stems, some 10 to 15 ft. in height or more, branching from the base and with no central trunk. Pinkish-purple blossoms, white-margined, open at or near the stem ends during May nights and close the following day. The spine-covered fruits are about the size and shape of a hen's egg. A native of southern Arizona and Mexico.

MACHAEROCEREUS ERUCA—Octopus Cactus, Creeping Devil. A prostrate cactus with ribbed stems 3 to 7 in. in diameter and densely spined. The branches die at one end and grow onward at the other end. It has tubular, 4 to 5 in. long, yellow, day-blooming flowers followed by globe-shaped fruit. It creeps on the ground like a huge spiny caterpillar.

MAMMILLARIA—Pin-Cushion Cactus, Fish-Hook Cactus. There are over 300 species of this low-growing usually dome-shaped or shortly

109. This picture, courtesy of the Desert Botanical Garden, Phoenix, Arizona, shows an octopus cactus *(Machaerocereus eruca)*. The branches die at one end and grow onward at the other, creeping on the ground like a huge spiny catepillar.

Barett Photo

cylindrical cactus, the solitary kinds are often so small they are overlooked except when in flower in late spring or early summer. The colorful blossoms which encircle the stems are brightly colored. Some species are shaped like pin-cushions, others are known as fish-hook cacti because of their long, slender, hooked spines. Several species are grown as house plants and used in desert dish gardens. Cacti fanciers and specialists develop extensive collections. Many of these small plants will flourish under the shade of larger plants as in their native habitat.

MEXICAN ORGAN-PIPE CACTUS—See *Lemaireocereus marginatus.*

MYRTILLOCACTUS GEOMETRIZANS—Garambullo, Myrtle Cactus. A very much branched, spiny tree-like cactus, grown in desert gardens for its interest or oddity. It grows up to 15 ft. in height with bluish-green, 5 to 6 ribbed branches about 4 in. thick. The whitish, day-blooming flowers are about 1 in. wide.

OCTOPUS CACTUS—See *Machaerocereus eruca.*

OPUNTIA—Prickly-Pear, Cholla. A very large genus of spined cacti with varying habits, some tree-like, and others prostrate or clambering trunkless plants. Perhaps the best known genus in that it is the most widely distributed in its native habitat, extending from Canada to the extremities of South America. There are many fine kinds suitable for both garden and indoor culture. Some have cylindrical stems, others have flat stems or pads, as the prickly-pear group.

These fantastic cacti are best used in a natural environment, their real beauty is found in the attractive flowers, some reminiscent of a water lily. The earliest of the cacti to be cultivated they do well with plenty of light and sun, sharp drainage and enough space so the roots can spread. Grown by fanciers in collections but many are too large for the ordinary collector. The tree-like species, with stem segments in the form of flat pads, need large pots or better still, where weather permits, should be planted in the ground.

O. bigelovi—Teddy Bear Cactus or Silver Cholla. A stocky bush with a short, sturdy trunk and compact, densely spined crown comon on hot rocky, south-facing hillsides. It has inconspicuous flowers and fruits but is noticeable any time of the year because of its short, heavy joints, densely covered with silvery spines which give it a silvery sheen and hence the name teddy bear. The joints drop from the plant and take root, the new plants forming dense thickets on desert hillsides.

O. compressa—The common, wild prickly pear of northeastern U. S.

O. fulgida. The jumping cholla is one of the most common of the chollas. It grows from 5 to 10 ft. tall or more, the main trunk being 3 to 8 ft. high and 6 in. in diameter. The bark is rough and dark gray. The branches or joints sometimes resemble links of sausages loosely strung together. The detached branch-tips become attached to clothing. Contact is so sudden and unexpected the cactus is said to jump at one.

O. versicolor—Staghorn or Tree Cholla. It has a definite trunk, seldom as high as 12 ft. with distinctive, intricately branched stems of a purplish or reddish color. The beautiful flowers vary from yellow and orange to bronze and red. The mature fruit is green tinged with purple and red.

O. whipplei—Whipple Cholla. The most widely distributed cholla in Arizona, it is low-growing, forming mats of short but erect stems, generally less than 2 ft. high. It blooms in June and July followed by yellow, fleshy fruits.

BRANCHING, CYLINDRICAL-JOINTED OPUNTIAS. Shrubby, they grow from 3 to 8 ft. tall. The better known include:

O. acanthocarpa—Buckthorn or Cane Cholla. The extreme variability of the flowers (in April and May) from yellow to red to purple makes this California desert plant difficult to identify at times. Sometimes sprawling.

O. imbricata. Bright red to purple flowers are attractive in May and June, the quite large yellow fruit is often mistaken for bloom at a distance.

O. spinosior. The walking stick or cane cholla has bright red to purple flowers in May and June followed by persistent clusters of yellow fruit. Those remain throughout the winter, at first glance giving the impression the shrubby cactus is in flower. It is very similar to the Texas *O. imbricata* but *O. spinosior* is native to Arizona. Stems of the dead plant leave a hollow long, straight cylinder of attractive wooden meshes used for making canes or walking sticks.

CHRISTMAS OR SHRUBBY CHOLLAS. These small, slender-stemmed much branched, shrubby chollas grow 2 to 4 ft. tall. The flowers are inconspicuous, both sparse and small. However the many scarlet, 1 in. long egg-shaped fruit attract immediate attention in late fall and during the winter months. In the open the plants are seldom more than 2 ft. high but in the thickets of northern Mexico some have become almost vine-like, growing to 12 ft. or more through mesquite or palo-verde trees.

O. leptocaulis is native to the Arizona and Texas deserts with green-yellow flowers in May and June and slender grayish-green stems bristling with spines.

O. ramosissima is similar but a California desert native.

PRICKLY PEARS. Perhaps the best known of the cacti throughout the Southwest, the flattened pods or stem joints grow into huge clumps, sometimes to 5 ft. high and 10 ft. in diameter. The flowers are large and spectacular followed by red to purple and mahogany pear-shaped fruits.

O. basilaris—Beaver Tail Prickly Pear. This is a low growing species not over 4 ft. with flat joint-pods, broadly oval, and bluish-green stems without spines. In their place are clusters of brownish spicules set in slight depressions in the wrinkled pads. A native of the California desert, attractive magenta to purple flowers bloom in March and April.

O. engelmanni—Engelmann Prickly Pear. A native of the Arizona and Texas deserts it is widely distributed. The plants are large and spreading from 3 to 5 ft. tall and to 15 ft. in diameter. The flower petals are bright yellow at first, turning to pink or rose with age and appearing from April to June. Mature fruits are purple to mahogany.

ORGAN-PIPE CACTI—See *Lemaireocereus*.

PACHYCEREUS. Much like *Cereus*, they are mostly Mexican treelike or columnar cacti with tall, deeply ribbed stems. The flowers are day blooming and not very showy. Suitable for tropical desert gardens, they are too large for greenhouse culture in the North.

P. marginatus—See *Lemaireocereus marginatus*.

P. pecten-aboriginum. The hairbrush cactus has a ribbed and spiny trunk 6 ft. long and a ft. in diameter and is crowned with many erect, ribbed branches up to 30 ft. in height. The 2 in. long flowers are white inside, purplish on the outside. The Indians used the bur-like fruits as combs.

P. pringlei is native to southern California. It is a huge columnar cactus to 25 ft. in height, with a woody trunk, often having upright many ribbed branches. The white flowers are about 3 in. long. Locally called the elephant cactus.

PENIOCEREUS GREGGI—Deerhorn Cactus. The beauty and fragrance of its flowers have earned it, in Mexico, a name meaning "queen-of-the-night", and in the Southwest it is often called night-blooming cereus. In early July buds, unfolding soon after sunset, perfume the desert air. The showy white flowers wilt soon after sunrise the next morning. The large tuberous root, which acts as a water-storage organ, usually weighs from 5 to 15 pounds, but some are 80 pounds or more. Bulbous fruits, red when mature, are very striking. When not in flower the plant is easily missed as the group of slender, fluted, gray-green stems may be hidden beneath a shrub or other taller growth.

PERESKIA. A tropical American shrubby or vine-like cactus, unlike others in that it bears true, broad, flat leaves persistent to the extent they may be said to be evergreen. The flowers also differ from those of other cacti in that they have stems (others are sessile) which appear either singly or in drooping clusters. The flowers resemble a wild rose. Hardy only in frost-free areas. They like a sandy well-drained soil and are useful for trellises. Easily propagated by cuttings and much used as stock for grafting.

P. aculeata—Barbados Gooseberry, Lemon Vine. At first it is shrubby and erect, but ultimately a woody sprawling vine from 10 to 20 ft. in length. The short-stalked oblongish leathery, thick leaves are 2 to 3 in. long, the curved spines usually 2 to a cluster. Fragrant white, pale yellowish or pink flowers, about 1½ in. across, are borne in clusters followed by yellow edible fruit like a lemon. There is a variety with crimson, yellow and green leaves.

P. bleo (P. grandiflora)—Bush Pereskia. Somewhat sprawling, usually not as tall as the above, 10 to 15 ft., from Brazil. The trunk is often 4 in. thick and spiny with spines solitary and straight. The oblong leaves are 3 to 6 in. long, white to pink and rose-purple flowers 1½ to 2 in. wide in large clusters are followed by pear-shaped 1 to 2 in. long fruit.

PIN-CUSHION CACTUS—See *Mammillaria.*

PRICKLY PEAR—See *Opuntia.*

SAGUARO—See *Carnegiea gigantea.*

SEA URCHIN CACTUS—See *Echinopsis.*

SILVER TORCH—See *Cleistocactus straussi.*

SUCCULENTS

Succulent, from the Latin word for juicy, refers to plants which have a capacity for water storage that makes drought-survival possible. It is the broader term and includes all cacti, but not all succulents are cacti. Drought-tolerance is much greater in succulents than in any other group of plants, making them capable of surviving long dry periods. Native to arid or semi-arid regions, many from South Africa, they possess fleshy moisture-storing leaves or stems or both.

Although generally most effective kept to themselves, the big bold kinds, often with odd and grotesque shapes in an endless variety of outlines and forms, are pleasing companions for plants with a similar style and similar drought-tolerant requirements, as species of the yuccas. They offer a decidedly individual contribution to the desert and semi-desert regions of the Southwest. Modern architecture with its stark and simple outlines makes an excellent setting for groups of large succulents. The fewer varieties used, the better the effect, and the various groups should be interrelated one to the other.

Succulents must have perfect drainage as on a slope or bank. Smaller kinds are well suited to the rock or wall garden or raised beds. They enjoy a porous soil, strong light, high day-time temperature and well regulated watering; all need a dry rest period. Their water-frugality and ease of culture make them popular house plants in the North. While there are frost-hardy plants among the succulents, including cacti, it is only in warm climates that the majority can be used outdoors the year around. Most are tender to cold.

AEONIUM—See *Sempervivum.*

AGAVE. An immense genus of the Amaryllis family containing many species of handsome plants, native to the warm arid and semi-arid regions of America. Tall, bare flower stems rise from long, stiff, fleshy evergreen leaves that form basal clumps, many of huge size on mature plants. Some flower annually, most at longer intervals. Some species die after flowering but new plants develop from suckers that arise from the base of the plant. Agaves like a thoroughly drained, sandy loam in which to grow.

Useful plants in dry, frost-free regions outdoors where they will grow into very large plants if given plenty of root space. Choose only the smaller types for garden use. Dwarf types are good cool greenhouse or house plants where there is ample sun. They can be planted

110. In the foreground are *Aloe marletti* and *Yucca elephantides.* In the raised border the small round plants are barrels *(Ferocactus wislizeni).*   Bool Photo

111. *Agave ferox* planted as a ground cover in very poor, dry soil in Balboa Park, San Diego. It must have occasional summer water. Plant dies after flowering but new plants are easily started by seeds or "pups" which are off-shoots at the base of the main rosette of leaves.

Cornell Photo

out in the North in the summer or used in tubs on the porch or terrace. The very decorative and striking large century plants, on the grand scale, offer a picturesque quality to the desert landscape.

Many species of agave are found in different parts of the Southwest. Their blossoms in general are various shades of yellow. The large species are commonly referred to as century plants or mescals, the small ones as lechuguillas. Lechuguillas cover miles of desert in Texas, New Mexico and northern Mexico. Perhaps the best known of the agave species is *A. americana.*

A. americana—Century Plant. It is grown as a house or porch plant in the North, especially the var. *marginata* which has white-margined leaves. It blooms only after it is 10 years old or more, then dies, but new plants develop from suckers at the base. Sometimes the leaves are 6 ft. long and a flower stalk may grow up to 40 ft. in height. Bell-shaped and upward-turned small, fragrant flower clusters are borne on branching flower stalks. The plant needs plenty of room and wide-open spaces. It should never be planted where there is any likelihood of having to be moved since the operation becomes more costly with each growing year.

ALOE. Succulent perennials of the lily family, these plants are native to the Cape of Good Hope. In a superficial way they somewhat resemble the American century plants. Attractive ornamentals, their stiff, fleshy, often large leaves are spiny along the edges and crowded together in picturesque basal rosettes. The leaves are so arranged as to give an irregular shade and texture to the plant. The flowers are mostly of reddish shades, a few yellow or orange, and produced in irregular finger-shaped showy spikes, sometimes over 20 ft. in height.

They will take little frost, and are found outdoors at their best in lower southern California where they grow freely under natural conditions. Although the aloes can stand considerable drought they will not survive long dry summers without some water, requiring enough to refresh and prepare them for the brilliantly colored candelabras which lift high to the winter suns.

Transplant bare-rooted with no attempt to salvage the feeding roots; propagate easily by suckers, or by cuttings in those producing stems. They enjoy a mild winter and a hot summer for best display and are easily grown in pots in the cool greenhouse like any other succulent. Choose from many species and fine new hybrids.

BESCHORNERIA YUCCOIDES. A succulent, desert plant for the warm coastal area of southern California, of the amaryllis family, related to and resembling the agave. Native to Mexico the plant is easily established in full sun on well-drained sandy soil. Great arching flower spikes arise from striking rosettes of sword-like rough-edged foliage covered with a whitish bloom. In June the green flowers with rose-red bracts hang down the length of the long curving spikes, rather like fuchsias. They bloom every year. Their tuberous rootstocks will stand a soil richer than agaves although the culture is similar. In colder regions they are grown as greenhouse plants.

BRYOPHYLLUM TUBIFLORUM. This succulent plant from Madagascar grows 12 to 18 in. tall. Fleshy cylindrical, 4 to 5 in. long, leaves are marked like a zebra with dark purple stripes and are in whorls of 3, the whorls about 1 in. apart, scalloped or notched on the upper side, the tip is 5 to 7 toothed. The handsome flowers are orange-red. Young plants sprout from the tips of the leaves and remain attached until roots are formed when they drop off. The plants grow quickly. Bryophyllum means "sprouting leaf" and the plants formerly listed under this heading are now also listed under *Kalanchoe*. *Kitchingia* is another former classification.

CARRION-FLOWER—See *Stapelia*.

CENTURY PLANT—See *Agave americana.*

CEROPEGIA WOODI—Rosary Vine. A popular tuberous, tropical, trailing vine of the milkweed family with variegated heart-shaped leaves and curious purple balloon flowers. It needs support if grown on walls. Related to the wax plant *(Hoya carnosa).*

CROWN-OF-THORNS—See *Euphorbia splendens.*

COTYLEDON. Sometimes offered under the name of *Umbilicus.* Low spreading, small shrubs or sub-shrubs, many from desert regions of South Africa. They thrive under the same treatment as the related sedums and other succulents and are useful in the rock garden with slight shade and considerable heat. The downy leaves are flattish, in rosettes, and the yellow flowers striped with red. They take both heat and drought.

C. *orbiculata.* A shrubby plant growing 2 to 4 ft. tall with thick, fleshy, light gray leaves, sometimes silvery-white with a red edge. Bell-shaped, golden-yellow flowers hang from a long stock. In restricted areas, as grown in pots in the greenhouse, it is very slow growing. Perhaps one of the best for use in dish gardens.

CRASSULA. .Succulent plants, mostly from South Africa, with extremely fleshy stem and leaf but with more normal uses in the garden then the description would imply. For plants of this nature, they have wide tolerances, but enjoy full sun and a sandy loam. During the growing season they like some water but during the rest period, keep on the dry side. Their crowns will rot during a long wet spell or in poorly drained ground, so porous soil and a good run-off are essential. Good massing material with cacti, they are grown outdoors in frost-free regions and are popular as greenhouse or house plants elsewhere.

C. *argentea*—Also offered as C. *portulacea.* Called jade plant, Japanese rubber plant and Japanese laurel and commonly offered by florists in the United States. It will take more abuse than most house plants but will not stand overwatering. As grown outdoors in California it is a thick-stemmed, branching shrub about 8 ft. tall. Oval, very thick and shining leaves seem merged with the stem. Makes an excellent natural hedge for dry ground and is a popular window-sill plant in the North.

C. *decipiens* is an erect leafy succulent for rockeries or use with cacti. It can take very little water as the roots rot readily.

C. impressa. Low succulent forming a bright mass of reddish leaves in winter; its flowers are red, excellent for bedding or the rock garden.

C. lactea. A shrubby plant 1 to 2 ft. tall with rather narrow thick fleshy leaves grown together at the base and white-spotted along the margins. Star-like white flowers in loose terminal clusters appear in winter. It is a popular window-sill plant in the North.

C. lycopodioides forms a spreading mass of tiny green leaves resembling a club moss. It is exceptionally drought-resistant and useful as a filler or ground cover in succulent plantings.

C. monticola. Slender stems are studded with small light gray, very thick leaves; it bears pink and white flowers in the winter. Useful for rock or wall plantings or collections.

C. perfossa. The necklace vine is a trailing succulent with the long stems drawn through disc-like leaves. Used for rock work or dry walls.

C. tetragona. An erect, brittle, shrubby plant with light green thick-curved leaves and white or crimson flowers in a few-flowered terminal cluster.

DASYLIRION — Sotol. An exceptionally ornamental short-trunked desert plant of the lily family, frequently confused with yuccas. Sotol has a basal cluster of many, pliant, ribbon-like, saw-toothed bluish-green leaves from which emerges an extremely tall, sand-colored flower stalk. At its upper end it bears a dense spike-head of tiny, creamy flowers which attract the bees. Blooming in May and June, the maturing flower clusters remain attractive throughout the summer.

The sotol makes a striking addition to the planting scheme and is particularly adaptable to the Spanish-type house, decorative when used judiciously. After the bloom stalk dies, the plant sends up several new shoots and the parent plant dies.

Outdoors the plants must have sandy or rocky soil, sun and much summer heat. They will stand very little frost and no slushy, wet winters. Sotols are quite similar to the yuccas in use and culture. Excellent specimen plants in tubs, for the lawn or the succulent collection.

D. glaucophyllum is a native of Mexico. The trunk is not tall, the leaves 3 to 4 ft. long and about ½ in. wide, the prickles yellowish-white. Small white flowers top 12 to 18 ft. high stalks.

D. texanum—Bear Grass. A native of Texas with a short trunk, partly underground, and glossay-green leaves 2 to 3 ft. long and about ½ in. wide. The flowering stalks are 9 to 15 ft. tall.

D. wheeleri—Wheeler Sotol. The trunk is not over 3 ft. high, but often absent under cultivation. The flower stalk grows to about 15 ft. in height, the leaves are nearly 3 ft. long and 1 in. wide at the spoon-shaped base. The stiff leaf bases, when pulled from the cluster, form the "desert spoons" sold in curio shops. Mexicans allow the sap of the succulent basal crowns to ferment to produce the alcoholic beverage, sotol.

DUDLEYA—See *Echeveria, Gormania.*

ECHEVERIA. Some are offered as *Dudleya.* A large genus of tropical American, chiefly Mexican, succulent perennials with small flowers usually in spikes and thick, flat, narrow to oval leaves in basal rosettes resembling the houseleek, *Sempervivum.* They enjoy a dry, sterile, rocky soil and are not hardy North, where they are used for summer bedding and grown in the cool greenhouse. The echeverias make a decorative group to collect. Their soft colors and varying shades of light green, bluish-gray, some margined reddish or pinkish, others white-hairy, make them interesting dish garden subjects. Easily increased by seed or offsets. *E. glauca* and *E. secunda* are hardy nearly as far north as Washington, D. C.

E. farinosa (Dudleya farinosa) has white-mealy, tongue-shaped leaves and yellow flowers on stems a ft. or more high.

E. glauca (E. secunda glauca) has basal, nearly round, pale bluish-green leaves, the terminal point purplish. The flowers are pink outside and yellowish inside.

E. pulverulenta (Dudleya pulverulenta) has rounded, thick, pointed, powdered white hairy leaves and red flowers on 2 ft. long stems in the spring.

E. secunda is similar to *E. glauca* but leaves are reddish along the margins and flowers are red on 15 in. stems.

EUPHORBIA. This large and diverse group includes hardy herbaceous perennials and annuals as well as tropical shrubs and some desert plants that assume a cactus-like form. The fleshy desert kinds are grown under conditions similar to those required by cacti, thriving in a porous, not very rich soil. Easily increased by cuttings which should be allowed to dry somewhat before being placed in a rooting mixture.

All euphorbias have milky juice and colorful bracts that are so conspicuous in some species (as the poinsettia) and so highly colored they function in place of the flower for display. Widely distributed in tropical and temperate regions, they thrive under varying conditions of soil and moisture. The annual snow-on-the-mountain (*E. marginata*) found from South Dakota to Texas and the tall branching cactus-like *E. lactea* from the East Indies are both in this genus.

E. fulgens—Scarlet Plume. A small Mexican shrub with slender, drooping branches and very decorative small orange-scarlet bracts. Cut branches, very lasting and showy, are grown in the North in greenhouse, as are poinsettias. Best grown from cuttings annually.

E. grandicornis—Much branched, shrubby or tree-like; grows 4 to 6 ft. high, usually leafless and striking in appearance. Adapted primarily to desert plantings, it is also a useful greenhouse subject.

E. lactea is much used for hedges in warm regions and generally leafless, the small leaves soon fall. A tall fast-growing cactus-like plant of candelabrum form, marked with a white band down the middle. It frequently grows to 20 ft. in height, unless clipped for hedges. Requires the same culture as the tree-like cacti. *E. hermentiana* is very similar but with wider branches and not so tall. Useful as a window sill plant in the North.

E. splendens—Crown-of-Thorns. A low creeping fleshy species, from Madagascar, with few leaves and arched flexible stems to 4 ft. long, armed with stout thorns, best trained over a small trellis. Bright red bracts are profusely produced during the winter months and will scatter out over the year. A greenhouse favorite.

FAUCARIA TIGRINA—See *Mesembryanthemum*.

GASTERIA. A genus of desert plants from South Africa of the lily family. Aloe-like plants, but smaller, they are essentially stemless with a dense basal rosette of 2-ranked flattish and pointed leaves, rather like a tongue, often dotted. The somewhat inflated red or pinkish tipped greenish flowers are borne in loose clusters on arching stems. Useful for the desert garden and grown in the greenhouse North, also found in collections. There are many showy hybrid gasterias. Increase these by cuttings or offshoots.

G. maculata makes a good house plant. It has shining green leaves to 6 in. long in rather twisted arrangements with large white spots. It thrives in light shade.

G. verrucosa—Conspicuously white-dotted dull gray leaves, 4 to 5 in. long, rought with many small white warts. The usually unbranched flower cluster is about 2 ft. long with pink flowers. A very good house plant, the several varieties differing mostly in the shape or wortiness of the leaves.

GORMANIA OBTUSATA. Also listed as *Sedum obtusatum* and *Dudleya brittoni*. Not over 6 in. high, found in western North America, related to and resembling the sedums.

GRAPTOPETALUM PARAGUAYENSIS. Fleshy succulent plant from Central America with bluish-green leaves in basal rosettes, frequently offered as *Sedum weinbergi* or as an *Echeveria*.

HAWORTHIA. Of the lily family, South African low, small rosette plants which may be rectangular instead of round. Either stemless or with the small thick, warty leaves crowding along the erect stem which does not show. Small white or greenish lily-like flowers are borne in a loose spire on a naked stalk. Uses are confined to small-scale gardening and more appropriately with rock, suiting the plant itself. The plants grow in the desert under bushy plants, so shade in extreme heat and use more sand than soil in ground preparation; some peat moss helps to hold the slight moisture they require. Easily increased by the many offsets which develop around the base. Much used in dish gardens with other succulents and cacti.

H. fasciata has white cross stripes, is decorative and makes a good house plant as does *H. truncata*. Choose small rosette plants with interestingly marked and fat pointed leaves.

HOUSELEEK—See *Sempervivum*

ICE PLANT—See *Mesembryanthemum crystallinum*

JADE PLANT—See *Crassula argentea*.

KALANCHOE. From damper climates than most succulents so they require more water than most. Best known as greenhouse and house plants although these succulents are grown in desert gardens in the far South. They are shrubby in form with soft fleshy, oval leaves usually toothed and with a profusion of small bright-colored, long-lasting flowers, in bright yellow, scarlet and purple. The flowers may be erect or drooping and appear mostly in the winter and on into spring. They will renew themselves by the rooting-in of fallen leaves or by seed to such an extent as to become a nuisance. Good pot plants, excellent quick fillers for color in the planter-box. Many new and interesting species are in cultivation.

K. blossfeldiana. This species from Madagascar and its hybrids are commonly found in the florist shops. A many-stemmed succulent about 10 in. tall, with ovalish scarlet flowers are borne in branched clusters in the winter time making it a good Christmas plant.

K. fedtschenkoi is not over 12 in. tall with nearly round, fleshy leaves with rounded marginal teeth and nodding purple flowers in terminal clusters. Much grown North as a house plant.

K. grandiflora is a small shrub with mauve-blue foliage which has pale yellow flowers in late winter.

K. laciniata, from South Africa, is one of the chief species in cultivation. Erect, it grows 1 to 2 ft. in height and has ovalish, wavy-margined leaves and fragrant pink flowers in terminal branched clusters.

K. tomentosa—Offered as *K. lanceolata* and *K. pilosa.* A handsome hairy stemmed, erect, branching plant 1 to 3 ft. tall, the furry leaves in terminal rosettes. Leaves are 1½ in. long and ¾ in. wide with chocolate-covered marginal teeth, the leaf surface white-felty. Inconspicuous, scant flowers are of no consequence.

KLEINIA. This genus of the composite family includes several succulent members now usually listed as *Senecio. K. repens* is a stiff finger-like plant of a striking blue-green color. *K. tomentosa* has stiff stems entirely covered with a snowy felt. *K. scaposa* has long cylindrical, sometimes flattened leaves; an intriguing plant. *K. stapeliaeformis* is reminiscent of some of the stapelias. They have fleshy angled stems and small rough leaves. All listed are worth considering as pot plants.

LECHUGUILLA—See *Agave.*

MESEMBRYANTHEMUM — Fig-Marigold. Splendid low growing, succulent, mostly desert plants from South Africa grown North as annuals for their showy flowers. They find many uses, as a cover for dry barren ground, for edging borders or paths, for bedding out or for the rock garden, excellent for poking into the crevices of dry walls but they are of no value for cutting. Also they make attractive trailing pot plants for summer flowering in the cool greenhouse. The flowers are daisy-like, full petaled, in many sizes and in all colors except blue. They close on dull days but when the weather is warm and sunny they make a gorgeous carpet of color.

Essentially arid country plants, they like an open sunny position, heat, and poor rather dry soil. North, sow indoors for an early start. With successive sowings until the end of May, they may be had in flower from June until September. To bloom freely in the East they need a long, hot summer, will take moisture in the garden without harm but must have good drainage.

M. crystallinum—Ice Plant. Also listed as *Cryophytum crystallinum*. Grown in warmer regions as a perennial but in the North as an annual. Runs wild on the seaside cliffs in California. On sunny days their pale green leaves glisten as though covered with minute chips of ice. The thick, fleshy, succulent leaves are covered with glistening white ice-like dots or globules. The plants are trailing or spreading, only about 6 in. in height with small, solitary white or rose colored flowers, nearly stalkless.

M. criniflorum—Also listed as *Dorotheanthus bellidiformis*. With little or no stem its prostrate branches form a low, dense mat of narrow succulent leaves thickly studded with 1 in. daisy-like flowers in pink, red, apricot, buff, orange, crimson or white.

M. lineare. Also found listed as *Dorotheanthus gramineus*. An even more attractive plant than the one described above. It forms dense tufts of narrow, cylindrical leaves covered with large white, pink, red or rose colored daisy-like flowers about 1½ in. across. In many of the cultivated forms the center of the flower is red or blue in color and surrounded by a broad white zone.

M. tigrinum. Also found listed as *Faucaria tigrina*. An almost stemless perennial with white spotted bluish-green, 1 to 2 in. long, leaves which have coarse marginal teeth tapering to fine hairs. Its yellow flowers are about 2 in. across. A good window-sill plant North.

PEDILANTHUS TITHYMALOIDES — Redbird Cactus. Native from Florida to Venezuela and of the spurge family this cactus-like succulent is an erect shrubby plant 4 to 6 ft. tall with fleshy zigzag stems, dark green leaves, the midrib being keeled below. Minute bright red or purple flowers are poised at the ends of the branches in dense clusters. There are varieties with white-edged leaves. Often grown in the greenhouse northward and easily propagated by cuttings.

PUYA ALPESTRIS. This is a Chilean desert plant of the pineapple family. It inhabits cool, dry, stony slopes of the upper Andes and while herbaceous it has somewhat woody stems in maturity. Yucca-like, the plant develops several low, thick leafy stems, of a clumpy character, but is picturesque with a mass of long grassy and spined leaves, 18 to 24 in. long and about 1 in. wide. Great close terminal spikes of dull steel-blue flaring flowers, accented by orange anthers, appear during the summer, the flower cluster much branched. Adaptable in the matter of climate and soils, the drier, cooler suit it best, but the plants will take some moisture and may even be grown indoors for a while in a planter or other container. It will take the most extreme exposure to weather and is easily propagated by stolons.

P. chilensis has a distinct stout stem 3 to 5 ft. high. The blue-green leaves are very narrow and about 4 ft. long. The greenish-yellow flowers are about 2 in. long, the cluster branching.

REDBIRD CACTUS—See *Pedilanthus.*

SCARLET PLUME—See *Euphorbia fulgens.*

SEMPERVIVUM—Houseleek, Hen-and-Chickens. There are many hybrids, mostly derived from a few basic species. The thick, fleshy leaves frequently form compact rosettes, often red spotted toward the tips. Flowers are borne in dense heads, but flowering is often erratic. Hardy ones are well suited for rock work and borders, tender kinds for summer bedding, and indoor pot plants; the smaller sorts are popular in dish gardens. Everlasting in ordinary good garden well-drained soil and full sun. Thrive even in sandy wastes. Their fleshy, often hairy leaves protect them against the hot noonday sun and drying summer winds. Excellent for covering dry banks or embedded in or on old walls or as edging plants. Shallow rooted, they enjoy a light mulch or humus during severe hot weather but do not need further feeding.

S. arachnoideum—Cobweb Houseleek. One of the most admired species with small rosettes of gray-green hairy leaves joined by a lacy, silvery web. Reddish flowers in June.

112. A section of the Huntington Botanic Garden featuring xerophytic plants only, those adapted to a deficiency of water. Earth paths are used. *Puya chilensis* is a bromeliad, of the same family as the pineapple, a Chilean desert plant with stiff, long, narrow leaves in a dense rosette and greenish-yellow flowers in terminal spikes.

Cornell Photo

S. *arenarium* forms tiny globe-shaped rosettes or clumps of bright green leaves; flowers are pale yellow. A sand-loving species.

S. *montanum* has tightly packed tiny leaf rosettes, scarcely 1¾ in. wide, and red-tipped. Bright purplish flowers in June on 6 in. stems.

S. *tectorum*—Common Houseleek. The best known and most grown species, with leafy rosettes to 4 in. across, hairy stems to 12 in. high and pink to red flowers 1 in. across. Occasionally escaping in the United States. It will practically live forever. There are several varieties, each offset or "chicken" will produce a new plant so easily increased.

By some S. *haworthi* and S. *spathulatum* and other related tender woody, stemmed and branching succulent species, popular in desert gardens, are considered as belonging to the genus *Aconium*. Here we have included them under *Sempervivum*. They need more moisture than the average succulent and do not succeed in extreme heat. Although they will withstand a great amount of drought they show it.

S. *haworthi*. This is a tender species from the Canary and Madeira Islands with a 1 to 2 ft. shrubby stem and short thick branches. The thick leaves are ovalish but sharp-pointed and the numerous yellowish-rose flowers are borne in a terminal cluster.

S. *spathulatum* is also a tender species from the Canary and Madeira Islands. Its thick and woody stems are 1 to 2 ft. tall, its leaves marked with red-brown and yellow flowers are borne in a profuse panicle.

SEDUM—Stonecrop. Mostly hardy succulent plants, erect and prostrate, including several useful for the wall and rock garden, carpet bedding, ground covers and borders. They do well in seashore gardens. Most are long-lived in sunny well-drained positions. Some are herbaceous perennials dying to the ground in winter, many are evergreen. Natives of the temperate and frigid zones, they are easy to grow in America. Like light, well-drained loamy soil in an open sunny position. After flowering increase by division of the tufts or from cuttings.

S. *acre*—Mossy Stonecrop. A fast spreader and useful ground cover where it can be contained. Yellow flowers in early summer. Especially suitable for dry places.

S. *kamtschaticum*—Evergreen, 6 to 9 in. high with dark glossy green foliage and orange-yellow flowers in July and August.

S. *lydium*. A dwarf, creeping, shapely evergreen, to 3 in. tall. The leaves are tipped red with tiny white or pink flowers in June. Used for carpet bedding or rock edgings.

S. *maximum atropurpureum*. Grows to 1½ ft. tall, has reddish purple leaves and rose-pink flowers during late summer.

S. *sieboldi*. A favorite trailing sedum, one of the most desirable. Roundish leaves 1 in. across in whorls of 3, pink-edged and grayish-green. Pink flowers, ½″ wide, in late fall. A handsome plant.

S. *spectabile*. One of the largest sedums because of its height, to 2 ft., it is grown largely in the border, frequently used as a pot plant. A robust, upright perennial with light grayish-green foliage and numerous rose-colored flowers ½″ across, in August and September. Several deeper forms are offered of which 'Brilliant' is best known. Indestructible but not invasive.

S. spurim. Often called *S. stoloniferum.* A strong growing, trailing evergreen 6 to 9 in. long. Dark red 'Dragon's Blood' is the preferred form with maroon leaves. A fast spreader. Pale pink flowers in summer.

SENECIO. A large and variable genus including some succulents interesting in mild climates and useful as pot plants or grown in succulent collections. Those formerly listed as *Kleinia* now generally considered part of the genus *Senecio. See Kleinia.*

SOTOL—See *Dasylirion.*

STAPELIA—Carrion-Flower. Strange, fleshy desert plants of reddish-brown and green coloring belonging to the milkweed family and native to South Africa. They are low-growing with curious, fleshy finger-like leaves that in reality are leafless stems ascending directly from the ground. The interesting, bizarre, star-shaped flowers are in smoky shades of yellow with red or purple to brown markings, tucked in at the base of the stubby stem, often with a disagreeable odor. The flowers may last for a week. Mostly used in desert gardens in California, in rock gardens and in succulent collections. Some are grown in pots in the cool greenhouse North. They need plenty of root room and are easily increased by cuttings. There are many different stapelias. The best known is *S. variegata* and there are several varieties of this species. Its flower is speckled and striped with dark chocolate-brown on pale yellow.

STONECROP—See *Sedum*

UMBILICUS—See *Cotyledon.*

VIII Plants for
Container Gardens

(Hardy plants and cacti and succulents are listed here without descriptions. They are described elsewhere; see index.)

With occasional root and top pruning and the renewal and enrichment of the potting mixture many trees and shrubs may be grown successfully in the same container for several years. Dwarf and slow-growing forms do not require frequent repotting and remain better scaled to container and site. More and more it is possible to buy container grown trees and shrubs in cans from the nursery. This contributes immeasurably to the success and ease of container gardening.

Evergreen species are attractive the year round, supplying good background material and they also blend and combine nicely with more colorful flowering kinds. Fastigiate forms of some of the junipers take up little space and make effective accent plants. Weeping forms of trees or shrubs are often attractive but require considerable space to show off to advantage.

POTTED TREES

Araucaria excelsa. The Norfolk-Island pine is widely grown in its juvenile stage by florists. Pyramidal, with horizontal branches and sharply pointed evergreen leaves, as usually grown it is a pot plant 2 to 10 ft. tall, very good indoors. It prefers partial shade.

Ficus carica. The common edible fig is often grown in conservatories in the North. It has large, handsome lobed leaves and an interesting gray bark.

Ficus elastica. The common rubber plant is widely potted and grown in the North, especially in the past. Variegated forms. Not as handsome as *F. lyrata.* Both will endure poorly lighted rooms and considerable abuse.

Ficus lyrata (F. pandurata). The fiddle-leaf fig is grown as a vigorous attractive pot plant in the North. It is more handsome when grown as a single stem plant and will grow to 1½ ft. in height with large handsome fiddle-shaped leaves showing more character than *F. elastica.*

Ficus retusa. The tender Indian laurel fig does well as a container plant and is attractive with glossy, dense, dark green foliage. It will take smoke, dust and the usually trying city conditions.

Palms. Palms are grown as decorative foliage plants in the North, a number of the small kinds are useful container plants and will take considerable neglect. *Collinia elegans (Chamaedorea elegans, Neanthe bella)* is commonly referred to as the parlor palm. It is a dwarf, pinnate-leaved palm quite tolerant of dim light and dry air. *Howea forsteriana,* the Kentia or paradise palm, has upright to horizontal dark green fronds, sometimes drooping from the central stem. It is the palm florists use for weddings and parties. *Phoenix roebelini,* the pigmy or miniature date palm, is slow growing, from 4 to 8 ft. tall with a 3 to 6 ft. spread. It has a short slender trunk and graceful lacy, arching fronds. *Raphia excelsa,* the lady palm, will grow from 5 to 10 ft. tall with a 3 to 6 foot spread, but it is slow growing. Straight bamboo-like stems from shrubby clumps. They bear a fibrous network of leaf sheaths. *Syagrus (Cocos) weddelliana,* the Weddell or cocos palm, is small in growth with graceful shiny bright green leaves, dull green underneath. It is ornamental and attractive as a young plant.

Pinus. Pines with their evergreen habit and ability to take dwarfing do well in containers. They will take considerable shearing and with careful pruning can be left in the same container for several years. *Pinus contorta,* the shore or beach pine, is symmetrical and narrow-crowned when young and takes dwarfing very well. A juvenile specimen of *P. strobus,* eastern white pine, may be used in a container until it grows too large and then transferred to the open ground. 'Fastigiata' has a columnar erect habit if that is preferred. The Japanese black pine, *Pinus thunbergi,* is much used by the Japanese for dwarf-tree purposes.

Sophora japonica—Japanese Pagoda Tree.

Styrax japonica—Japanese Snowbell.

Tilia cordata 'Swedish Upright'—Small or Little-Leaved Linden.

POTTED SHRUBS

Many tender tropicals are grown under glass or as house plants in the North and taken outdoors only when danger of frost is over. Types that do not object to the restrictions of pot culture, those that will do well when their roots are restricted, dwarf forms or juvenile specimens that do not grow too large for the area, and plants that will take hard pruning will be most successful. Some suggestions follow.

Abelia grandiflora sherwoodi—Glossy Abelia.

Cotoneasters.

Cytisus—Brooms.

Elaeagnus pungens—Silverberry.

Fatisa japonica — Tender tropical-looking shrub of rapid growth reaching 4 to 6 ft. or more and with a wide spread. It has bold, dark green glossy, deeply lobed, fan-shaped leaves and is grown as a foliage plant in the North.

Ilex cornuta—Chinese or Horned Holly.

Juniperus—Low prostrate forms of juniper are adaptable for container gardening. Choose from several species. The low arching forms of the Chinese juniper *(J. chinensis)* not over 2 ft. high, look like small Pfitzer junipers. Shore juniper *(J. conferta)* forms a low 1 to 2 ft. uneven mat of blue-green foliage, excellent used with stone. Creeping juniper *(J. horizontalis)* is prostrate with long spreading branches and bluish-green or grayish-blue needle-like leaves. Tamarix juniper *(J. sabina tamariscifolia)* is another low form with ascending branches and usually not over 2 ft. high.

Lavandula spica (L. officinalis)—English Lavender.

Ligustrum japonicum rotundifolium (L. coriaceum)—Japanese Privet.

Lippia citriodora. Lemon verbena is a popular old favorite grown by florists. A South American tropical shrub it is grown northward as a greenhouse subject or summer bedding plant. Lemon-scented leaves are lance-shaped, 2 to 3 in. long.

Nerium oleander. For years oleander has been grown as tubbed plants for northern summers and as conservatory plants. Slim dark green evergreen foliage is bamboo-like, showy flowers in terminal clusters are fragrant and appear in April through summer.

Pinus mugo mughus—Mugho Pine. To keep the plant from spread- and getting out of hand pinch back new, soft green shoots about an inch each spring.

Pittosporum tobira, Japanese pittosporum, is a useful pot plant in the North. Thick leathery, 4 in. long, dark green, lustrous leaves are blunt toward the tip. Creamy white flowers in terminal custers appear in May and are fragrant like orange blossoms. The shrub is wide spreading but can be held back by judicious pruning. *P. t.* 'Variegatum' has gray-green leaves outlined in white.

Podocarpus elongata is tender and prized in its young state as a foliage plant. Likes a little acid peat in the soil and is not hardy north of zone 6. The plant can be kept to 8 ft. in a tub. Graceful with pendulous branches and dark green, rather, thin pointed narrow soft willowy leaves. Sometimes called the fern pine. *P. macrophyllus,* the yew pine, is slower growing although similar, its leaves lighter green and wider. Dependable and useful as a house plant while young. 'Maki' is smaller with more crowded leaves.

Punica granatum 'Nana'. Improved forms of the dwarf pomegranate are grown in the cool greenhouse North where they make attractive bushy, compact plants 3 ft. tall and will bear fruit when still quite young. The tiny orange fruits are dry and not edible. Double flowered forms and several color variations from yellow to orange. Keep the plants pinched back for handsome specimens.

Rosmarinus officinalis—Rosemary.

Taxus cuspidata 'Nana'—Japanese Yew.

POTTED ANNUALS

Many annuals make excellent pot plants. With their shallow roots they are well adapted to container gardening techniques. Easily and quickly grown from seed or young seedlings they supply a wealth of color. With an early start it is possible to have flowering annuals a month or so in advance of the regular season. In warm climates many of the northern summer outdoor annuals are grown as winter plants.

To keep the annuals looking well and in good condition they will need regular care. Pinch back to encourage good branching, remove all faded blossoms for continued flowering and water regularly as necessary so the roots will not dry out and die. During the heat of July and August they will need daily attention. Although this should not take many minutes of one's time it should become routine so plants are never allowed to completely dry out. Choose those annuals that best suit your needs. The amount of water required will not be great.

Many of the low growing kinds are excellent for edging or carpeting the soil at the foot of taller tubbed plants and the trailing forms are useful for spilling over the sides of tubs or for hanging arangements. Interesting groupings of potted annuals banked in tiers can be highly decorative supplying a mass of bright color. They are especially effective combined with potted bulbs. At the end of the season bring indoors any that have further use and simply discard the annual, temporary kinds.

Anagallis arvensis caerulea. The poor-man's weatherglass has trailing stems with blue flowers and is much used in window boxes and hanging baskets or for cascading over the edge of a planter.

Browallia speciosa. Browallia is excellent for pot culture or hanging baskets. The plant bears numerous small violet-blue, white throated flowers and glossy green foliage, enjoying a long blooming period through most of the summer. It is particularly useful for partially shaded areas.

Calendula officinalis.

Campanula isophylla. The Ligurian bellflower is a trailing plant useful for window boxes and hanging baskets. It has handsome small oval to heart-shaped leaves and shallow bell-shaped, starry pale blue flowers 1 in. across, close to and intermingling with the foliage. There is also a white form. It has a long blooming period and does well in partial shade. It may be wintered over as a house plant in the North.

Convolvulus tricolor (C. minor). The dwarf or bush morning glory is useful for hanging baskets, raised beds and container gardening. The low-growing, trailing plants grow about a ft. high but will spread 2 ft. or more. Constantly in bloom, the miniature flowers resemble those of the tall climbing morning glory. Usually the main part of the flower is blue, pink or purple; the center yellow with a band of white between the center and the expanded part. The flowers are open all day in good weather.

Dimorphotheca aurantiaca—Cape Marigold, African Daisy.

Eschscholtzia californica—California Poppy.

Lantana camara—Lantana.

Lobularia maritima—Sweet Alyssum. Invaluable as an edging plant or a ground cover for a planter.

Mesembryanthemum.

Pelargonium hortorum—Geranium.

Petunia hybrids. Unequalled for container use. With the wide color range, prolific bloom over a long period of time and the many types— tall, dwarf and compact, or trailing—it is one of the most versatile of annuals.

Phlox drummondi.

Portulaca grandiflora.

Sanvitalia procumbens.

Tagetes — Marigold. Dwarf marigolds are useful as container plants. The smallest is the signet marigold *(T. teniufolia pumila).* The single French marigold *(T. patula)* is also fairly drought-tolerant.

Tropaeolum. Nasturtium

Verbena hybrida.

Vinca rosea.

Zinnia. The dwarfer types listed as Mexican hybrids and often cata- logued under Haageana are good container subjects. *Z. linearis* the only single zinnia, is fairly drought-resistant.

POTTED PERENNIALS

Most perennials enjoy a cold-winter dormancy and do not reach their maximum beauty or size the first year. They also require a larger root space, so as container plants they do not give the quick returns and present more problems than do annuals. At the end of the season in the North, if you have no place to carry perennials over for the winter they can be planted out in the garden.

Also when the perennial border becomes overcrowded it is possible to lift some from the garden that need to be divided and pot them up for terrace decoration. Give the perennials a couple of weeks to adjust and recuperate from the shock of transplanting. Place the plants in the shade and keep the roots moist enough so they will not dry out. Treat only perennials that do not resent transplanting in this manner.

With many perennials as asters, phlox and chrysanthemums pinch- ing out the tips in late spring and early summer will aid in developing compact, better branching plants. Although it will delay blooming somewhat, and the flowers will be smaller they will be far more numerous.

Aster novae-angliae (New England Aster) and *A. novi-belgi* (New York Aster)—Michaelmas Daisy.

Gaillardia aristata.

Heuchera sanguinea—Coral Bell. When dividing every third year or so pot up some plants for the terrace.

Kniphofia uvaria—Torch Lily.

Liatris—Button Snakeroot.

Monarda didyma. Bee-balm grows to 3 ft. with scarlet flowers and has a long blooming season. Pot up some plants when they need to be divided for decorating the breezeway or terrace. There are white, rose and yellowish-pink kinds available.

Rudbeckia hirta—Gloriosa Daisy Selections.

Salvia superba. This outstanding salvia grows 2 ft. tall or more, has a broad, bushy habit and a long flowering period with deep purple flowers. Pot up a plant for the porch or patio when dividing an old clump.

Sedum spectabile.

Vinca minor—Periwinkle.

Yucca smalliana. Separate a small plant from the parent's base and try growing it in a container.

POTTED CACTI AND SUCCULENTS

Cacti and succulents are among the best container plants for indoor and outdoor use. Many are extremely well suited to the dry atmosphere of present day living rooms. Not as sensitive to neglect as many other container plants, their prime need is perfect drainage.

Most are easy to grow, thriving on a lean soil with warmth, in a sunny or well lighted situation. They do best in restricted containers, an asset when pot gardening. Shallow clay pots, low wooden boxes, hollowed out tree trunks, tufa or lava rock and strawberry jars are all useful for displaying succulents which are usually interesting the year round and comparatively long-lived.

The fascination of their foliage and pattern forms intrigue many people. There is a wide range of attractive plants from which to choose in many delightful soft shades of green, gray, gray-green and blue-green as well as a variety of heights, shapes and sizes. See Chapter on Desert Flora, including Cacti and Succulents.

IX Conservation
is Everyone's Problem

Aside from air, water is our most abundant natural resource and, unlike most other natural resources, is practically indestructible. In fact, geologists believe that most of the earth's original supply of water, hundreds of millions of years old, is still in use as part of an everrecurring process referred to as the hydrologic or water cycle. Energy provided by the sun causes water from the land and ocean to evaporate. The resulting vapor is carried in the air, to fall somewhere as rain or snow. The water, draining down through soil or rock structure, eventually returns to the land and ocean, and the cycle begins all over.

Although there is plenty of water available for the world's needs, it is not always in the right place at the time when it is needed. Shortages occur regionally because facilities for collection, storage, treatment and delivery of water are inadequate. Some of these facilities can be expanded or improved but it would be impossible to transport water economically to many arid places of the world, and on 35 per cent of the land surface of the earth, water shortage must be considered as permanent.

SEEDING THE CLOUDS

The subject of rainmaking has been a matter of controversy. An authoritative pamphlet entitled "Weather and Climate Control", issued by the National Science Foundation, appraises current opinion: "There is increasing but still somewhat ambiguous statistical evidence that precipitation from some types of cloud and storm systems can be modestly increased or redistributed by seeding techniques. . . . Present indications, if taken at face value, are that local precipitation can be increased in many situations in the order of 10 per cent by seeding. These positive results are obtained in cases where rain would have fallen anyway without seeding; there is no evidence that seeding can induce rain to fall when normally there would be none. Thus, seeding is of limited value in relieving drought situations."

SALT WATER CONSERVATION

The supply of usable water would be practically limitless if the salt could be easily and inexpensively removed. But at the present time there is no cheap method to convert salty ocean water to fresh, or to build pumping stations and pipelines to transport the converted water. The cheapest method to date would cost farmers two hundred times more than present irrigation costs.

On seacoasts and islands that have no fresh water it is sometimes cheaper to remove the salt than bring in fresh water by ship. Naval and passenger ships now use a distilling or evaporating process as standard equipment. A distilling machine boils the salt water and by means of the membrane process salt water flows through narrow sheets or membranes electrically charged so that the sodium and chloride in the salt are separated from the water. Up-to-date lifeboat equipment includes a "desalting kit" consisting of a plastic bag to be filled with sea water. A solid chemical which is dropped into the salt water changes the soluble material into insoluble substances which are filtered out at the bottom of the bag, leaving behind relatively pure water. Until more economical methods are found for converting salt water and transporting it, the idea is not practical for gardening purposes.

ARE DROUGHTS INEVITABLE?

In years gone by, water was relatively abundant and inexpensive, and most of us thought of the supply as endless. But with the population increase and industrial expansion, demands have multiplied. Our increased standards of living and sanitation, with multiple bathrooms, home laundries, dishwashing machines, and garbage grinders have greatly increased household requirements. For example, no water is required to put garbage in a can, but it takes a couple of gallons each day to flush garbage down the drain. A dishwasher uses twice as much water as handwashing; and so it goes.

Dr. Raymond L. Nace of the U.S. Geological Survey, has summed up the problem: "World population, technology, economic activity and water demands all are growing at geometric rates, but the supply of fresh water is not growing at all. . . . We should continue to prepare for the future droughts that will inevitably return. Drought is a natural phenomenon and we cannot control nature. We have to learn better how to work with nature."

WATER POLLUTION IS A FACTOR

Although the quantity of water has remained constant, its quality has deteriorated, and much of our country's supply is in danger of contamination by chemicals and sewage. Some legislation to control the pollution of our precious rivers and lakes has been passed, but it must be extended and enforced. Every citizen should inform himself about local practices on garbage and waste disposal, and on spraying of nearby streams and natural water sources.

CAN WATER BE REUSED?

An interesting question was asked recently by a gardener who wished to know if laundry and dish rinse water could be used on plants. The answer is by Herbert Fordham, Waltham Field Station (Mass.) extension horticulturist: "I think you will find it would be safe to use waste water (laundry and dish) on vegetables as on flowers with one exception. There are a few laundry detergents which contain borax. Any laundry or dish water containing borax should not be applied to plant growth since harmful residues will build up in the soil and cause serious injury to the plants."

With the exception noted, reuse of water from baths, dishes and laundry is feasible. Keep a water bucket handy for collecting waste water. By doing so, you may save some plants which would otherwise die of thirst during severe droughts.

METERED WATER

Water in the reservoirs during wet periods must be conserved for use during droughts. Yet for the most part, consumers pay little attention to water conservation in normal times. Kenneth Holum, an Assistant Secretary of the U.S. Deptment of the Interior writes: "The only conservation measure that we have found to be effective at [non-drought] times arises from an awareness of the economic cost of waste. Installation of meters on the lines of previously unmetered consumers has demonstrated that most people will conserve water when they are penalized financially for wasting it. Lawn watering, for instance, will be more carefully controlled; the tendency to turn on lawn sprinklers and forget them or to tolerate leaky plumbing will rapidly dissipate. ... Without adopting a full-time rationing system, meaningful conservation of water by individuals is limited practically to metering....

COMMUNITY PARTICIPATION IN WATER CONSERVATION

Interested garden club and conservation groups have been effective, at local, regional and national levels, in working for education and legislation affecting water. If your club does not have a program on the subject, here are some ideas for helping:

Why not include a class at your next flower show calling for entries of drought-resistant plants?

Feature sand gardens at every exhibition and explain their value to arid sites.

Help the local library plan a display of books dealing wholly or partly with water conservation. The same book display can then be exhibited at your club meeting.

Plan a series of lecture-demonstrations pertinent to water conservation. Some topics: Selection of plants for drought-resistant qualities; Use of mulches; Good watering techniques in the garden; New watering equipment; Drip, Drip, Drip adds up to Drought.

Send a release to local newspapers, radio and TV stations at least once each year, pointing out the need to conserve water during periods of plenty for periods when the rainfall is below normal.

Work through poster and essay contests in schools, scout movements, church groups, and other young-people organizations to dramatize the need to conserve water.

Why not sponsor a tour to a local reservoir as part of an educational program?

Assign members to give talks on pertinent topics such as local water costs, local methods of sewage disposal, local reservoir facilities, local rainfall data, etc.

Support and fight for good water legislation; get out the vote when such legislation is pending.

INDEX

A CATALOGUE OF SELECTED DOVER BOOKS
IN ALL FIELDS OF INTEREST

A CATALOGUE OF SELECTED DOVER BOOKS
IN ALL FIELDS OF INTEREST

AMERICA'S OLD MASTERS, James T. Flexner. Four men emerged unexpectedly from provincial 18th century America to leadership in European art: Benjamin West, J. S. Copley, C. R. Peale, Gilbert Stuart. Brilliant coverage of lives and contributions. Revised, 1967 edition. 69 plates. 365pp. of text.

21806-6 Paperbound $3.00

FIRST FLOWERS OF OUR WILDERNESS: AMERICAN PAINTING, THE COLONIAL PERIOD, James T. Flexner. Painters, and regional painting traditions from earliest Colonial times up to the emergence of Copley, West and Peale Sr., Foster, Gustavus Hesselius, Feke, John Smibert and many anonymous painters in the primitive manner. Engaging presentation, with 162 illustrations. xxii + 368pp.

22180-6 Paperbound $3.50

THE LIGHT OF DISTANT SKIES: AMERICAN PAINTING, 1760-1835, James T. Flexner. The great generation of early American painters goes to Europe to learn and to teach: West, Copley, Gilbert Stuart and others. Allston, Trumbull, Morse; also contemporary American painters—primitives, derivatives, academics—who remained in America. 102 illustrations. xiii + 306pp.

22179-2 Paperbound $3.50

A HISTORY OF THE RISE AND PROGRESS OF THE ARTS OF DESIGN IN THE UNITED STATES, William Dunlap. Much the richest mine of information on early American painters, sculptors, architects, engravers, miniaturists, etc. The only source of information for scores of artists, the major primary source for many others. Unabridged reprint of rare original 1834 edition, with new introduction by James T. Flexner, and 394 new illustrations. Edited by Rita Weiss. 6⅝ x 9⅝.

21695-0, 21696-9, 21697-7 Three volumes, Paperbound $15.00

EPOCHS OF CHINESE AND JAPANESE ART, Ernest F. Fenollosa. From primitive Chinese art to the 20th century, thorough history, explanation of every important art period and form, including Japanese woodcuts; main stress on China and Japan, but Tibet, Korea also included. Still unexcelled for its detailed, rich coverage of cultural background, aesthetic elements, diffusion studies, particularly of the historical period. 2nd, 1913 edition. 242 illustrations. lii + 439pp. of text.

20364-6, 20365-4 Two volumes, Paperbound $6.00

THE GENTLE ART OF MAKING ENEMIES, James A. M. Whistler. Greatest wit of his day deflates Oscar Wilde, Ruskin, Swinburne; strikes back at inane critics, exhibitions, art journalism; aesthetics of impressionist revolution in most striking form. Highly readable classic by great painter. Reproduction of edition designed by Whistler. Introduction by Alfred Werner. xxxvi + 334pp.

21875-9 Paperbound $3.00

VISUAL ILLUSIONS: THEIR CAUSES, CHARACTERISTICS, AND APPLICATIONS, Matthew Luckiesh. Thorough description and discussion of optical illusion, geometric and perspective, particularly; size and shape distortions, illusions of color, of motion; natural illusions; use of illusion in art and magic, industry, etc. Most useful today with op art, also for classical art. Scores of effects illustrated. Introduction by William H. Ittleson. 100 illustrations. xxi + 252pp.
21530-X Paperbound $2.00

A HANDBOOK OF ANATOMY FOR ART STUDENTS, Arthur Thomson. Thorough, virtually exhaustive coverage of skeletal structure, musculature, etc. Full text, supplemented by anatomical diagrams and drawings and by photographs of undraped figures. Unique in its comparison of male and female forms, pointing out differences of contour, texture, form. 211 figures, 40 drawings, 86 photographs. xx + 459pp. 5⅜ x 8⅜.
21163-0 Paperbound $3.50

150 MASTERPIECES OF DRAWING, Selected by Anthony Toney. Full page reproductions of drawings from the early 16th to the end of the 18th century, all beautifully reproduced: Rembrandt, Michelangelo, Dürer, Fragonard, Urs, Graf, Wouwerman, many others. First-rate browsing book, model book for artists. xviii + 150pp. 8⅜ x 11¼.
21032-4 Paperbound $3.50

THE LATER WORK OF AUBREY BEARDSLEY, Aubrey Beardsley. Exotic, erotic, ironic masterpieces in full maturity: Comedy Ballet, Venus and Tannhauser, Pierrot, Lysistrata, Rape of the Lock, Savoy material, Ali Baba, Volpone, etc. This material revolutionized the art world, and is still powerful, fresh, brilliant. With *The Early Work,* all Beardsley's finest work. 174 plates, 2 in color. xiv + 176pp. 8⅛ x 11.
21817-1 Paperbound $3.75

DRAWINGS OF REMBRANDT, Rembrandt van Rijn. Complete reproduction of fabulously rare edition by Lippmann and Hofstede de Groot, completely reedited, updated, improved by Prof. Seymour Slive, Fogg Museum. Portraits, Biblical sketches, landscapes, Oriental types, nudes, episodes from classical mythology—All Rembrandt's fertile genius. Also selection of drawings by his pupils and followers. "Stunning volumes," *Saturday Review.* 550 illustrations. lxxviii + 552pp. 9⅛ x 12¼.
21485-0, 21486-9 Two volumes, Paperbound $10.00

THE DISASTERS OF WAR, Francisco Goya. One of the masterpieces of Western civilization—83 etchings that record Goya's shattering, bitter reaction to the Napoleonic war that swept through Spain after the insurrection of 1808 and to war in general. Reprint of the first edition, with three additional plates from Boston's Museum of Fine Arts. All plates facsimile size. Introduction by Philip Hofer, Fogg Museum. v + 97pp. 9⅜ x 8¼.
21872-4 Paperbound $2.50

GRAPHIC WORKS OF ODILON REDON. Largest collection of Redon's graphic works ever assembled: 172 lithographs, 28 etchings and engravings, 9 drawings. These include some of his most famous works. All the plates from *Odilon Redon: oeuvre graphique complet,* plus additional plates. New introduction and caption translations by Alfred Werner. 209 illustrations. xxvii + 209pp. 9⅛ x 12¼.
21966-8 Paperbound $5.00

DESIGN BY ACCIDENT; A BOOK OF "ACCIDENTAL EFFECTS" FOR ARTISTS AND DESIGNERS, James F. O'Brien. Create your own unique, striking, imaginative effects by "controlled accident" interaction of materials: paints and lacquers, oil and water based paints, splatter, crackling materials, shatter, similar items. Everything you do will be different; first book on this limitless art, so useful to both fine artist and commercial artist. Full instructions. 192 plates showing "accidents," 8 in color. viii + 215pp. 8⅜ x 11¼.   21942-9 Paperbound $3.75

THE BOOK OF SIGNS, Rudolf Koch. Famed German type designer draws 493 beautiful symbols: religious, mystical, alchemical, imperial, property marks, runes, etc. Remarkable fusion of traditional and modern. Good for suggestions of timelessness, smartness, modernity. Text. vi + 104pp. 6⅛ x 9¼.
                            20162-7 Paperbound $1.25

HISTORY OF INDIAN AND INDONESIAN ART, Ananda K. Coomaraswamy. An unabridged republication of one of the finest books by a great scholar in Eastern art. Rich in descriptive material, history, social backgrounds; Sunga reliefs, Rajput paintings, Gupta temples, Burmese frescoes, textiles, jewelry, sculpture, etc. 400 photos. viii + 423pp. 6⅜ x 9¾.   21436-2 Paperbound $5.00

PRIMITIVE ART, Franz Boas. America's foremost anthropologist surveys textiles, ceramics, woodcarving, basketry, metalwork, etc.; patterns, technology, creation of symbols, style origins. All areas of world, but very full on Northwest Coast Indians. More than 350 illustrations of baskets, boxes, totem poles, weapons, etc. 378 pp.
                            20025-6 Paperbound $3.00

THE GENTLEMAN AND CABINET MAKER'S DIRECTOR, Thomas Chippendale. Full reprint (third edition, 1762) of most influential furniture book of all time, by master cabinetmaker. 200 plates, illustrating chairs, sofas, mirrors, tables, cabinets, plus 24 photographs of surviving pieces. Biographical introduction by N. Bienenstock. vi + 249pp. 9⅞ x 12¾.   21601-2 Paperbound $4.00

AMERICAN ANTIQUE FURNITURE, Edgar G. Miller, Jr. The basic coverage of all American furniture before 1840. Individual chapters cover type of furniture—clocks, tables, sideboards, etc.—chronologically, with inexhaustible wealth of data. More than 2100 photographs, all identified, commented on. Essential to all early American collectors. Introduction by H. E. Keyes. vi + 1106pp. 7⅞ x 10¾.
              21599-7, 21600-4 Two volumes, Paperbound $11.00

PENNSYLVANIA DUTCH AMERICAN FOLK ART, Henry J. Kauffman. 279 photos, 28 drawings of tulipware, Fraktur script, painted tinware, toys, flowered furniture, quilts, samplers, hex signs, house interiors, etc. Full descriptive text. Excellent for tourist, rewarding for designer, collector. Map. 146pp. 7⅞ x 10¾.
                            21205-X Paperbound $2.50

EARLY NEW ENGLAND GRAVESTONE RUBBINGS, Edmund V. Gillon, Jr. 43 photographs, 226 carefully reproduced rubbings show heavily symbolic, sometimes macabre early gravestones, up to early 19th century. Remarkable early American primitive art, occasionally strikingly beautiful; always powerful. Text. xxvi + 207pp. 8⅜ x 11¼.   21380-3 Paperbound $3.50

ALPHABETS AND ORNAMENTS, Ernst Lehner. Well-known pictorial source for decorative alphabets, script examples, cartouches, frames, decorative title pages, calligraphic initials, borders, similar material. 14th to 19th century, mostly European. Useful in almost any graphic arts designing, varied styles. 750 illustrations. 256pp. 7 x 10.   21905-4 Paperbound $4.00

PAINTING: A CREATIVE APPROACH, Norman Colquhoun. For the beginner simple guide provides an instructive approach to painting: major stumbling blocks for beginner; overcoming them, technical points; paints and pigments; oil painting; watercolor and other media and color. New section on "plastic" paints. Glossary. Formerly *Paint Your Own Pictures*. 221pp.   22000-1 Paperbound $1.75

THE ENJOYMENT AND USE OF COLOR, Walter Sargent. Explanation of the relations between colors themselves and between colors in nature and art, including hundreds of little-known facts about color values, intensities, effects of high and low illumination, complementary colors. Many practical hints for painters, references to great masters. 7 color plates, 29 illustrations. x + 274pp.
                                                          20944-X Paperbound $2.75

THE NOTEBOOKS OF LEONARDO DA VINCI, compiled and edited by Jean Paul Richter. 1566 extracts from original manuscripts reveal the full range of Leonardo's versatile genius: all his writings on painting, sculpture, architecture, anatomy, astronomy, geography, topography, physiology, mining, music, etc., in both Italian and English, with 186 plates of manuscript pages and more than 500 additional drawings. Includes studies for the Last Supper, the lost Sforza monument, and other works. Total of xlvii + 866pp. 7⅞ x 10¾.
                                       22572-0, 22573-9 Two volumes, Paperbound $11.00

MONTGOMERY WARD CATALOGUE OF 1895. Tea gowns, yards of flannel and pillow-case lace, stereoscopes, books of gospel hymns, the New Improved Singer Sewing Machine, side saddles, milk skimmers, straight-edged razors, high-button shoes, spittoons, and on and on . . . listing some 25,000 items, practically all illustrated. Essential to the shoppers of the 1890's, it is our truest record of the spirit of the period. Unaltered reprint of Issue No. 57, Spring and Summer 1895. Introduction by Boris Emmet. Innumerable illustrations. xiii + 624pp. 8½ x 11⅝.
                                                          22377-9 Paperbound $6.95

THE CRYSTAL PALACE EXHIBITION ILLUSTRATED CATALOGUE (LONDON, 1851). One of the wonders of the modern world—the Crystal Palace Exhibition in which all the nations of the civilized world exhibited their achievements in the arts and sciences—presented in an equally important illustrated catalogue. More than 1700 items pictured with accompanying text—ceramics, textiles, cast-iron work, carpets, pianos, sleds, razors, wall-papers, billiard tables, beehives, silverware and hundreds of other artifacts—represent the focal point of Victorian culture in the Western World. Probably the largest collection of Victorian decorative art ever assembled—indispensable for antiquarians and designers. Unabridged republication of the Art-Journal Catalogue of the Great Exhibition of 1851, with all terminal essays. New introduction by John Gloag, F.S.A. xxxiv + 426pp. 9 x 12.
                                                          22503-8 Paperbound $5.00

A HISTORY OF COSTUME, Carl Köhler. Definitive history, based on surviving pieces of clothing primarily, and paintings, statues, etc. secondarily. Highly readable text, supplemented by 594 illustrations of costumes of the ancient Mediterranean peoples, Greece and Rome, the Teutonic prehistoric period; costumes of the Middle Ages, Renaissance, Baroque, 18th and 19th centuries. Clear, measured patterns are provided for many clothing articles. Approach is practical throughout. Enlarged by Emma von Sichart. 464pp. 21030-8 Paperbound $3.50

ORIENTAL RUGS, ANTIQUE AND MODERN, Walter A. Hawley. A complete and authoritative treatise on the Oriental rug—where they are made, by whom and how, designs and symbols, characteristics in detail of the six major groups, how to distinguish them and how to buy them. Detailed technical data is provided on periods, weaves, warps, wefts, textures, sides, ends and knots, although no technical background is required for an understanding. 11 color plates, 80 halftones, 4 maps. vi + 320pp. 6⅛ x 9⅛. 22366-3 Paperbound $5.00

TEN BOOKS ON ARCHITECTURE, Vitruvius. By any standards the most important book on architecture ever written. Early Roman discussion of aesthetics of building, construction methods, orders, sites, and every other aspect of architecture has inspired, instructed architecture for about 2,000 years. Stands behind Palladio, Michelangelo, Bramante, Wren, countless others. Definitive Morris H. Morgan translation. 68 illustrations. xii + 331pp. 20645-9 Paperbound $3.00

THE FOUR BOOKS OF ARCHITECTURE, Andrea Palladio. Translated into every major Western European language in the two centuries following its publication in 1570, this has been one of the most influential books in the history of architecture. Complete reprint of the 1738 Isaac Ware edition. New introduction by Adolf Placzek, Columbia Univ. 216 plates. xxii + 110pp. of text. 9½ x 12¾. 21308-0 Clothbound $12.50

STICKS AND STONES: A STUDY OF AMERICAN ARCHITECTURE AND CIVILIZATION, Lewis Mumford.One of the great classics of American cultural history. American architecture from the medieval-inspired earliest forms to the early 20th century; evolution of structure and style, and reciprocal influences on environment. 21 photographic illustrations. 238pp. 20202-X Paperbound $2.00

THE AMERICAN BUILDER'S COMPANION, Asher Benjamin. The most widely used early 19th century architectural style and source book, for colonial up into Greek Revival periods. Extensive development of geometry of carpentering, construction of sashes, frames, doors, stairs; plans and elevations of domestic and other buildings. Hundreds of thousands of houses were built according to this book, now invaluable to historians, architects, restorers, etc. 1827 edition. 59 plates. 114pp. 7⅞ x 10¾. 22236-5 Paperbound $3.50

DUTCH HOUSES IN THE HUDSON VALLEY BEFORE 1776, Helen Wilkinson Reynolds. The standard survey of the Dutch colonial house and outbuildings, with constructional features, decoration, and local history associated with individual homesteads. Introduction by Franklin D. Roosevelt. Map. 150 illustrations. 469pp. 6⅝ x 9¼. 21469-9 Paperbound $5.00

THE ARCHITECTURE OF COUNTRY HOUSES, Andrew J. Downing. Together with Vaux's *Villas and Cottages* this is the basic book for Hudson River Gothic architecture of the middle Victorian period. Full, sound discussions of general aspects of housing, architecture, style, decoration, furnishing, together with scores of detailed house plans, illustrations of specific buildings, accompanied by full text. Perhaps the most influential single American architectural book. 1850 edition. Introduction by J. Stewart Johnson. 321 figures, 34 architectural designs. xvi + 560pp.
22003-6 Paperbound $4.00

LOST EXAMPLES OF COLONIAL ARCHITECTURE, John Mead Howells. Full-page photographs of buildings that have disappeared or been so altered as to be denatured, including many designed by major early American architects. 245 plates. xvii + 248pp. 7⅞ x 10¾.
21143-6 Paperbound $3.50

DOMESTIC ARCHITECTURE OF THE AMERICAN COLONIES AND OF THE EARLY REPUBLIC, Fiske Kimball. Foremost architect and restorer of Williamsburg and Monticello covers nearly 200 homes between 1620-1825. Architectural details, construction, style features, special fixtures, floor plans, etc. Generally considered finest work in its area. 219 illustrations of houses, doorways, windows, capital mantels. xx + 314pp. 7⅞ x 10¾.
21743-4 Paperbound $4.00

EARLY AMERICAN ROOMS: 1650-1858, edited by Russell Hawes Kettell. Tour of 12 rooms, each representative of a different era in American history and each furnished, decorated, designed and occupied in the style of the era. 72 plans and elevations, 8-page color section, etc., show fabrics, wall papers, arrangements, etc. Full descriptive text. xvii + 200pp. of text. 8⅜ x 11¼.
21633-0 Paperbound $5.00

THE FITZWILLIAM VIRGINAL BOOK, edited by J. Fuller Maitland and W. B. Squire. Full modern printing of famous early 17th-century ms. volume of 300 works by Morley, Byrd, Bull, Gibbons, etc. For piano or other modern keyboard instrument; easy to read format. xxxvi + 938pp. 8⅜ x 11.
21068-5, 21069-3 Two volumes, Paperbound $10.00

KEYBOARD MUSIC, Johann Sebastian Bach. Bach Gesellschaft edition. A rich selection of Bach's masterpieces for the harpsichord: the six English Suites, six French Suites, the six Partitas (Clavierübung part I), the Goldberg Variations (Clavierübung part IV), the fifteen Two-Part Inventions and the fifteen Three-Part Sinfonias. Clearly reproduced on large sheets with ample margins; eminently playable. vi + 312pp. 8⅛ x 11.
22360-4 Paperbound $5.00

THE MUSIC OF BACH: AN INTRODUCTION, Charles Sanford Terry. A fine, nontechnical introduction to Bach's music, both instrumental and vocal. Covers organ music, chamber music, passion music, other types. Analyzes themes, developments, innovations. x + 114pp.
21075-8 Paperbound $1.50

BEETHOVEN AND HIS NINE SYMPHONIES, Sir George Grove. Noted British musicologist provides best history, analysis, commentary on symphonies. Very thorough, rigorously accurate; necessary to both advanced student and amateur music lover. 436 musical passages. vii + 407 pp.
20334-4 Paperbound $2.75

JOHANN SEBASTIAN BACH, Philipp Spitta. One of the great classics of musicology, this definitive analysis of Bach's music (and life) has never been surpassed. Lucid, nontechnical analyses of hundreds of pieces (30 pages devoted to St. Matthew Passion, 26 to B Minor Mass). Also includes major analysis of 18th-century music. 450 musical examples. 40-page musical supplement. Total of xx + 1799pp.

(EUK) 22278-0, 22279-9 Two volumes, Clothbound $17.50

MOZART AND HIS PIANO CONCERTOS, Cuthbert Girdlestone. The only full-length study of an important area of Mozart's creativity. Provides detailed analyses of all 23 concertos, traces inspirational sources. 417 musical examples. Second edition. 509pp.   21271-8 Paperbound $3.50

THE PERFECT WAGNERITE: A COMMENTARY ON THE NIBLUNG'S RING, George Bernard Shaw. Brilliant and still relevant criticism in remarkable essays on Wagner's Ring cycle, Shaw's ideas on political and social ideology behind the plots, role of Leitmotifs, vocal requisites, etc. Prefaces. xxi + 136pp.

(USO) 21707-8 Paperbound $1.75

DON GIOVANNI, W. A. Mozart. Complete libretto, modern English translation; biographies of composer and librettist; accounts of early performances and critical reaction. Lavishly illustrated. All the material you need to understand and appreciate this great work. Dover Opera Guide and Libretto Series; translated and introduced by Ellen Bleiler. 92 illustrations. 209pp.

21134-7 Paperbound $2.00

BASIC ELECTRICITY, U. S. Bureau of Naval Personel. Originally a training course, best non-technical coverage of basic theory of electricity and its applications. Fundamental concepts, batteries, circuits, conductors and wiring techniques, AC and DC, inductance and capacitance, generators, motors, transformers, magnetic amplifiers, synchros, servomechanisms, etc. Also covers blue-prints, electrical diagrams, etc. Many questions, with answers. 349 illustrations. x + 448pp. 6½ x 9¼.

20973-3 Paperbound $3.50

REPRODUCTION OF SOUND, Edgar Villchur. Thorough coverage for laymen of high fidelity systems, reproducing systems in general, needles, amplifiers, preamps, loudspeakers, feedback, explaining physical background. "A rare talent for making technicalities vividly comprehensible," R. Darrell, *High Fidelity*. 69 figures. iv + 92pp.   21515-6 Paperbound $1.35

HEAR ME TALKIN' TO YA: THE STORY OF JAZZ AS TOLD BY THE MEN WHO MADE IT, Nat Shapiro and Nat Hentoff. Louis Armstrong, Fats Waller, Jo Jones, Clarence Williams, Billy Holiday, Duke Ellington, Jelly Roll Morton and dozens of other jazz greats tell how it was in Chicago's South Side, New Orleans, depression Harlem and the modern West Coast as jazz was born and grew. xvi + 429pp.

21726-4 Paperbound $3.00

FABLES OF AESOP, translated by Sir Roger L'Estrange. A reproduction of the very rare 1931 Paris edition; a selection of the most interesting fables, together with 50 imaginative drawings by Alexander Calder. v + 128pp. 6½x9¼.

21780-9 Paperbound $1.50

AGAINST THE GRAIN (A REBOURS), Joris K. Huysmans. Filled with weird images, evidences of a bizarre imagination, exotic experiments with hallucinatory drugs, rich tastes and smells and the diversions of its sybarite hero Duc Jean des Esseintes, this classic novel pushed 19th-century literary decadence to its limits. Full unabridged edition. Do not confuse this with abridged editions generally sold. Introduction by Havelock Ellis. xlix + 206pp. 22190-3 Paperbound $2.50

VARIORUM SHAKESPEARE: HAMLET. Edited by Horace H. Furness; a landmark of American scholarship. Exhaustive footnotes and appendices treat all doubtful words and phrases, as well as suggested critical emendations throughout the play's history. First volume contains editor's own text, collated with all Quartos and Folios. Second volume contains full first Quarto, translations of Shakespeare's sources (Belleforest, and Saxo Grammaticus), Der Bestrafte Brudermord, and many essays on critical and historical points of interest by major authorities of past and present. Includes details of staging and costuming over the years. By far the best edition available for serious students of Shakespeare. Total of xx + 905pp. 21004-9, 21005-7, 2 volumes, Paperbound $7.00

A LIFE OF WILLIAM SHAKESPEARE, Sir Sidney Lee. This is the standard life of Shakespeare, summarizing everything known about Shakespeare and his plays. Incredibly rich in material, broad in coverage, clear and judicious, it has served thousands as the best introduction to Shakespeare. 1931 edition. 9 plates. xxix + 792pp. 21967-4 Paperbound $4.50

MASTERS OF THE DRAMA, John Gassner. Most comprehensive history of the drama in print, covering every tradition from Greeks to modern Europe and America, including India, Far East, etc. Covers more than 800 dramatists, 2000 plays, with biographical material, plot summaries, theatre history, criticism, etc. "Best of its kind in English," New Republic. 77 illustrations. xxii + 890pp. 20100-7 Clothbound $10.00

THE EVOLUTION OF THE ENGLISH LANGUAGE, George McKnight. The growth of English, from the 14th century to the present. Unusual, non-technical account presents basic information in very interesting form: sound shifts, change in grammar and syntax, vocabulary growth, similar topics. Abundantly illustrated with quotations. Formerly Modern English in the Making. xii + 590pp. 21932-1 Paperbound $4.00

AN ETYMOLOGICAL DICTIONARY OF MODERN ENGLISH, Ernest Weekley. Fullest, richest work of its sort, by foremost British lexicographer. Detailed word histories, including many colloquial and archaic words; extensive quotations. Do not confuse this with the Concise Etymological Dictionary, which is much abridged. Total of xxvii + 830pp. 6½ x 9¼. 21873-2, 21874-0 Two volumes, Paperbound $7.90

FLATLAND: A ROMANCE OF MANY DIMENSIONS, E. A. Abbott. Classic of science-fiction explores ramifications of life in a two-dimensional world, and what happens when a three-dimensional being intrudes. Amusing reading, but also useful as introduction to thought about hyperspace. Introduction by Banesh Hoffmann. 16 illustrations. xx + 103pp. 20001-9 Paperbound $1.25

POEMS OF ANNE BRADSTREET, edited with an introduction by Robert Hutchinson. A new selection of poems by America's first poet and perhaps the first significant woman poet in the English language. 48 poems display her development in works of considerable variety—love poems, domestic poems, religious meditations, formal elegies, "quaternions," etc. Notes, bibliography. viii + 222pp.
22160-1 Paperbound $2.50

THREE GOTHIC NOVELS: THE CASTLE OF OTRANTO BY HORACE WALPOLE; VATHEK BY WILLIAM BECKFORD; THE VAMPYRE BY JOHN POLIDORI, WITH FRAGMENT OF A NOVEL BY LORD BYRON, edited by E. F. Bleiler. The first Gothic novel, by Walpole; the finest Oriental tale in English, by Beckford; powerful Romantic supernatural story in versions by Polidori and Byron. All extremely important in history of literature; all still exciting, packed with supernatural thrills, ghosts, haunted castles, magic, etc. xl + 291pp.
21232-7 Paperbound $2.50

THE BEST TALES OF HOFFMANN, E. T. A. Hoffmann. 10 of Hoffmann's most important stories, in modern re-editings of standard translations: Nutcracker and the King of Mice, Signor Formica, Automata, The Sandman, Rath Krespel, The Golden Flowerpot, Master Martin the Cooper, The Mines of Falun, The King's Betrothed, A New Year's Eve Adventure. 7 illustrations by Hoffmann. Edited by E. F. Bleiler. xxxix + 419pp. 21793-0 Paperbound $3.00

GHOST AND HORROR STORIES OF AMBROSE BIERCE, Ambrose Bierce. 23 strikingly modern stories of the horrors latent in the human mind: The Eyes of the Panther, The Damned Thing, An Occurrence at Owl Creek Bridge, An Inhabitant of Carcosa, etc., plus the dream-essay, Visions of the Night. Edited by E. F. Bleiler. xxii + 199pp. 20767-6 Paperbound $1.50

BEST GHOST STORIES OF J. S. LEFANU, J. Sheridan LeFanu. Finest stories by Victorian master often considered greatest supernatural writer of all. Carmilla, Green Tea, The Haunted Baronet, The Familiar, and 12 others. Most never before available in the U. S. A. Edited by E. F. Bleiler. 8 illustrations from Victorian publications. xvii + 467pp. 20415-4 Paperbound $3.00

MATHEMATICAL FOUNDATIONS OF INFORMATION THEORY, A. I. Khinchin. Comprehensive introduction to work of Shannon, McMillan, Feinstein and Khinchin, placing these investigations on a rigorous mathematical basis. Covers entropy concept in probability theory, uniqueness theorem, Shannon's inequality, ergodic sources, the E property, martingale concept, noise, Feinstein's fundamental lemma, Shanon's first and second theorems. Translated by R. A. Silverman and M. D. Friedman. iii + 120pp. 60434-9 Paperbound $2.00

SEVEN SCIENCE FICTION NOVELS, H. G. Wells. The standard collection of the great novels. Complete, unabridged. *First Men in the Moon, Island of Dr. Moreau, War of the Worlds, Food of the Gods, Invisible Man, Time Machine, In the Days of the Comet.* Not only science fiction fans, but every educated person owes it to himself to read these novels. 1015pp. (USO) 20264-X Clothbound $6.00

LAST AND FIRST MEN AND STAR MAKER, TWO SCIENCE FICTION NOVELS, Olaf Stapledon. Greatest future histories in science fiction. In the first, human intelligence is the "hero," through strange paths of evolution, interplanetary invasions, incredible technologies, near extinctions and reemergences. Star Maker describes the quest of a band of star rovers for intelligence itself, through time and space: weird inhuman civilizations, crustacean minds, symbiotic worlds, etc. Complete, unabridged. v + 438pp. (USO) 21962-3 Paperbound $2.50

THREE PROPHETIC NOVELS, H. G. WELLS. Stages of a consistently planned future for mankind. *When the Sleeper Wakes,* and *A Story of the Days to Come,* anticipate *Brave New World* and *1984,* in the 21st Century; *The Time Machine,* only complete version in print, shows farther future and the end of mankind. All show Wells's greatest gifts as storyteller and novelist. Edited by E. F. Bleiler. x + 335pp. (USO) 20605-X Paperbound $2.50

THE DEVIL'S DICTIONARY, Ambrose Bierce. America's own Oscar Wilde— Ambrose Bierce—offers his barbed iconoclastic wisdom in over 1,000 definitions hailed by H. L. Mencken as "some of the most gorgeous witticisms in the English language." 145pp. 20487-1 Paperbound $1.25

MAX AND MORITZ, Wilhelm Busch. Great children's classic, father of comic strip, of two bad boys, Max and Moritz. Also Ker and Plunk (Plisch und Plumm), Cat and Mouse, Deceitful Henry, Ice-Peter, The Boy and the Pipe, and five other pieces. Original German, with English translation. Edited by H. Arthur Klein; translations by various hands and H. Arthur Klein. vi + 216pp. 20181-3 Paperbound $2.00

PIGS IS PIGS AND OTHER FAVORITES, Ellis Parker Butler. The title story is one of the best humor short stories, as Mike Flannery obfuscates biology and English. Also included, That Pup of Murchison's, The Great American Pie Company, and Perkins of Portland. 14 illustrations. v + 109pp. 21532-6 Paperbound $1.25

THE PETERKIN PAPERS, Lucretia P. Hale. It takes genius to be as stupidly mad as the Peterkins, as they decide to become wise, celebrate the "Fourth," keep a cow, and otherwise strain the resources of the Lady from Philadelphia. Basic book of American humor. 153 illustrations. 219pp. 20794-3 Paperbound $2.00

PERRAULT'S FAIRY TALES, translated by A. E. Johnson and S. R. Littlewood, with 34 full-page illustrations by Gustave Doré. All the original Perrault stories— Cinderella, Sleeping Beauty, Bluebeard, Little Red Riding Hood, Puss in Boots, Tom Thumb, etc.—with their witty verse morals and the magnificent illustrations of Doré. One of the five or six great books of European fairy tales. viii + 117pp. 8⅛ x 11. 22311-6 Paperbound $2.00

OLD HUNGARIAN FAIRY TALES, Baroness Orczy. Favorites translated and adapted by author of the *Scarlet Pimpernel.* Eight fairy tales include "The Suitors of Princess Fire-Fly," "The Twin Hunchbacks," "Mr. Cuttlefish's Love Story," and "The Enchanted Cat." This little volume of magic and adventure will captivate children as it has for generations. 90 drawings by Montagu Barstow. 96pp. (USO) 22293-4 Paperbound $1.95

THE RED FAIRY BOOK, Andrew Lang. Lang's color fairy books have long been children's favorites. This volume includes Rapunzel, Jack and the Bean-stalk and 35 other stories, familiar and unfamiliar. 4 plates, 93 illustrations x + 367pp.
21673-X Paperbound $2.50

THE BLUE FAIRY BOOK, Andrew Lang. Lang's tales come from all countries and all times. Here are 37 tales from Grimm, the Arabian Nights, Greek Mythology, and other fascinating sources. 8 plates, 130 illustrations. xi + 390pp.
21437-0 Paperbound $2.75

HOUSEHOLD STORIES BY THE BROTHERS GRIMM. Classic English-language edition of the well-known tales — Rumpelstiltskin, Snow White, Hansel and Gretel, The Twelve Brothers, Faithful John, Rapunzel, Tom Thumb (52 stories in all). Translated into simple, straightforward English by Lucy Crane. Ornamented with headpieces, vignettes, elaborate decorative initials and a dozen full-page illustrations by Walter Crane. x + 269pp.
21080-4 Paperbound **$2.00**

THE MERRY ADVENTURES OF ROBIN HOOD, Howard Pyle. The finest modern versions of the traditional ballads and tales about the great English outlaw. Howard Pyle's complete prose version, with every word, every illustration of the first edition. Do not confuse this facsimile of the original (1883) with modern editions that change text or illustrations. 23 plates plus many page decorations. xxii + 296pp.
22043-5 Paperbound $2.75

THE STORY OF KING ARTHUR AND HIS KNIGHTS, Howard Pyle. The finest children's version of the life of King Arthur; brilliantly retold by Pyle, with 48 of his most imaginative illustrations. xviii + 313pp. 6⅛ x 9¼.
21445-1 Paperbound $2.50

THE WONDERFUL WIZARD OF OZ, L. Frank Baum. America's finest children's book in facsimile of first edition with all Denslow illustrations in full color. The edition a child should have. Introduction by Martin Gardner. 23 color plates, scores of drawings. iv + 267pp.
20691-2 Paperbound **$2.50**

THE MARVELOUS LAND OF OZ, L. Frank Baum. The second Oz book, every bit as imaginative as the Wizard. The hero is a boy named Tip, but the Scarecrow and the Tin Woodman are back, as is the Oz magic. 16 color plates, 120 drawings by John R. Neill. 287pp.
20692-0 Paperbound $2.50

THE MAGICAL MONARCH OF MO, L. Frank Baum. Remarkable adventures in a land even stranger than Oz. The best of Baum's books not in the Oz series. 15 color plates and dozens of drawings by Frank Verbeck. xviii + 237pp.
21892-9 Paperbound $2.25

THE BAD CHILD'S BOOK OF BEASTS, MORE BEASTS FOR WORSE CHILDREN, A MORAL ALPHABET, Hilaire Belloc. Three complete humor classics in one volume. Be kind to the frog, and do not call him names . . . and 28 other whimsical animals. Familiar favorites and some not so well known. Illustrated by Basil Blackwell. 156pp. (USO) 20749-8 Paperbound $1.50

EAST O' THE SUN AND WEST O' THE MOON, George W. Dasent. Considered the best of all translations of these Norwegian folk tales, this collection has been enjoyed by generations of children (and folklorists too). Includes True and Untrue, Why the Sea is Salt, East O' the Sun and West O' the Moon, Why the Bear is Stumpy-Tailed, Boots and the Troll, The Cock and the Hen, Rich Peter the Pedlar, and 52 more. The only edition with all 59 tales. 77 illustrations by Erik Werenskiold and Theodor Kittelsen. xv + 418pp. 22521-6 Paperbound $3.50

GOOPS AND HOW TO BE THEM, Gelett Burgess. Classic of tongue-in-cheek humor, masquerading as etiquette book. 87 verses, twice as many cartoons, show mischievous Goops as they demonstrate to children virtues of table manners, neatness, courtesy, etc. Favorite for generations. viii + 88pp. $6\frac{1}{2}$ x $9\frac{1}{4}$. 22233-0 Paperbound $1.50

ALICE'S ADVENTURES UNDER GROUND, Lewis Carroll. The first version, quite different from the final Alice in Wonderland, printed out by Carroll himself with his own illustrations. Complete facsimile of the "million dollar" manuscript Carroll gave to Alice Liddell in 1864. Introduction by Martin Gardner. viii + 96pp. Title and dedication pages in color. 21482-6 Paperbound $1.25

THE BROWNIES, THEIR BOOK, Palmer Cox. Small as mice, cunning as foxes, exuberant and full of mischief, the Brownies go to the zoo, toy shop, seashore, circus, etc., in 24 verse adventures and 266 illustrations. Long a favorite, since their first appearance in St. Nicholas Magazine. xi + 144pp. $6\frac{5}{8}$ x $9\frac{1}{4}$. 21265-3 Paperbound $1.75

SONGS OF CHILDHOOD, Walter De La Mare. Published (under the pseudonym Walter Ramal) when De La Mare was only 29, this charming collection has long been a favorite children's book. A facsimile of the first edition in paper, the 47 poems capture the simplicity of the nursery rhyme and the ballad, including such lyrics as I Met Eve, Tartary, The Silver Penny. vii + 106pp. (USO) 21972-0 Paperbound $2.00

THE COMPLETE NONSENSE OF EDWARD LEAR, Edward Lear. The finest 19th-century humorist-cartoonist in full: all nonsense limericks, zany alphabets, Owl and Pussycat, songs, nonsense botany, and more than 500 illustrations by Lear himself. Edited by Holbrook Jackson. xxix + 287pp. (USO) 20167-8 Paperbound $2.00

BILLY WHISKERS: THE AUTOBIOGRAPHY OF A GOAT, Frances Trego Montgomery. A favorite of children since the early 20th century, here are the escapades of that rambunctious, irresistible and mischievous goat—Billy Whiskers. Much in the spirit of Peck's Bad Boy, this is a book that children never tire of reading or hearing. All the original familiar illustrations by W. H. Fry are included: 6 color plates, 18 black and white drawings. 159pp. 22345-0 Paperbound $2.00

MOTHER GOOSE MELODIES. Faithful republication of the fabulously rare Munroe and Francis "copyright 1833" Boston edition—the most important Mother Goose collection, usually referred to as the "original." Familiar rhymes plus many rare ones, with wonderful old woodcut illustrations. Edited by E. F. Bleiler. 128pp. $4\frac{1}{2}$ x $6\frac{3}{8}$. 22577-1 Paperbound $1.00

TWO LITTLE SAVAGES; BEING THE ADVENTURES OF TWO BOYS WHO LIVED AS INDIANS AND WHAT THEY LEARNED, Ernest Thompson Seton. Great classic of nature and boyhood provides a vast range of woodlore in most palatable form, a genuinely entertaining story. Two farm boys build a teepee in woods and live in it for a month, working out Indian solutions to living problems, star lore, birds and animals, plants, etc. 293 illustrations. vii + 286pp.

20985-7 Paperbound $2.50

PETER PIPER'S PRACTICAL PRINCIPLES OF PLAIN & PERFECT PRONUNCIATION. Alliterative jingles and tongue-twisters of surprising charm, that made their first appearance in America about 1830. Republished in full with the spirited woodcut illustrations from this earliest American edition. 32pp. 4½ x 6⅜.

22560-7 Paperbound $1.00

SCIENCE EXPERIMENTS AND AMUSEMENTS FOR CHILDREN, Charles Vivian. 73 easy experiments, requiring only materials found at home or easily available, such as candles, coins, steel wool, etc.; illustrate basic phenomena like vacuum, simple chemical reaction, etc. All safe. Modern, well-planned. Formerly *Science Games for Children*. 102 photos, numerous drawings. 96pp. 6⅛ x 9¼.

21856-2 Paperbound $1.25

AN INTRODUCTION TO CHESS MOVES AND TACTICS SIMPLY EXPLAINED, Leonard Barden. Informal intermediate introduction, quite strong in explaining reasons for moves. Covers basic material, tactics, important openings, traps, positional play in middle game, end game. Attempts to isolate patterns and recurrent configurations. Formerly *Chess*. 58 figures. 102pp. (USO) 21210-6 Paperbound $1.25

LASKER'S MANUAL OF CHESS, Dr. Emanuel Lasker. Lasker was not only one of the five great World Champions, he was also one of the ablest expositors, theorists, and analysts. In many ways, his Manual, permeated with his philosophy of battle, filled with keen insights, is one of the greatest works ever written on chess. Filled with analyzed games by the great players. A single-volume library that will profit almost any chess player, beginner or master. 308 diagrams. xli x 349pp.

20640-8 Paperbound $2.75

THE MASTER BOOK OF MATHEMATICAL RECREATIONS, Fred Schuh. In opinion of many the finest work ever prepared on mathematical puzzles, stunts, recreations; exhaustively thorough explanations of mathematics involved, analysis of effects, citation of puzzles and games. Mathematics involved is elementary. Translated bv F. Göbel. 194 figures. xxiv + 430pp. 22134-2 Paperbound $3.50

MATHEMATICS, MAGIC AND MYSTERY, Martin Gardner. Puzzle editor for Scientific American explains mathematics behind various mystifying tricks: card tricks, stage "mind reading," coin and match tricks, counting out games, geometric dissections, etc. Probability sets, theory of numbers clearly explained. Also provides more than 400 tricks, guaranteed to work, that you can do. 135 illustrations. xii + 176pp.

20335-2 Paperbound $1.75

MATHEMATICAL PUZZLES FOR BEGINNERS AND ENTHUSIASTS, Geoffrey Mott-Smith. 189 puzzles from easy to difficult—involving arithmetic, logic, algebra, properties of digits, probability, etc.—for enjoyment and mental stimulus. Explanation of mathematical principles behind the puzzles. 135 illustrations. viii + 248pp.
20198-8 Paperbound $1.75

PAPER FOLDING FOR BEGINNERS, William D. Murray and Francis J. Rigney. Easiest book on the market, clearest instructions on making interesting, beautiful origami. Sail boats, cups, roosters, frogs that move legs, bonbon boxes, standing birds, etc. 40 projects; more than 275 diagrams and photographs. 94pp.
20713-7 Paperbound $1.00

TRICKS AND GAMES ON THE POOL TABLE, Fred Herrmann. 79 tricks and games— some solitaires, some for two or more players, some competitive games—to entertain you between formal games. Mystifying shots and throws, unusual caroms, tricks involving such props as cork, coins, a hat, etc. Formerly *Fun on the Pool Table*. 77 figures. 95pp.
21814-7 Paperbound $1.25

HAND SHADOWS TO BE THROWN UPON THE WALL: A SERIES OF NOVEL AND AMUSING FIGURES FORMED BY THE HAND, Henry Bursill. Delightful picturebook from great-grandfather's day shows how to make 18 different hand shadows: a bird that flies, duck that quacks, dog that wags his tail, camel, goose, deer, boy, turtle, etc. Only book of its sort. vi + 33pp. 6½ x 9¼. 21779-5 Paperbound $1.00

WHITTLING AND WOODCARVING, E. J. Tangerman. 18th printing of best book on market. "If you can cut a potato you can carve" toys and puzzles, chains, chessmen, caricatures, masks, frames, woodcut blocks, surface patterns, much more. Information on tools, woods, techniques. Also goes into serious wood sculpture from Middle Ages to present, East and West. 464 photos, figures. x + 293pp.
20965-2 Paperbound $2.00

HISTORY OF PHILOSOPHY, Julián Marias. Possibly the clearest, most easily followed, best planned, most useful one-volume history of philosophy on the market; neither skimpy nor overfull. Full details on system of every major philosopher and dozens of less important thinkers from pre-Socratics up to Existentialism and later. Strong on many European figures usually omitted. Has gone through dozens of editions in Europe. 1966 edition, translated by Stanley Appelbaum and Clarence Strowbridge. xviii + 505pp.
21739-6 Paperbound $3.50

YOGA: A SCIENTIFIC EVALUATION, Kovoor T. Behanan. Scientific but non-technical study of physiological results of yoga exercises; done under auspices of Yale U. Relations to Indian thought, to psychoanalysis, etc. 16 photos. xxiii + 270pp.
20505-3 Paperbound $2.50

Prices subject to change without notice.
Available at your book dealer or write for free catalogue to Dept. GI, Dover Publications, Inc., 180 Varick St., N. Y., N. Y. 10014. Dover publishes more than 150 books each year on science, elementary and advanced mathematics, biology, music, art, literary history, social sciences and other areas.